Race in Space

The Representation of Ethnicity in *Star Trek* and *Star Trek: The Next Generation*

Micheal C. Pounds

The Scarecrow Press, Inc.
Lanham, Maryland, & London
1999

SCARECROW PRESS, INC.

Published in the United States of America
by Scarecrow Press, Inc.
4720 Boston Way
Lanham, Maryland 20706

4 Pleydell Gardens, Folkestone
Kent CT20 2DN, England

British Library Cataloguing in Publication Information Available

Library of Congress Cataloging-in-Publication Data

Pounds, Micheal C., 1950–
    Race in space : the representation of ethnicity in Star trek and Star trek,
the next generation / Micheal C. Pounds.
        p.   cm.
    Includes bibliographical references and index.
    ISBN 0-8108-3322-0 (cloth : alk. paper)
    1. Star trek (Television program) 2. Star trek, the next generation
(Television program) 3. Minorities in television. I. Title.
PN1992.77.S73P68   1999
791.45'72—dc21   97-9554

⊗ ™ The paper used in this publication meets the minimum requirements of
American National Standard for Information Sciences—Permanence of
Paper for Printed Library Materials, ANSI Z39.48–1984.
Manufactured in the United States of America.

For my father,
who supported his son's dreaming about space, the future, and the fantastic
with a patient ear and a quiet, knowing sense of humor
and who was my first teacher about machines and technology.

And my mother,
whose work made the dream of flight through air and space
come true each and every day.

And for Francis R. Scobee, Michael J. Smith, Ronald E. MacNair, Ellison S. Onizuka,
Judith A. Resnik, Gregory B. Jarvis, and Sharon Christa McAuliffe
who are now enrolled among the honored who have given their full measure
to advance the dream of equality across its next frontier:
space.

Contents

Figures

Tables

Acknowledgments

I would like to thank Peter H. Salus, who tolerated my need to discuss my ideas and encouraged me to continue to develop them. I thank Thomas R. Cripps, who first introduced me to the study of popular culture and whose own work in the history of African-American images in American media is a continuing example of good scholarship. I owe Carlton Moss so much for allowing me to ask him so many questions and for his easy manner in teaching me how to look at things with relentless objectivity and sensitivity. I owe more to these three colleagues than I can ever repay.

I would like to express my appreciation to the librarians and staff members of Doheny Library of the University of Southern California, University Research Library and the Dixon Art Library of the University of California at Los Angeles, and the Library of the Academy of Motion Picture Arts and Sciences for their patience with all my questions and for helping me to navigate their collections. In particular, I want to single out Miki Goral, UCLA reference librarian, for her indispensable assistance with research related to this study. Brigitte Kueppers of UCLA's URL-Special Collections facilitated my research of unique materials under her supervision and care and I thank her very much. I owe Elizabeth Brenner, librarian for the Writers Guild/West, much for her cooperation and generous assistance in locating resources within the guild's collection.

Race, Media, and Coming of Age: A Personal Introduction

Race,[1] as W. E. B. Dubois cautioned, is this century's central problem, its final frontier of understanding. Despite a hundred years of communications advances expanding our modes of expression and exposing diverse audiences to common experiences, the golden age of social harmony has yet to dawn. Film, phonography, photography, telegraphy, and broadcast media, in turn, trumpeted their capacities to reinvigorate learning by easing the storage and retrieval of information even over distance and time. Each in this succession of media promised heightened scientific approximation of observable reality and the creation of riveting mediated experiences based on the symbolic representation of characters, situations, and general emotions. However, looking back, we can see that many of the claims about mass media's social benefits—its capacity to bring "to life" aspects of the human experience that may be removed by time, distance, or culture—remain unfulfilled. Nowhere is this lack more telling than in the area of race relations.

Indeed, biased and demeaning depictions of African Americans reemerged within the context of each new medium, thereby undermining racial amelioration and understanding. Against this background, media scholars and proponents of racial equality have examined mass media treatments of race and formulated one of the longest and most relentlessly consistent critiques of these cultural products. Nevertheless, civil rights activists and sympathetic

1

media producers continue to regard film and broadcast media as particularly important creative activities. These media are all the more important because of audience size, the durability and portability of mass media products, and the ability of these audiovisual mass media to articulate alternative models of social relations.

The gathering momentum of the post-World War II civil rights movement and the accelerating evolution of telecommunication technologies were two of the major forces reshaping American society as I was born in 1950. My earliest memories are of sitting on the living room floor in my parents' home in a segregated, working-class town outside Baltimore, Turners' Station, and being mesmerized by the marvels of radio and television, through which the world entered our home. As my family struggled to grasp middle-class status and security, my parents believed that these media would contribute to their two sons' education—they would serve as an important adjunct to our formal public education by bringing the larger world into our home.

I remember that as a child I turned the pages of an illustrated two-volume encyclopedia of World War II while listening to radio or watching television and eavesdropping on the conversations of grown-ups as I sat on the floor of the combination living/dining room of our two-story, two-bedroom, brick house. That encyclopedia was one of my first primers. Its black-and-white photos and matter-of-fact captions taught me about aerial bombardment, infantrymen slogging through knee-deep mud, female French collaborators (in close-up shots with their heads shaven), war refugees in long lines with their possessions strapped to their backs, Nazi criminals hanging from gallows, and the aftermath of Nazism (the macabre neat rows of bleached human skulls, stacks of limbs, and the odd hills of dead naked bodies in German concentration camps). A whole codex of human tragedy spread out before me while I attended to distant romances, mysteries, comedies, and adventures broadcast into our home and heard my parents and neighbors talk about the equally horrid human tragedies occurring then, in my contemporary world and not at some oceanic distance: Emmett Till's murder, the wave of black men lynched by white mobs, and the ways seemingly benign social interactions could erupt, like landmines, and cause embarrassment, or injury, or even death in our racialized American world.

I grew up in the warm embrace of family and neighbors who encouraged me to learn and expand my horizons but offered sharp cautions about the harsh reception that awaited me in the wider world dominated by white privilege and segregation. My consciousness formed around the issue of belonging. I puzzled over the question of where I fit in. This is what DuBois meant in *The Souls of Black Folk* by the term *double consciousness:* being a sentient being conscious of being a social problem. My neighbors responded by creating a community of "us," black, brown, and tan folk, who freely shared their common experiences of discrimination as they negotiated racism's obstacle course. (How often my elders would report wearily, "You won't believe what devilment white folks are up to now.") As a youngster, I learned that one definition of racism was the anonymous threat that "they" could strike out at any moment, in any situation, with devastating cruelty. My neighbors formed a familiar and comfortable cocoon of steady support and certain discipline. Beyond lay a terribly flawed world, fractured by a lack of moral logic, and frightening in its senseless brutality. I learned early on the need to always be on guard for whites who used the color of their skin as a warrant to humiliate, terrorize, maim, and kill.

Even as *Brown v. Board of Education* promised to change society at large, even as I prepared myself to live in its wider world, I lived under segregation's intimidation and uncertainty. Throughout my adolescence, the world, as I understood it, could not be fully predictable and trustworthy. The irrational logic of discrimination formed no reliable barometer of how white people would treat me. Travel with my family—whether embarking on a family vacation or rushing south to attend ill grandmothers or family funerals—was laced with worry about whether our family would reach its destination unmolested. Far from ending discriminatory public policies, the postwar civil rights movement and the school desegregation decision destabilized our already fragile existence and haunted my parents. They desperately sought wider horizons of opportunity for their children but knew we would have to live in an often hostile society and face adult-size hatreds as integration dissolved protective social and institutional membranes of the black community.

I turned for pleasure to the small set of institutions within our community (Methodist church, church choir and youth fellowship group, YMCA, Boy Scouts, organized sports, NAACP youth chapter, the public library, and recreation opportunities) for the secure fellowship they afforded. Outside our community, I selected an equally small set of institutions such as circuses, professional sports, repertory theater, broadcast media, and motion pictures in which I could rely on being alone in a crowd for some degree of safety as I sought entertainment, culture, and pleasure. Although this range of activities may seem fairly diverse, running through them is the fact that my choices were contextualized by my racial identity. I wanted both to express my African American racial identity (as a vital part of who I was) when I chose and to participate in other leisure activities as a full-fledged American citizen without others stigmatizing me because of my race. As an African American, I knew that the selection of any activity for pleasure that took me outside my community—whether physically or psychologically—was contaminated by at least the equally strong possibilities that I could be singled out, embarrassed, or terrorized because of my ethnic identity.

However, I could not isolate myself within my small, working-class black township, like a hermit, in the hope of being protected there from racism and its effects. Racism was delivered by messenger to our neighborhood motion picture house and beamed into our lives by radio and television. As exciting as these simulations of reality were—with their capacity to traverse time and space—they betrayed our curiosity, patronage, and loyalty by presenting representations of ethnic characters that traded on racialized stereotypes. Make no mistake—I spent many an afternoon at the movies because black actors were among a film's featured players, and many were the times that I came running to the television set (or cried out to my family to come see) because there were "colored on TV!" However, I clearly remember my parents and neighbors taking pains to point out that these were actors who were being paid to "act the fool." In other words, I was taught to compare media depictions of blacks with the blacks in my life (my parents, relatives, and neighbors) for dimensionality, common sense, and humanity. With these criteria in mind, I could easily make distinctions between media's black images and the black people I knew as family, neighbors, and historical heroes. All of this presented quite a daunting situation for a young person. I had to learn to negotiate a larger world where I was not reflected, and I could not fully understand why.

Why was there such dissonance between my two worlds, black and white?

My parents struggled under segregation's limitations, and from their efforts to foster their family I saw two different examples of coping. My father expressed his farm-bred self-reliance by risking self-employment as an independent owner-operator in the interstate carrier industry that was just poised to expand with the federal highway program. My mother was able to extend her World War II employment in military aircraft manufacturing into a career in the aerospace industry of the cold war. Their experiences modeled an ability to calculate and accept risk, an interest in and facility with existing and advancing technologies, a willingness and aptitude for engaging with people from different regions and backgrounds, and a fascination with travel (though their itineraries did not extend beyond the United States).

Their examples of courage helped me know that I could chart a course among the crosscurrents of school integration (hostile teachers and students), forced school busing, and interaction with white adults outside my community, and could learn to expand my world to include Baltimore City (its downtown stores, museums, theaters, and Enoch Pratt Free Library) and many of the other cities of the Northeast. Looking back now, I realize my parents' attitudes and endeavors influenced so many of my personal choices. Outside of school and sports, for instance, my reading and media entertainment tended toward adventure, sword and sorcery, and science fiction genres. From today's vantage point, these selections seem only too logical: they clearly reinforced my parents' examples (and family-centered experiences and lessons that emphasized hard work, perseverance, a hope for the future) and allowed the chance to construct a romance of my own desire to experience change in preparation for a life of still greater change.

It should come as no surprise that science fiction figured prominently among my personal choices of divertissements. Perhaps its appeal for me was to be expected, considering the cold war's threat of nuclear annihilation was a palpable fact of life growing up, as I did, in a region that was among the highest targeting priorities for Soviet ICBMs. In other words, science fiction was that literary genre in which war-inspired advanced technology, its hideously destructive and miraculous liberating potentials, could be imagined and played out in a thousand directions that harmed no one. It was admittedly small comfort to read about trying to break the light-speed barrier, or how even microbes could defeat invaders from Mars, or how souls could be collected by interstellar vampires against the terrors of real-world scientists' latest doomsday weapons. But it was comforting at some basic level to be able to use the language of science and the technology of Armageddon (nuclear power, rockets, computers, and space sciences) for amusement; it was a way to gain some measure of control (for knowledge is a form of control) over forces beyond the ordinary individual's influence.

However, other reasons lay behind science fiction's appeal for me. I was particularly drawn to stories in which the moral position triumphed, travel to exotic distant worlds was depicted as adventure, fantastic and alien technology and science challenged the mind, and a calculated risk of personal danger permeated throughout. In addition, one of the major themes in science fiction is whether humans can control technology and events to mollify their impact to benefit individuals and society. Another frequent theme deals with valorizing rationality and morality over baser human drives, such as personal greed and intergroup hatreds. Other writers' stories survey the more global question of the perfectibility of humanity and assert that humanity could indeed have a future—beyond warfare, scarcity, and disease—one in which a primary goal would be tackling two of nature's greatest unfinished creations: human beings and human society.

These are some of the major themes in contemporary science fiction literature, and they are equally the major social issues that confronted America in the second half of this century, though often transmogrified to alien worlds. This was the world I was born to and would grow to maturity in. Growing up under official segregation, but being encouraged to prepare myself for competition in a society free of racial discrimination, set me up as an excellent candidate to consume science fiction's cultural products: books, television series, movies, and comics. I responded to science fiction's themes, dramas, characters, and plots because they were metaphors for my social reality. I am a charter member of that group of African American boy and girl "firsts": real-world, earthbound equivalents of astronauts who accepted the mantle of integration to represent the race in new social settings and "to boldly go where no blacks have gone before." Science fiction allowed me to fantasize what it would be like to be a daring hero unfettered by biased racialized attitudes—a hero that others could depend on, trust, respect, and love, someone willing to serve the greater good, by becoming a living example, against evil villains, war, and limitations natural and social.

Moreover, one of science fiction's basic qualities is that it offers an essentially moral universe, albeit overpopulated with machines, where right and order prevail. At the heart of these narratives is the challenge to the hero to assert the best qualities (mental/physical, conscious/unconscious, and emotional/intellectual) in just the right combination to overcome adversity. Then, too, science fiction expands on the human potential by allowing different definitions of life and culture to coexist. For a young person in the middle of a national morality play, science fiction seemed to confirm not only my drive for self-esteem but the idea that my personal drama fit into a greater moral tale in which nothing less than the nature of society would be determined as well.

As my youthful, wide-eyed fascination with being the exotic vagabond (by first being bused to school and then going away to a predominantly white college) and cultural cosmonaut, cooled with the first years of being an adult, I came to regard science fiction more cautiously. As a self-conscious college student, an active participant in civil rights protests, and extracurricular tutor for a Student Nonviolent Coordinating Committee after-school program, I began to view science fiction with increasing skepticism, because I could not find among its heroes any characters that looked like me, my family, hometown neighbors, or heroes from the civil rights movement.

Then, in the late 1960s, something novel was introduced onto the American popular culture stage when the National Broadcasting Company broadcast a new kind of science fiction program each week. The program, created by a Korean War veteran bomber pilot, who was also an ex-Los Angeles police officer, was called *Star Trek*. Suddenly, every week in millions of American homes there was a character, Lieutenant Uhura, who was clearly black and who was completely integrated into the life of her shipmates. *Star Trek* stood out and attracted my attention (beyond the casting of an attractive actress in the Lieutenant Uhura role or the fact that she wore a miniskirt) because the series displayed no apparent hesitancy in dealing with themes, plots, situations, and characters that centered on ethnicity.

What did *Star Trek* matter in the larger scheme of things? Was it just another episodic television program, only set in outer space? Whether I watched on our home black-and-white television or on the college student union color set, I sensed that *Star Trek* was more than mere escapism. For me it confirmed my hope for blacks, and other ethnic groups, of a better future world.

During this period, broadcast networks redrew their schedules in seeming deference to, or at least acknowledgment of, contemporary race politics. Network series such as *The Mod Squad, Mission: Impossible, I Spy, Hogan's Heroes, Julia, Mannix, The Bill Cosby Show, Room 222, Flip Wilson Show, Rowan and Martin's Laugh-In, McCloud, Ironside, On the Silent Force, The Young Rebels, The Young Lawyers, The Partners,* and *Sing Along with Mitch* were built around or featured a black actor among the principal cast (e.g., Clarence Williams III, Greg Morris, Bill Cosby, Ivan Dixon, Diahann Carroll, Lloyd Haynes and Denise Nicholas, Flip Wilson, Sammy Davis, Jr., Terry Carter, Abbey Lincoln, Don Mitchell, Percy Rodrigues, Louis Gossett, Jr., Judy Pace, Rupert Crosse, Leslie Uggams). In addition, other network programs, such as *Make Room for Granddaddy, All in the Family, Matt Lincoln,* and *The Mary Tyler Moore Show* featured blacks as recurring, supporting characters (Roosevelt Grier, Isabel Sanford, Sherman Hemsley, Mike Evans, and John Amos). Then, too, network series such as *Bonanza, East Side/West Side, The Bold Ones, The Name of the Game, Rawhide, The Outer Limits,* and *Wild Wild West* from time to time crafted a story line that brought a black presence into the established social setting of the show. Moreover, throughout the same period, each of the three networks' news divisions produced numerous documentary and special reports that focused a televisual eye on America's civil rights movement and related topics, like housing and employment discrimination.

Something seemed to be changing American television, allowing it to reflect on the social change taking place in American race relations. National television networks and local broadcasters seemed to acknowledge black America (albeit under pressure from civil rights groups), inaugurating community affairs programming and producing their own investigations of the local state of race matters. Broadcasters adopted a self-conscious attitude about reflecting contemporary race politics and produced some programs that presented historical facts, current sociology, and fierce, often militant analysis and emotions in an unabashed manner without any veneer of social politeness (something surprising for a medium in which careers rose or plummeted on sponsors' often swift reactions to programs their advertising supported).

Encouraged by the general discrediting of race-based discriminatory policies, television writers and producers created network shows that freely refashioned many of the central issues of race relations that were being debated in city councils and cocktail parties across America into either situation-comedy or episodic program formats. If ever there was a "golden age of television," surely the period when programming responded to a major shift in racial attitudes and laws could lay claim to the title.

I have chosen to examine one genre of television programming, science fiction, and within that genre two television series: *Star Trek*, which premiered in the mid-1960s, and *Star Trek: The Next Generation*, which premiered twenty years later in the mid-1980s. I selected *Star Trek* and *Star Trek: The Next Generation* for several reasons. Since the end of its network run, *Star Trek*, the original series, has continued to generate popular interest, in the forms of more than 400 annual conventions held in different locations around the country; an animated series; seven feature-length motion pictures; two network specials; three weekly, hour-long syndicated sequels; a comic book; action figurines; and a number of novels that feature the original, principal characters. By pairing *Star Trek* with its first, direct television descendant, I hope to make comparisons between these programs to determine how the events and attitudes of the intervening decades are reflected in the new series' stylistic changes.

Star Trek and *Star Trek: The Next Generation* are Gene Roddenberry's utopian vision of the future. In his utopia, planetary, regional, and local politics; hostilities; monetary crises; criminal behavior; mental illness; physical diseases; educational inequities; unemployment; homelessness/housing; urban renewal; religious warfare; poverty; and racial bias and prejudice purportedly do not exist. The promise of *Star Trek* and *Star Trek: The Next Generation* is a world where social problems are no longer an impediment to individual success.

Roddenberry's vision of the future coincides with the changing political and social realities of America in the 1960s. By 1961, the

nation had a new, young president who faced seemingly insur-
mountable domestic and international challenges: protests against
racially inspired murders of black citizens, civil actions in favor of
civil rights reforms, cold war tensions between American and Soviet interests and their satellite nations, economic competition between communism and capitalism, and the Soviet Union's superiority in missile technology. President Kennedy saw in some of
these problems opportunities for American renewal and publicly
urged the nation to greet these challenges with enthusiasm. Rather
than fear change, the new president urged Americans to reaffirm
the nation's pioneering spirit. Of one of the most technologically
arduous of these subjects, the missile gap, Kennedy expressed this
theme of rising to adversity by incorporating the nation's space
program as a crucial component of his administration's vision of
America's potential as "the new frontier."

During the 1960s, America's other watchword was *change*. The
nation's values of small-town social stability, religious parochial-
ism, insular family life, and white male privilege and advancement came into conflict with the emerging values of urban centers
that stressed social reform, racial tolerance, ecumenism, and responsibility and duty beyond the nuclear family. Out of this tension, self-realization (the individual's identity defined as a con-
catenation of attitudes, values, and beliefs) was reformulated as
functioning within self-selected, politically oriented, direct-action
groups. American youth were encouraged to dedicate themselves
to effect changes in society by participating in public policy
through organizations such as the political parties, Peace Corps,
and newly emerging grassroots, citizen-action group. As the second third of the twentieth century ended, American youth stood
on the threshold of a new vision of society with an explicit, outwardly directed mandate of social reform and improving ethnic
relations domestically and abroad which print, broadcast news,
and entertainment media trumpeted as the last frontier of human
understanding.

American institutions responded to the imperative for change
in race relations in different ways. For example, the United States
Armed Forces, beginning with the Korean War, was among the
first to accommodate civil rights pressure by slowly integrating its
units and, much, much later, its command structure. The federal
judiciary addressed some of the nation's race issues, such as equal

educational opportunities, by recommending a passive, timorous, and unfocused agenda for integration. Consequently, civil rights groups and allied activists shifted a portion of their attention to monitoring whether other aspects of society were deserting the old patterns of discriminatory behavior. Mass media institutions, like motion pictures and television, came under rigorous scrutiny for their employment trends and images. Unlike print media, in which the relatively lower costs of ownership allowed minority publishers to establish themselves and flourish, electronic media, in which the cost of operation and production was prohibitively high, presented a formidable barrier for minority ownership, participation, and creative expression. Rights groups focused on film and television in part because they had a record of using demeaning stereotypes and in part because their popularity gave additional weight to their social images and messages.

Since *Star Trek* first appeared on network television, the United States has undergone unprecedented social reforms in the area of race (e.g., in public housing, retail sales, fashion and cosmetics, banking, fire and public safety, publicly appointed administrative and publicly elected county, city, and state office holders, many federal agencies). In the nation's public life, there seemed no returning to the old ways of blatant discrimination. However, when the focus turns to the private sector (e.g., private housing sales, private social clubs, corporate executive echelons), resistance to racial amelioration persists.

The fact that social values do not change uniformly across all of society's institutions but at the same time are not static must present media producers with fearsome choices. This must be particularly true when one instance of a series that is being "sequeled" is regarded as the model for developing an entire media franchise (including television, film, comic books, theme park attractions, clothing, videocassettes, posters, and CD-ROMs) and when any deviation from its initial parameters may be considered a violation, at best, or breaking faith with consumers and jeopardizing any chance for obtaining future audiences/consumers, at worst. Given the media's abhorrence of tampering with success, one would suspect that further developments of *Star Trek* would jealously guard and continue its future social vision. The vastness of space's canvas of uncharted realms obviously presents producers with an ample variety of alien civilizations and situations, such as exploring cultural, class, and ethnic differences. But how far can media producers pursue themes like ethnicity, diversity, and social equality before they find themselves ahead of society? How often can they revisit these ideas without jeopardizing audience loyalty? Against society's shifts in its social agenda on culture, diversity, and ethnicity, how do *Star Trek* and *Star Trek: The Next Generation* depict their specific social contexts? Can the way race is treated by these series be detected? If any difference in attitudes toward ethnicity arises how can changes be accounted for? Implied in all these questions is a more fundamental question: What in *Star Trek's* depiction of race relation can attract, hold, and build audiences over more than twenty-five years and from one version of the series to another? Is the political environment as the nation transitioned from the Kennedy/Johnson era to the Reagan/Bush years significant in understanding *Star Trek* and *Star Trek: The Next Generation*?[2]

I have tried to describe my own particular relationship to science fiction and some of the reasons that I take it seriously. Science fiction has an established relationship with television that dates back to the founding moments of network broadcasting. In addition, throughout the more than forty years of broadcast television in the United States, approximately fifty different science fiction programs have been broadcast over America's networks and ad hoc syndication broadcast systems. Science fiction programming was there at the inauguration of the new medium and has never been off television schedules for very long. Moreover, science fiction programs could not be simply dismissed as mere escapist fare because they carry an association with the imagination, the intellect, and the development of scientific and televisual technology. Then, too, there is the fact that at its center science fiction offered a society threatened by cold war tensions a vision that there would be a future.

More than twenty years later, I return to reconsider one of the most popular programs from that period to understand the period's influence, for example, on casting decisions that resulted in ethnic, national, and gender diversity among crew members on that series and its current progeny—*Star Trek* and *Star Trek: The Next Generation*, respectively—and to reassess the ways that era's great constitutional and moral crisis and the social conflicts it set into motion shaped the fundamental creative assumptions and dynamics of these series. Another purpose in revisiting *Star Trek* and *Star Trek: The Next Generation* is to assay the contribution of these programs toward improving the sadly checkered record of the televisual representation of ethnicity. My objective throughout this current project is to determine the narrative situations and circumstances in which ethnic characters may be depicted and the cultural attitudes, values, and beliefs invested in these symbolic formulations.

Another goal is to create a space, open a dialogue, about fictional Africanist characters and their employment in dramatic material. I want to determine whether setting television series in the distant future can free them of the historical categories of racist stereotypes and the current system of misogynist, homophobic, and xenophobic truncation that has been noted in various American media products. I propose to evaluate ethnic image making in these television series against African America's unique historical and societal circumstances to further the larger project of developing multicultural environments and cultural products that appreciate the commonalities of life as experienced at the individual and societal dimensions.

I propose to investigate *Star Trek* and *Star Trek: The Next Generation* in several steps. First, in chapter 1, I examine the historical background, the social, business, creative, and cultural issues, that constituted the larger environment of American television as the nation struggled to respond to challenges from the civil rights movement for racial fairness. In chapter 2, the three broadcast networks of the 1960s are situated within American broadcasting's competitive business structure; how they face technological and creative changes, Roddenberry's vision of a future of technological and social change, and *Star Trek's* emergence from this environment are described. In chapter 3, the focus shifts to American television in the 1980s and the way technological change and audience patterns led to the off-network production of a sequel series, *Star Trek: The Next Generation.* Chapter 4 identifies the principal, recurring characters in these *Star Trek* series, their character profiles, and the relationships among them, especially as these reflect values about culture, ethnicity, or gender. Chapter 5 selects from the entire repertoire of these television series those episodes that either feature identifiably ethnic characters (black American, African, Indian, and extraterrestrial aliens) or that deal specifically with story lines that are developments of racialized themes.

Chapter 6 analyzes these episodes to elicit, or release, the symbolic codes surrounding and constituting these depictions of ethnicity from the narrative and plot that they appear in. In addition, this chapter addresses the manner in which these television series represent ethnicity both within individual episodes and across time in other episodes from both series within the sample. Chapter 7 returns to these findings to draw from them the cultural attitudes, values, and beliefs that underscore *Star Trek*'s vision of the future and the ways ethnicity functions therein.

Chapter 1

The Changing Social Context
of Broadcasting

In the 1960s, American broadcasting was a competition largely between Columbia Broadcasting System (CBS) and National Broadcasting Company (NBC) with American Broadcasting Company (ABC) playing the role of the spoiler. However, as the decade progressed, a new force was added to the normal business pressures. American broadcasting, along with other business sectors, came increasingly under the critical attention of civil rights organizations such as the National Association for the Advancement of Colored People (NAACP) and the Congress on Racial Equality (CORE). With the authority of the federal Fair Employment Act, civil rights groups gained a statutory means to bring studios, network executives, and media guilds to public account for their poor records on black employment and lack of racial sensitivity in programming content. Just as creative developments transformed the conventional forms of television during the decade, these forces from outside the industry were stimulating different, equally profound changes. These groups were aimed at nothing short of changing the face (or, rather, the complexion) of television.

For civil rights groups, there was a sense of urgency about bringing show business into rapport with the movement's moral vision. If the nation's entertainment industry, which was still mired in a tradition of negative racial stereotypes, could be enlisted on the side of social reform, then civil rights groups and African Americans might win direct and indirect benefits. Not only might African American employment in the media increase, but a commitment to improve public images of African Americans could conceivably ripple throughout entertainment venues, such as advertising, film, television, and stage production, in a multiplier effect. In this way, the entertainment industry's position of high visibility and respect could work for civil rights.[1]

Reforming minority images and increasing minority employment in the media meant gaining the support of Hollywood creative elites: writers, craft guilds, casting directors, producers, and executives. Partly because every media production begins with the written word and partly because Hollywood had a well-organized and liberal writers' union, one of the first groups that drew the attention of civil rights reformers was the Writers Guild of America/West (WGA/W).

At the heart of the issue were the biased attitudes and formulas used to depict African Americans that dated back to the earliest studio days. Unfortunately, any prospect of using the WGA/W as a wedge to improve the range of African American portrayals was undercut by the facts that before 1960, WGA/W records showed that African American membership was negligible and that throughout the 1960s the new African American members that joined WGA/W ranks never brought the total African American membership above a few percent of the full membership.[2] The downside of this situation was that there was no African American block within the WGA/W that could agitate for change. The upside was that civil rights groups could press their case by relying on moral suasion.

Nate Monaster, WGA/W president, declared that his organization should give its "allout [*sic*] support [to] virtually any demands made by CORE and NAACP."[3] Going still further, Monaster stated unequivocally, "our Guild should lead the way, I have a hunch. The Guild should flatly declare this is a conspiracy we have all been a part of, that it's a disgrace to humanity . . . that we'll do everything we can."[4] With these kinds of endorsements, civil rights reformers and African American writers might have thought they were on the threshold of a new era of acceptance in Hollywood.

As sterling as Monaster's sentiments may have been, the real impetus for the reform of African American images had to originate from something more substantial than a confession. Liberal initiatives for racial fairness were up against a media business culture that had more than fifty years' experience with managing change. Realistically, the WGA/W could contribute to reform efforts in two ways: by encouraging greater minority membership and employment of minority writers and by developing new techniques for presenting the minority experience and encouraging the training of writers in those techniques.

Unfortunately, never more than a few minority WGA/W members were working in Hollywood during the 1960s. Moreover, the likelihood of Hollywood's few African American media writers impacting minority images was severely circumscribed by the way they worked within the industry.[5] When African American writers found work in Hollywood companies, they worked mostly as freelancers. As freelance writers, minorities received fewer assignments than their white counterparts. Throughout this period minority writers were not found on studio and network staffs. It is important to realize that staff writing and story editor positions are key to developing stories, beyond the pilot, and introducing featured characters. In addition, the experiences gained in these positions are considered essential to moving on to jobs as producers and executive producers and into the executive suites of studios and independents. In an industry that ran on connections culled from these middle echelon positions, minority writers were simply outsiders.

During the 1960s, the membership of the WGA/W increased dramatically, reflecting the growth of independent film and, especially, television.[6] Writers who had sold a literary work to film or television or who wanted to try their luck in another medium came to Hollywood in search of the keys to the new media kingdom. Annual new WGA/W membership, based on their ability to obtained qualifying employment, increased by eighty writers in 1960 and reached a rate of 150 new writers by the end of that decade.[7] Nonetheless, for any given year, new African American members remained as a single-digit percentage.[8]

These new Hollywood writers needed orientation to the special techniques of writing for film and television. The guild, sensing that there was a need to introduce aspiring writers to writers who were established and had expert knowledge of Hollywood's ins and outs and the various forms of media writing, brought out its own primer in 1958 entitled *TV and Screen Writing*.[9] The guild's book took the quite logical approach of organizing its presentation of media writing according to production categories, such as novel to screenplay, the western, comedy, science fiction, factual television, and business film. However, it was silent about the American media's legacy of demeaning representations of African Americans or the way the brewing turmoil of civil rights was challenging accepted industry norms for depicting American society even as the book was being written.

In 1960, Lajos Egri, a Hungarian immigrant, revised his 1942 primer on media writing entitled *The Art of Dramatic Writing* for this new audience of writers.[10] However popular this guide may have been among Hollywood professionals for its concise reduction of dramatic writing to technique, it had little to offer writers on the central social issue of the post-world war era: race relations. In his outline, or "bone structure," of character development, Egri lists race and nationality as interchangeable terms without further definition or elaboration by politics or economics.[11]

The unhappy reality for writers in Hollywood is that producers and studios control the screenplay and teleplay development process. However enthusiastic writers may have been about redressing Monaster's media conspiracy against African Americans, they worked in an environment that allowed them little authority and no ownership over what they wrote. Writers, like Hollywood's other culture workers, were part of a production system that regarded creative talent as interchangeable commodities and reduced writing to a technical skill that did not require any special experiences or outlook.[12]

John Howard Lawson, the prize-winning writer and founding member of the Writers Guild in Hollywood, described the result of this system for the representation of African Americans when a generation before, in the late 1930s, he wrote:

> The virtual exclusion of the Negro is part of a code that prohibits the presentation of wide areas of American life: poverty cannot be shown, because it is "depressing." Workers cannot be portrayed in terms of jobs or trade-union activity, because these things suggest criticism of the *status quo*. Women are derided, to prove that their place is in the kitchen, or the bedroom.
>
> Restrictions on content necessarily impoverish the screen-structure and force reliance on meretricious social concepts and false motivations. Characters tend to become increasingly stereotyped, weak willed, emotionally unstable.[13]

The point here is that the writing process in film and television is defined not by writers but by the studio executives, television executives, and independent producers.[14] The possibility of writers weaving more varied and less stereotypical parts for African Americans into their scripts was effectively circumscribed. Within this media culture, the writer adapts established dramatic conventions to meet the tastes and expectations of the largest possible audience.[15] The writing process as defined by Hollywood is aimed at producing films and television programs for a mass audience of millions and does not affirm ethnicity or race as an area of technical expertise or special experience.

The prospects for African Americans making inroads into the behind-the-camera craft unions looked no better as the 1960s dawned. In fact, the California Department of Labor Statistics reported that employment among members of the International Alliance of Theatre and Stage Employees (IATSE) fell to 39,700 in December 1961 from 44,200 in the same month a year earlier.[16] Notwithstanding these figures, which IATSE Vice President George Flaherty referred to optimistically, the last half of 1960 was one of the union's worst on record, with no general industry corrective trend in view.[17] Two years earlier, *Daily Variety* found African Americans almost nonexistent in Hollywood production jobs. A tightening job market meant little or no improvement of this dismal situation.[18]

Expanding on the period cited by the industry journal, *Daily Variety*, Herbert Hill, national labor secretary of the NAACP, characterized the twenty-five-year record of industry negotiations over minority images and hiring since the 1940s as an "exercise in futility" with no "tangible gains."[19] Referring to a recent study, he declared that "'less than one percent' of all Hollywood craft unions were Negroes . . . that 15 IATSE shops were 'lilly-white' . . . and that ad agencies were responsible for less use of the Negro thesp [thespians] on tv . . . out of 'fear and fantasy' over potential loss of southern markets."[20] To counter Hollywood's recalcitrance, Hill announced a two-part NAACP strategy aimed at forcing industrywide improvements: "decertification proceedings" against unions and public protest demonstrations against media corporations that failed to hire minorities.[21]

Despite the cloudy economic horizon and the increased unemployment among his union, Zeal Fairbanks, IATSE international representative, claimed that the situation for African Americans was improving.[22] Going still further, Richard Walsh, IATSE president, later told *Daily Variety* that "no discrimination exists within IA ranks" and that he had "nothing to meet with the NAACP on."[23]

During the summer of 1963, following the WGA/W's dramatic concession to Hollywood discrimination against African Americans, other media organizations began to consider their own histories and whether to be publicly associated with the NAACP's position. Among the group of Hollywood professional craft unions, several local chapters balked at the NAACP's pressure tactics. One IATSE chapter, Scenic Artists Local 816, continued its opposition to integration and warned that it had no intention of waiving its long-standing requirement that applicants to apprenticeship have two to four years of art school training. Following this lead, IA Film Technicians Local 638, Cameraman's Local 659, Teamsters Local 399, and other locals questioned whether the NAACP's demands to put on minorities might constitute "featherbedding," or violate union seniority rules, or make them guilty of discriminating against white members.[24] Curtis W. Walker, secretary-treasurer of the American Federation of Guards Local 1, vowed that his union would file a grievance against any union that hired an African American in preference to a union member.[25]

Several unions objected to Hill's blanket condemnation and went on record about their chapter's integration status. Larry Kilty, business agent for Cartoonist Local 839, reported that the union local was integrated and did not discriminate. Harry Martinez, business agent for Plasterers Local 755, reported two African American members. Another integrated union was Local 724 International Hod Carriers, according to its business agent, Norval D. Jarrard. Two other business agents, Max Krug, Office Employees Local 174, and John A. Buchanan, Local 278 Janitors, went on record that their chapters were integrated.[26] IATSE Propman's Local 44 pointed out that their chapter had never barred African Americans and had been completely integrated for years.[27] By the end of the summer of 1963, two more Hollywood union locals, IA Teachers 884 and Waitress Union 639, spoke out about their minority membership and rejected the NAACP's program for change.[28] This brought the number of Hollywood locals that positioned themselves against the NAACP to ten.[29] Moreover, other television and film union locals, such as IATSE Lamp Operators Local 728, said their members felt integration was not a value that they were prepared to embrace, or that they believed adopting it as a policy would conflict with the employment prospects of their white members.[30]

Union denials were undercut by their own records. A review of the employment rolls of Grips Local 80, Electrical Workers Local 40, and Soundmen Local 695 revealed that there were no African American members among these Hollywood IASTE chapters.[31] Among the unions cited by Hill as having no African American members were Cameraman's Local 659, Cine-Technicians Local 789, Grip's Local 80, Painters Local 720, Projectionists Local 165, Propman Local 44, Script Supervisors 847, Soundmen Local 695, Story Analysts Local 854, and Costumers Local 705. Later in June 1963, Herbert Hill added Studio Projectionist 165 and Electrical Technicians 659 to the list of IATSE locals with few or no African American members.[32] Less than a month later, Hill added Script Supervisors Local 871 and Story Analysts Local 854 to the list of craft unions that were accused of having no African American members.

The IATSE position became more tenuous when twenty-seven-year-old, ex-Navy projectionist Robert McKnight became the moving party in a suit charging racial discrimination filed against IATSE Moving Picture Machine Operators Local 162 by Commissioner C. L. Dellums, vice president of the Brotherhood of Sleeping Car Porters. The suit charged IATSE with rejecting his June 1962 application for membership while accepting three whites.[33] What was significant here was the fact that while on active naval duty, McKnight trained and qualified as a projectionist. This incident pointed to the validity of NAACP claims that even when qualified African Americans applied for employment in Hollywood, they faced rejection as a matter of course.

Indeed, on 1 August 1963, James Tolbert, NAACP–Hollywood branch president, announced that IATSE Set Designers Local 847 had been targeted by his organization as the first Hollywood union to face charges of discrimination before the National Labor Relations Board. The NAACP, according to Tolbert, had filed a formal complaint on behalf of an African American whose application for membership had not been acted upon for three years.[34]

Then, in early August, IATSE Publicists Association Local 818

broke ranks with IATSE hard-liners and released a statement sig-
naling their "sympathy" with NAACP objectives and stated ". . .
that we believe that integration should be based on the basic right
of all qualified persons of any race, creed, or religion to belong to
any union." Going still further, the publicists' statement endorsed
the NAACP proposal of establishing an industry-wide committee
to supervise the transition to integration.[35]

Throughout that summer's negotiations, the NAACP consistently rejected the three main union objections to its integration
program. To the first point, that low industry employment
should exempt craft guilds from aligning themselves positively
with integration, the NAACP's leaders stated flatly that that was
not a sufficient reason. Instead, they pointed to a Texas state
court decision against Hughes Tool Company that stated that
even though not hiring, the company's proven past record of discrimination justified the imposition of precedent setting remedi-
ation: hiring African Americans preferentially. The second point
related to the diminished employment opportunities unions
faced when productions left the Hollywood area to reduce production costs. Union officials asserted that if the NAACP wanted
to make inroads into the craft professions, the organization
should speak out against these "runaway" productions. The
NAACP answered that it was not right to ask it to fight runaway
production, because African Americans to that point had no
stake in industry. Union officials' third charge was that the
NAACP's proposal to add one minority to each production crew
was a form of "featherbedding." NAACP officials replied that
unions should be very careful about making that specific charge
and countered that their proposal should rather be thought of as
a cost of doing business that comes under the heading of correcting a past mistake.[36]

During the summer of 1963 the members of the Hollywood-
NAACP branch expressed concern that conferences and negotiations might not be sufficient and began to actively consider more
public action.[37] This sentiment was expressed by Hollywood-
NAACP President James Tolbert in a letter dated 11 June to
Charles Boren, Association of Motion Picture Producers (AMPP)
executive vice president, that threatened "a massive program of
demonstrations, possible legal actions and grievance petitions."[38]
Boren responded to the possibility of direct action by saying that

his group was "particularly" anxious to cooperate.[39] Echoing Boren's sentiment, Tolbert agreed that "[t]he attention drawn to the situation has made men of goodwill more cognizant of the problem and has prompted them to act in a positive manner. . . . Still there remains a hard core of men who are not going to be swayed by the facts. They aren't going to retreat from their position if nothing more than moral pressure is applied."[40]

In that letter to Boren, Tolbert charged that film and television producers do not engage in "equitable across-the-board hiring" of African Americans. In addition to pointing out that acting, writing, directing, technicians, crafts unions, and sales departments resisted African American hiring, Tolbert called attention to the recent "poetic license" in casting white actors to play historical people of color, including Anita Ekberg as Zenobia, Gina Lollobrigida as the Queen of Persia, Elizabeth Taylor as Cleopatra, and Victor Mature as Hannibal.[41]

On the heels of this letter and the NAACP participation in a suit against IATSE Moving Picture Machine Operators Local 162, Tolbert corresponded with Boren and requested his assistance in setting up a meeting on 18 July between the NAACP and "selected representatives of the motion picture and television industries" including ad agencies.[42] Obviously, one of the objectives of such a meeting was to avoid taking this issue into the costly arena of litigation, to circumvent the prospect of costly and protracted legal action that the unions' stubbornness seemed destined to force upon the NAACP.

Before that meeting, Hollywood stars including James Whitmore, Marlon Brando, Robert Wise, Nate Monaster, and John Frankenheimer convened a meeting of the Arts Division of the American Civil Liberties Union (ACLU) on 12 July at the Beverly Hilton to present a three-point program to combat discrimination in Hollywood.[43] Their plan urged employers and employees to insist on fair employment for African Americans, to present honest and realistic images of African Americans in contemporary society, and to champion integration through "speaking, writing, singing, acting, composing and demonstrating."[44]

By mid-July, the NAACP's campaign of moral suasion seemed to be achieving positive results. It was no longer possible to dismiss its claims about unfair employment and skewed representations. Civil rights activists had gotten the attention of studio, network, and union management; increasingly the agendas of these groups was being set by the NAACP-Hollywood branch.

In response, several media executives participated in a hastily conducted survey of minority employment.[45] Harry Ackerman, Screen Gems executive producer; Basil Grillo, Bing Crosby Productions' president; Jerry Thorpe, representing Desilu Studios; Dominick Dunne, Four Star executive producer; Bob Wood, manager of broadcast standards; and unnamed ABC-TV and CBS-TV executives reported that minority hiring had been trending up for the past eighteen months to two years without NAACP pressure. These media executives credited the change to several factors, including Kennedy Administration support for civil rights, greater willingness of casting directors and producers to use minority actors as extras, and increased sensitivity of some producers to featuring minority themes and characters in dramatic situations built around civil rights issues. Tolbert joined in the spirit of appreciating these industry responses to racial fairness but understandably traced their inauguration to his organization's efforts.[46]

Ironically, at summer's end, while the NAACP was facing an uphill battle with labor unions that should logically have been its liberal allies, it seemed poised for success with film and television producers, the group of Hollywood professionals who had the reputation for being tough-minded negotiators and fiscally conservative.[47] However, not every level of media management greeted the NAACP's demands with unqualified approval. Television producers seemed rather ambivalent about integration. Although they generally backed the ideas of using African Americans in their programs and eschewed biased representations in favor of more realistic portrayals, they balked at the notion that every television program, regardless of concept or setting, should feature an African American character.[48]

Taken at face value, these optimistic projections should have translated into thousand of opportunities in studio, independent, and network television for African American actors. Unfortunately, Screen Actors Guild (SAG) statistics showed that there were only 150 to 200 African American actors among its 9,500 Hollywood members (14,000 nationwide). While employment of African Americans as extras may have increased by 100 percent during the previous six weeks, the total membership of the Screen Extras Guild (SEG) was 185. The small numbers of African American actors may be traced to the industry lack of hospitality toward minorities and its poor employment record.[49] One statement from a group of well-known producers, who are frankly remote from the work-a-day world of the actor, would hardly be enough to persuade African American actors that Hollywood had reformed.

As if to underline the need to go beyond the producers' statement, Marlon Brando suggested, at a 12 July evening meeting of the ACLU Arts Division at the Beverly Hilton, that Hollywood stars boycott any production company that maintained discriminatory hiring practices.[50] Speaking with what must have been considerable passion and prescience, Brando urged his fellow actors that "[w]e can refuse to work in a picture if the Negro is not represented in it. Somebody said it was going to be a long, hot summer. Somebody said it was going to be an incredible summer. We can do something now or let the situation get away from us and have it end tragically."[51]

Quietly, as media unions and production executives hammered out their positions on civil rights in public forums and the pages of trade papers, television advertisers pursued a far less public decision-making process on race relations. On 2 August 1963, *Daily Variety* signaled that sector of the media industry's acceptance of the inevitable when it reported that Lever Brothers, the British soap company, requested that three African Americans be planted in Art Linkletter's *House Party* audience and that one, Lena Cooper, be drawn into the commercial: a first in television history.[52] One gesture, however, does not translate into blanket reform, especially if that gesture remains unique.

A week later on 9 August, when the NAACP met with broadcasters in Hollywood, Johnny Otis, chairman of the association's television-radio committee and bandleader-drummer, blasted the industry for appreciating the existence and economic importance of the African American market, while simultaneously practicing "systematic exclusion" of minorities when it came to jobs. Otis accused sponsors and agencies of being "equally guilty of perpetuating racial discrimination in the broadcast industry."[53] Roy Wilkins, NAACP national executive secretary, told the meeting, "While there have been meetings, promises, discussions, indications of awareness of what the Negro is after, but there has also been what we believe to be deliberate confusions of the Negro's aims and goals."[54] Wilkins's comment highlighted his appreciation of the importance of advertising within the media economy and his intention not to let agencies and sponsors side-step their responsibilities.

A week later, Tolbert, president of the NAACP–Hollywood branch, announced that advertising agency executives, "the men who make the wheels go round," would be the group's next target.[55] Wilkins's assessment was confirmed by Lil Cumber's experiences as head of Hollywood's largest African American talent agency as she reported that "[a]dditional work for Negro performer stems from efforts of those 'upstairs'—the producers rather than the casting directors."[56]

If media culture was going to change, its engine, its relationship with sponsors and advertising agencies, had to be retuned. Advertising and commercials needed to face the civil rights groups' agenda and the revision of American media sociology that it implied squarely. Perhaps the experience of the advertisers and manufacturers who had successfully marketed to the African American community showed the more general advertising industry a new business opportunity that integration would allow.

Marlon Brando's prediction of summertime civil unrest that year was circumvented to some extent by the announcement of a general agreement between the NAACP and more than 100 media representatives at AMPP headquarters on 18 July.[57] The theme of the conference was the inclusion of African Americans in "virtually every television and motion picture production" and "fully integrated technical crews."[58] After a two-hour conference, Charles Boren, AMPP executive vice president, announced that an "area of agreeableness" had been established.[59] Based on this "area of agreeableness," Herbert Hill announced that the NAACP would suspend any national demonstrations and would not sponsor any boycotts against Hollywood film and television productions until enough time had passed for a determination to be made of the results of industry performance in hiring and other areas. Instead, Hill stated the focus of NAACP attention would shift to the AFL-CIO craft unions which "in terms of civil rights records are among the most backward and reactionary to be found anywhere in the U.S."[60] He offered unions the option of aggressively making affirmative efforts to recruit African Americans into apprenticeship programs to cover lost ground and to revisit the propriety of relying upon seniority lists as the sole source of employment referrals.

In a similar vein, less than two weeks later both the 2,300-member Hollywood chapter and 1,500-member New York chapter of the TV Academy went on record favoring integration of minorities into all aspects of the television business.[61] Royal Blakeman, president of the New York chapter, urged all those working in television to appreciate that "[a]s a medium which has a tremendous impact on the lives of most Americans, television should be in the vanguard in giving proper representation to all groups. . . . This applies especially to the Negro. There are in America Negro ambassadors, Negro judges, Negro doctors and Negro lawyers as well as Negro housewives and workers."[62]

By the end of August, the NAACP's position seemed to be gathering adherents and irreversible momentum. The Screen Producers Guild (SPG) joined IATSE Publicist Local 818 in endorsing the Hollywood NAACP's aims. SPG president Larry Weingarten conceded that "maybe we have been lax. In the past we haven't been too concerned with the problem." Then a few days later, George Flaherty, IATSE Projectionist Local 165 West Coast vice president, announced that several applications by African Americans were under "serious consideration" and volunteered that apprenticeship programs would soon been started.[63]

The next bit of encouragement came from Hollywood's Central Casting. According to Charles Boren, AMPP executive vice president, African American registrations with Central Casting had increased in July and August from 45 to 106 in 1963.[64] Boren related that "[t]he studios have ordered their people wherever possible to use more Negroes in motion pictures and on television."[65] Producer Robert Cohn and director John Rich's feature motion picture *The New Interns* accounted for the hiring of seventeen African American actors, including Greg Morris and Anita Poree.[66]

By mid-October, the NAACP's Hollywood negotiations and strategies produced important developments on both the studio and union fronts. Six of the major studios, Paramount Pictures, Revue, 20th Century-Fox, M-G-M, Disney, and Columbia, and the minor studio Warner Brothers pledged their cooperation with the civil rights organization's program of integration of the media industry.[67] Less than a month later, IATSE Grips Local 80 and Film Technicians Local 683 yielded. Grips Local 80 admitted five African Americans, and Film Technicians Local 683 accepted the applications of five African Americans. When these two unions accepted the NAACP's policy, only two unions, IATSE Sound-men's Local 695 and IATSE Cameramen Local 659, remained to be won over.[68]

That December the NAACP could look back over a highly public and largely effective campaign to reform Hollywood's relation to African Americans. The Joint Labor-Management Committee, launched by the AMPP in response to NAACP pressure, had been in existence for several months and was working toward improved minority employment. Hollywood's Central Casting and its talent agencies began actively representing and referring minority actors for commercials, film, and television. Otis Greene, an African American Hollywood actor, looked back over the civil rights organization's campaign with appreciation and said, "For the first time the young Negro can look to Hollywood with acting aspirations."[69] With this phase of its program gaining momentum, the NAACP turned its attention to monitoring the actual content of American television and motion pictures.[70]

From the early 1960s, groups sympathetic with civil rights began to urge the television industry to make a commitment to improving their corporate employment and entertainment development for African Americans. In 1962, for example, the committee on integration of the New York Society on Ethical Culture conducted a two-week long study of the three networks' programming.[71] Monitors divided the programming into 398 half-hour units and found African Americans absent from 309 of them. In twenty-seven of the remaining eighty-nine half-hour segments, African Americans appeared "mostly transiently as singers, dancers or musicians." The majority of the other sixty-two half-hour segments were news, discussion, or other information programs. Researchers concluded that African American participation in general television entertainment programming and children's television was "negligible and psychologically damaging."[72]

When a new federal Fair Employment Act became law on 2 July 1965, civil rights groups gained a statutory means to bring network executives and media guilds to public account for their poor records on black employment and promoting racial sensitivity in programming content. Davis Roberts, chairman of the labor industry committee of the Hollywood chapter of the NAACP, expressed "disappointment with the negligible results" that had been achieved in previous rounds of conferences with networks, studios, and independent producers on their employment practices.[73] In fact, statistics developed by the Academy of Motion Picture Arts and Sciences (AMPAS) showed that industry employment of blacks in "above-the-line" categories, defined as actors working in front of the camera, actually fell from its 1963 peak. Ironically, even when producers refrained from casting blacks in roles as menial workers, the result was white actors getting work and black actors being underemployed.[74]

Pressure on the television industry about its African American employment record continued to mount when in April 1966 the results of a special television monitoring project were announced at a press conference at the Statler Hotel in New York City. Session speakers included Henry Talbert, western regional director of the National Urban League; Eason Monroe, executive director of the ACLU; and Sy Gomberg, film writer and chairman of the ACLU's arts division. Fred Schmidt, industrial relations researcher at UCLA, prepared and presented the monitoring report on local Los Angeles broadcast programming, entitled "A Guest in The House: A Survey of Television and The American Negro."[75] The survey included musicals, dramatic, variety, news, and advertising programming. In summary, Schmidt reported that among noncommercial programming, African Americans represented less than 4 percent of the speaking roles. When nonspeaking roles were counted, African American parts amounted to almost 8.5 percent of the total. Television advertising was highlighted by the report for its very poor record: about 0.65 percent speaking and 1.30 percent nonspeaking roles.[76] Panelists warned broadcasters that if population trends pointing to at least a dozen cities becoming at least 50 percent African American within fifteen years held true, profits from television programming would increasingly be tied to racial sensitivity.[77]

However, Hollywood insiders did not necessarily respond well to this kind of pressure. For example, Herb Aller, president of the IATSE Cameramen's Local 659, rejected NAACP executive Herbert Hill's charges that Hollywood labor unions had done little to increase the presence of African Americans within their memberships.[78] Aller retorted that IATSE performance was not at issue; that the union observed its membership rules; and that once the union's seniority list is exhausted, television producers have the right to hire whomever they want.[79] Then, too, Sheldon Leonard,

independent producer behind *I Spy*, deflected criticism that his
program had not gone far enough to revise the African American
male image by saying that "the majority of tv viewers will sleep
through message programs. No matter how eloquent, no one is
going to hear us."[80]

The stakes seemed particularly high in 1965. In the previous two
years, the nation's stumbling advances on race relations suffered
staggering setbacks. Cambridge on the eastern shore of Maryland
in 1964, Watts in southern California in 1965, and other urban centers around the country erupted in conflagrations that were fueled
by frustration with the slow pace of social change. The atmosphere
of continuing violence against civil rights—such as the assassinations of Malcolm X, Andrew Goodman, James Chaney, and
Michael Schwerner, three Mississippi Freedom Summer workers,
the death of Jimmie Lee Jackson, and a racially motivated bomb-
ing campaign that saw twenty-four black churches destroyed between June and October—was brought to the consciousness of the
entire nation via television's nightly news programs.

Turmoil over civil rights not only brought the struggle for social
reform into every American home but engendered resistance. In
some cases, entertainment producers such as Gerald Puccell and
Peter Rachtman, who had mounted LeRoi Jones's plays *The Toilet*
and *The Dutchman* in Los Angeles and San Francisco, were effectively banned following the riots because the language and style
of the plays were judged too shocking in the aftermath of the Los
Angeles riots.[81] Even the Los Angeles tour of the Ringling Brothers and Barnum and Bailey Circus, which featured neither controversial language nor racial themes, suffered a $300,000 box-office
loss as audiences stayed close to home following the L.A. riots.[82]

Chapter 2

Launching *Star Trek*

By the mid-1960s, it was clear that American network television faced dramatic social, technical, and business changes. Civil rights groups' agitation highlighted the need for firm commitments on hiring minorities, at all levels, and eliminating racial stereotypes. Color television and videotape emerged from network research laboratories, where they had languished for years, to reshape the medium. Color television, though costly, promised larger audiences. Videotape offered greater flexibility in production and programming but spelled the beginning of the end of live programming. The business side of television was rocked to its core assumptions by quiz show scandals that ended sponsor- and advertising agency-developed programs that accounted for between 70 and 78 percent of American programming.[1] In addition, collusion among agencies, sponsors, and producers led to renewed FCC regulation and oversight of the industry.

Social and business issues, production technology and costs, the effects of scandal, and business and creative cycles combined to complicate American television. However, media producers knew that change was vital to their business, something to be managed and turned to profit. Failure to spot a change or trend could damage the corporate bottom line, if not spell outright disaster in television, because the competition keyed on these shifts and was prepared to risk millions on its judgments. Misreading television or its audiences could be very expensive and result in tides of red ink, too. In this climate, broadcast executives and producers revisited a program genre with a considerable history in literature, radio, and early television: science fiction. They were prepared to gamble that science fiction and the new production technologies would form a seamless match and again attract audiences, especially if it were properly produced.

Science fiction, whether in literature, radio, film, or early television drama, had proven appeal. As a genre, it is the unique speculative domain where the future of the human condition is addressed, though in romanticized and popularized form.[2] Its pedigree stretches back to writers such as Robert Louis Stevenson, Edgar Allan Poe, Mark Twain, Jules Verne, H. G. Wells, and, conceivably, as far back as James Fenimore Cooper's tales about a technologically advanced culture's clashes with the indigenous inhabitants of a distant "new world." If we consider philosophers, writers, and politicians such as Thomas Jefferson, Ralph Waldo Emerson, James Madison, and Henry David Thoreau with their interests in testing the limits of individual freedom, then the roots of this literary genre are deep in the American soil. No other literary form can boast the sheer reach of science fiction, which includes adventure fantasy, time travel, physical and psychical transmigration, occult mysticism, ecopolitics, and fantasies about the limits of political power and technology.

Whereas literary artistry and political freedom were the reactants that helped bring about science fiction, the rapid progress and dissemination of scientific research were the essential reagent. Science promised to revolutionize humanity's relation with the world. Coleridge, for example, believed that mathematics could conjure the physical and noncorporeal mysteries of existence. Galvani and Watt, Volta and Olm, Ampère, Bunsen, Morse, and Davy pried from nature such a flow of electrochemical secrets that popular opinion held that all of nature could be reduced to discernible, verifiable facts and that the most basic fact was that nature was fundamentally electrical. Herchel, Mesmer, and Maxwell linked electrical and neural phenomena. By the end of the nineteenth century, science held out the prospect that humans could understand nature's most sublime secrets. This knowledge would give humanity complete control over nature's forces, subtle and awesome. The goal: to achieve one harmonious sphere of life under direct human dominion, all for the greater glory of Christianity's God and the redemption of humanity from the fall.

The ideas of utopia and dystopia are at the center of a considerable portion of science fiction literature, motion pictures, and broadcast programs. In science fiction, humanity's long desire for maximum individual freedom is conceptualized as attainable once the creative engine of science is loosened from economic and political constraints. The background of science fiction may be traced to Enlightenment theories about government, particularly the relationship between politics and religion, and the law's role in creating and limiting the conditions that nurture individual rights and the common good and protecting the individual soul's right to commune with its god. Viewed in this way, the religious sects that fled European intolerance and braved uncharted seas to colonize the New World were this nation's common space-traveling ancestors, as were the Africans who voyaged across time and space in chains, squeezed together in the bottoms of ships surrounded by filth, sickness, and death, in fear for their lives. The persistent reemergence of experimental religious and secular utopian communities and the consistently recurring theme of social reform and personal fulfillment in this country's history suggest that America is the natural legatee of Thomas More's vision and the natural launching point for a literary genre that revisits that voyage theme and the desire for the perfect model of human harmony: God's bright shining city on the hill, the new Jerusalem.

However, a future with no nationalistic foment nor competitive markets based on scarcity no longer contains the elements many hold crucial to propelling social, not to mention literary, development. In other words, strife, on both the social and personal levels, "stirs the pot," adds the energy necessary to keep society from devolving into a steady state or entropy. In science fiction, the possibilities for dramatic conflict thus arise when the intuitive and the intellectual, the emotional and the rational, the mind and the machine compete for control in its technologically dominated societies. Therefore, at the heart of science fiction is the promise that if only troublesome human flaws were eliminated, a golden age would emerge.

The focal point of these utopian and dystopian dramas is the heroic person. Typically this is someone, or some being, whose identity is indeterminate. Heroes are suspended between the past and present, between existence as they know it with its limitations, and a fearsome unknown where self-actualization awaits. They twist and wattle. They are heroic, in part, because they are willing to forswear the comfortable markers of identity that are encrusted within social conventions as part of the established hierarchy. Instead, they forge their own sense of self by facing the unknown and testing themselves by ordeal. Their battle ribbons are the emblems of their courage. In this way, heroic characters are known by their actions and not, according to the suspect and limiting traditions of an older society, where their parents' identities or their family status in the social order outweigh personal integrity. Inheritance may supply the genetic makeup, but it is the way the specific person meets and deals with a specific challenge that defines the hero.

The example of the hero demonstrates humanity's moral vision and the potential to excel under pressure. Part of the attraction of science fiction and its heroes may be the way it presents readers with eldritch characters, fantastic phenomena, and other-worldly settings. But another part of its appeal is the ways it finds to express the resilience and triumph of the human spirit, intellectual cunning, and courage. The first action that defines the hero is, of course, his or her willingness to step outside the familiar, leave behind comforts of family and community, and roam the frontier for the affirmation of identity through moral acts. Clearly, the heroic character is idealized as the avatar of the best values of the individual and society. However, the hero's final act brings closure and is definitive, too. Therefore, the hero's return as the narrative ends is more than a simple homecoming for an errant scion. While the hero's experiences are personally transformative, they have social consequences, too. The hero does not just return to society but cuts through mere social formalities, discovers vital social truths, and is welded with them. Society, in the mythic hero tradition, is not just renewed but reformulated, reoriented, and reinvigorated.

Postwar America faced crises and opportunities both domestic and international. Every part of American society contributed to the war effort, but to enjoy the boons that victory held out meant coming to terms with vast social change, voyaging into uncharted realms. As global empires collapsed, the racial theories that created and supported them shredded. Liberation movements among the world's colored races gained encouragement and momentum. American society faced a future where its relation to the world and to significant portions of its own society was in flux. Creaters of cultural products must have recognized in science fiction an intriguing metaphor and vehicle for media productions that could be shaped to resonate in contemporary affairs for audiences.

> Space, the final frontier. These are the voyages of the starship *Enterprise* its five-year mission to explore strange new worlds, to seek out new life and new civilizations . . . to boldly go where no man has gone before.[3]

In the 1990s, this motto is familiar to television viewers around the world, but in the fall of 1966, it introduced NBC-TV's primetime audience to a new, untried, hour-long, episodic, dramatic series set aboard a futuristic spaceship. The name of the series was *Star Trek,* and the name of the starship setting was the *Enterprise,* serial number NCC-1701.[4] The *Enterprise,* the flagship of an armada under the authority of a combined-services, quasimilitary organization known as Starfleet, and its crew pursue a heroic, even Homeric mission to explore space, contact intelligent alien life forms, and expand humanoid knowledge and power. Starfleet, in turn, is an arm of the United Federation of Planets defined by those early programs as a congress of planets drawn together by the ideals of peaceful coexistence, scientific research, colonization of space, and the propagation of life and promulgation of civilization by applying advanced technology to insure survival. Moreover, Starfleet offers the galaxy's "best and brightest" the challenge of rising to their potential against the backdrop of interstellar adventure, unique opportunities for scientific research, and the excitement of contact with alien civilizations.[5]

Star Trek represented more than the usual gamble that a television network takes in launching a new program because NBC had little faith in science fiction. In the past, when science fiction had found a place on network schedules, it was largely as children's programming.[6] Now, *Star Trek* proposed to develop science fiction as a forum for contemporary themes for a grown-up audience (see figure 2.1). To break away from science fiction television's "kiddy" image and to create an appealing image for an older audience, the program's producers planned to attract some of the best science fiction writers of the day with a budget that would be bigger than

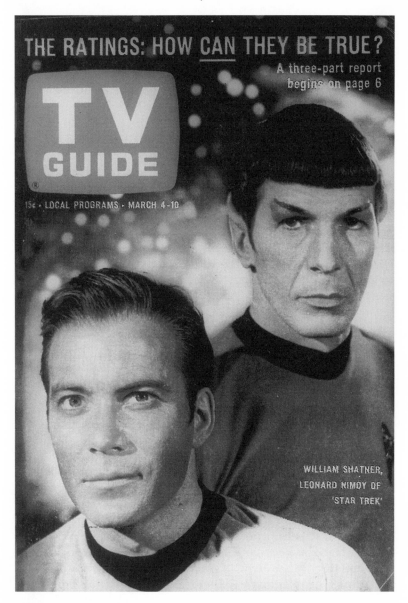

Figure 2.1: *TV Guide* marks the launch of Star Trek (March 4–10, 1967).

typical hour-long episodic programs and that would be large enough to bring their visions to televisual life.

Star Trek as utopian fiction was exemplary. In its world, science and technology enjoyed the highest official approval, economic affairs between worlds were rarely major problems, and brilliant creativity was instantly rewarded. *Star Trek* was in many ways a unique program that offered a public well informed about international conflicts and the constant threat of nuclear holocaust a vision of a hopeful future based not on nation-states and regional rivalries but multicultural cooperation and the spirit of individual excellence, attitudes spawned by the nation's recent run of successes and euphoria about its space program.

As if to signify the spirit of American technological can-do and the hope of a brighter future, *Star Trek's* production designers turned to the nation's space program as they developed the series' uniforms and central emblem: the Starfleet logo. From at least 1964, the National Aeronautics and Space Administration (NASA) emblazoned its official documents and so forth with its own logo. This logo consisted of the following three elements: the organization's name arranged in a complete circle; a starfield and two planetary bodies, graphics depicting the orbit of the smaller body; and an inverted V, the legs of which straddled the larger globe (see figure 2.2). These simple elements crystallized President Kennedy's challenge to the nation's space program: to rocket people to the moon and return them safely to Earth. As his production staff geared up for producing a pilot for the series, Roddenberry wrote Pato Gusman, chief of art direction, suggesting, "Let's give some thought to a distinctive emblem for our ship and the uniforms of our crew."[7]

Star Trek's production designers "borrowed" the inverted V symbol (perhaps symbolizing rocket flight or the pattern of compressed air that a high-speed projectile makes as it accelerates) and the circle sign for orbit. Combined, these produced the emblem for Paramount's new series.

Nearly thirty years after its premier, *Star Trek*—its theme music, the starship *Enterprise,* and its crew—is recognized by television and film audiences around the world and is now one of Paramount Pictures' most valuable trademarks and franchises. *Star Trek* remains, for millions of devotees, one of the most widely disseminated symbols popularizing space exploration and offering a hopeful vision of the future.

National Aeronautics and Space Administration
Logo from 1964

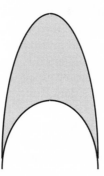

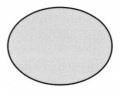

Rocket Trajectory

Orbital Ellipse

Components of NASA Logo in Starfleet logo

Figure 2.2

However, the program's first run was not universally acclaimed or successful by media industry standards.[8] Unfortunately, it was canceled during its third season, before the producers could accumulate enough episodes to satisfy the requirements of the post network syndication market.[9] *Star Trek*'s failure to find the kind of first-run, prime-time mass audience networks demand must have come as quite a surprise to the program's creator, Gene Roddenberry. Roddenberry, a television writer during the 1950s and early 1960s, envisioned his first science fiction series as an extension of one of the most popular television genres of the time, the western. Although there was no mass audience for a grown-up, prime-time television science fiction program, he hoped that audiences already familiar with the western, which had proven audience appeal, would accept his new series, which he described to network officials as a "*Wagon Train* to the stars."[10]

In this new series, Roddenberry saw the chance to engage a younger audience and to distinguish science fiction on television from prior prime-time programs such as *Captain Video and His Video Rangers* (Dumont, 1949-1955), *Space Patrol* (ABC-TV, 1951), *Tom Corbett, Space Cadet* (CBS-TV, 1950; ABC-TV, 1951-1952; NBC-TV, 1951), and *Flash Gordon* (Syndicated, 1953-1954), by producing well-written teleplays by established science fiction writers and dealing with current social issues, thinly disguised by extraterrestrial settings.

If science fiction was problematic as a television genre, American networks had already experimented with anthology series that featured the supernatural and bizarre. During America's first two decades of broadcasting, network television had already featured the anthology format, in which separate and different stories were presented to viewers each week. Science fiction, in addition to stories of the supernatural, found a home on anthology shows. Science fiction writers were able to place their stories with regularity on such programs as *Out There* (CBS-TV, 1951-1952), *Tales of Tomorrow* (ABC-TV, 1951-1953), *Science Fiction Theatre* (Syndicated, 1955-1957), *Men Into Space* (CBS-TV, 1959-1960), *Way Out* (CBS-TV, 1961), *UFO* (Syndicated, 1972), *My Favorite Martian* (CBS-TV, 1963-1966), *The Twilight Zone* (CBS-TV, 1959-1987), *The Outer Limits* (ABC-TV, 1963-1965), and *Alcoa Presents: One Step Beyond* (ABC-TV, 1959-61). Roddenberry clearly thought of *Star Trek* as a logical development of the earlier examples of this kind of program.[11] Moreover, *Star Trek* promised those writers and other established science fiction writers a forum where they could tell full-fledged science fiction tales with no apologies.

Star Trek's Network History

In fact, as new program schedules premiered in fall 1966, it became clear that the three networks and their program suppliers took the criticisms of the last few years seriously and were reformulating the way minorities were depicted on American television (see table 2.1). CBS brought to audiences an espionage thriller, in the vein of NBC's previous season hit, *I Spy*, called *Mission: Impossible* and introduced the African American actor Greg Morris as the Impossible Mission team's engineering genius.[12] On Thursday nights, ABC introduced *The Green Hornet* to counter NBC's *Batman* and in the process introduced the naturalized Chinese martial arts expert, Bruce Lee. On Friday nights, ABC rolled out its new angle on the police drama, *Hawk,* which featured a full-blooded Iroquois detective, Burt Reynolds, partnered with an African American detective, Wayne Grice. On NBC, *I Spy* returned with its mixture of hip irreverence, international intrigue, and interracial pairing of stars Robert Culp and Bill Cosby. Among its new programs, NBC premiered a revamped *Tarzan* that featured Rockne Tarkington as Tarzan's black friend and Manuel Padilla, Jr., as the Earl of Greystoke's young, orphaned Mexican buddy.

Table 2.1

Families on Television: Ethnic/Racial Composition by Decade

Decade	White %	Black %	Hispanic %	Native American %	Asian %	Other/ Mixed %	N
1950s	97	0	2	1	0	0	85
1960s	97	1	0	0	0	2	98
1970s	84	14	1	0	1	0	139
1980s	87	6	2	1	0	4	175
Total	90	6	1	<1	<1	2	497

(Source: S and R, in *Journal of Broadcast Education* 38: 456)

That season's most ambitious reformulation of televisual sociology was presented in NBC's new science fiction series, *Star Trek,* which quite self-consciously included as members of its regular cast Leonard Nimoy as an extraterrestrial Other science officer, George Takei as a Chinese-American physicist turned helmsman, and Nichelle Nichols as an African communications officer.[13]

However, *Star Trek,* as well as the other network programs with integrated casts, was launched with a sense of trepidation. In the previous season, several southern NBC affiliates refused to carry *I Spy* because it featured Culp and Cosby as interracial partners and leads.[14] The southern defection was secured by the beginning of the next season, and the show opened with a lineup of 204 stations, covering 98 percent of the nation. Unfortunately, as the networks' first drafts of their fall schedules were released, it became clear that *The Sammy Davis Jr. Show* was nowhere to be found. Just why the show was dropped was not clear. Southern broadcasters, contrary to their previous attitude, were reportedly exhilarated with the prospect of a variety show hosted by Davis, despite the fact that the show got off to a rough start because Davis had to bail out of hosting his own program for its first three shows to keep his prior commitment to ABC. This circumstance meant that he had to engage three substitute hosts: Sean Connery, Johnny Carson, and Jerry Lewis. These last-minute changes aside, Nielsen ratings for the show even with substitute hosts were better than the Friday night show it replaced. Nonetheless, at a time when African American performers were forecast to be breaking into television, *The Sammy Davis Jr. Show* vanished from NBC television.

Therefore, as *Star Trek* prepared for its maiden voyage on network television, the climate for its kind of experimentation with interracial regular cast members and themes was unsettled. The previous season's new shows raised general questions about what formulas would succeed on network broadcast television. According to the Home Testing Institute's preseason survey, the new network shows of 1965 were alike in engendering low audience appeal.[15] And, in the recent past, these new shows had not fared well. For example, of the new 1961-62 shows, 66 percent (22 of 33) were not renewed. In 1962-63, 73 percent of the new shows (19 of 26) were replaced. The rate of successful shows improved slightly in 1963-64 to 60 percent and in 1965-66 to 59 percent. The institute's survey produced a PiQ rating (an industry measure that predicted program popularity) of 11 for the 1965-66 season's new shows, which mirrored its rating of 10.6 in 1961-62 and the 10.2 in 1962-63 and predicted that at least two-thirds of the new shows would fail to find an audience.

Little direct evidence pointed to what kind of season 1966-67 would be for a series like *Star Trek*. But some information existed about how other, perhaps tangentially related, shows fared. For example, new action-adventure dramas set within the world of international espionage had disappeared from all three networks' 1965-66 program schedules.[16] Despite the continuing popularity of *Mission: Impossible,* even CBS West Coast Programming Vice President Perry Lafferty commented, "I believe the [spy] trend is going downhill."[17] The espionage genre—which had spawned programs such as *The F.B.I.* on Sunday, *Run for Your Life* on Monday, *Girl from U.N.C.L.E.* on Tuesday, *Man Who Never Was* and *I Spy* on Wednesday, *Jericho* on Thursday, *Man from U.N.C.L.E.* and *Wild, Wild West* on Friday, *Get Smart* and *Mission: Impossible* on Saturday—was being phased out because domestic ratings were lackluster and international distributors feared that cold war tensions would stymie overseas sales.[18]

In the competition for ratings, NBC and ABC determined that CBS's ratings reign could be attributed to its schedule of movies and could be counterprogrammed with western and western-like programs.[19] *Star Trek* figured as part of NBC's strategy to bring the network back into contention for Thursday night.[20] Moreover, there was speculation that the fading espionage genre might segue neatly into science fiction. As one Hollywood observer put it, "Those watching the future course of the snoop-intrigue-murder-mayhem-politico field envision new permutations in the spy form. Instead of an earth enemy, the antagonist will come from other planets."[21]

Among network watchers, CBS was generally thought to own its "first" position without any real competition from NBC or ABC. As the 1966 television season unfurled, the question around network executive suites was whether NBC would be able to open any daylight between it and ABC.[22] Although NBC could not hope to oust CBS from its position of dominance, it could hope to make a good showing, place a strong second, and garner the choicest demographics: males between eighteen and thirty-five years old.[23]

NBC's strategies for besting its rival ABC included exploiting the new technology of color television. While other hour-long episodic television programs were still shot for black-and-white broadcast, Roddenberry lobbied for *Star Trek* to be shot only in color. Two years before the program aired, he and staff art directors were figuring ways to use color effects that would add a sense of excitement and scientific accuracy to their show. In a July 1964 letter to Grant Tinker, NBC president, Roddenberry built a case for *Star Trek* being one of the network's color programs.

> Still another plus [for color photography]—the art designer and I have been puzzling over such problems as creating the illusion of the remarkable speeds necessary to the U. S. S. Enterprise. . . . One answer is suggested in the *Journal of British Interplanetary Society*, an article by Dr. I. E. Sanger, "Some Optical and Kinematical Effects in Interstellar Astronautics." . . . The point being, speeds exceeding light can be suggested by graduated changes in colorations of the ship and of space bodies ahead and behind. This, along with some appropriate new sound, could create not only an illusion of extraordinary acceleration but also give our series vessel an imagination and completely unique effect.[24]

Inaugural overnight ratings and ratings compilations for the first month of the new season seemed to bear out NBC's faith that *Star Trek* would help it secure the audience it wanted so much. As the series rolled out its first sixteen episodes, attention focused on whether it would attain and hold a 30 percent share of audience as reported in the A. C. Nielsen Company's survey of television shows. A 30 share or better would earn NBC's confidence and lead it to order additional episodes to round out the season schedule. Earning much less than a 30 share would signal trouble to network officials and might lead to the series' cancellation. First reports disclosed that the new science fiction program had captured a 19.8 rating and a 40.6 share of audience for the premiere episode. The next week the program averaged a 15.8 rating and a 30 share. Initially, *Star Trek* looked like a hit (see tables 2.2, 2.3). However, it was the next few weeks that were critical. Network executives would review the statistics from two months of the season and decide about ordering additional episodes to fill out the season.

Unfortunately, starting around the end of September of its first season, *Star Trek* began to slip in the ratings (see table 2.4).[25] Those

Table 2.2

Comparative Scores: Nielsen and Trendex[28]

Through 8 September 1966		*Episode: "Man Trap"*	
Rating Service	*Network/Program*	*Rating*	*Share*
	8:30 p.m		
Trendex-26 City	NBC/*Star Trek*	19.2	40.6
	ABC/*Tammy Grimes Show*	14.7	31.1
	CBS/*My Three Sons*	10.1	21.4
	9:00 p.m.		
	NBC/*Star Trek*	20.4	40.6
	ABC/*Bewitched*	16.5	33.3
	CBS/ Movie	10.9	21.5
Rating Service	*Network/Program*	*Rating*	*Share*
	8:30 p.m		
Nielsen-30 City	NBC/*Star Trek*	25.2	46.7
	ABC/*Tammy Grimes Show*	14.1	26.1
	CBS/*My Three Sons*	9.4	17.4
	8:45 p.m.		
	NBC/*Star Trek*	24.1	43.3
	ABC/*Tammy Grimes Show*	15.1	27.1
	CBS/*My Three Sons*	10.9	19.6
	9:00 p.m.		
	NBC/*Star Trek*	24.4	42.2
	ABC/*Bewitched*	15.8	27.6
	CBS/Movie	10.7	18.7
	9:15 p.m.		
	NBC/*Star Trek*	23.0	39.8
	ABC/*Bewitched*	17.2	29.8
	CBS/Movie	11.0	19.0

(Source: UCLA-Special Collections)

were the first indications that the program, after its excellent initial ratings, was having a problem holding its audience. If the program fell much further, it would land below the 25-share floor that was that period's cutoff point that meant certain cancellation of television programs. It was a clear warning signal to NBC of a possible downward audience trend (see table 2.5).

Table 2.3

Comparative Scores: Nielsen and Trendex[29]

Through 15 September 1966		*Episode: "Charley X"*	
Rating Service	*Network/Program*	*Rating*	*Share*
		8:30 p.m	
Trendex-26 City	NBC/*Star Trek*	19.1	35.9
	ABC/*Tammy Grimes Show*	11.9	2.4
	CBS/*My Three Sons*	19.2	36.0
		9:00 p.m.	
	NBC/*Star Trek*	12.3	22.8
	ABC/*Bewitched*	15.6	29.0
	CBS/Movie	24.0	44.6
Rating Service	*Network/Program*	*Rating*	*Share*
		8:30 p.m	
Nielsen-30 City	NBC/*Star Trek*	NA	32.0
	ABC/*Tammy Grimes Show*	NA	21.4
	CBS/*My Three Sons*	NA	33.4
		8:45 p.m.	
	NBC/*Star Trek*	NA	31.5
	ABC/*Tammy Grimes Show*	NA	20.0
	CBS/*My Three Sons*	NA	35.1
		9:00 p.m.	
	NBC/*Star Trek*	NA	29.2
	ABC/*Bewitched*	NA	25.0
	CBS/Movie	NA	36.0
		9:15 p.m.	
	NBC/*Star Trek*	NA	26.6
	ABC/*Bewitched*	NA	28.9
	CBS/Movie	NA	36.2

(Source: UCLA-Special Collections)

Audience levels are the *sine qua non* of American broadcasting following the quiz show scandals. That is, when networks relinquished their system of producing television programs under direct full corporate sponsorship, they instituted a new system that tied profits to the auctioning of advertising time within programs. Networks predict and guarantee audiences to advertisers based on

Table 2.4

Arbitron Overnight Ratings[30]

Through 15 September 1966	*"Episode: Charley X"*
Network/Program	*Rating*
	8:00 p.m.
NBC/*Star Trek*	32.0
ABC/*Tammy Grimes Show*	21.0
CBS/*My Three Sons*	34.0
	8:30 p.m.
NBC/*Star Trek*	38.0
ABC/*Bewitched*	29.0
CBS/Movie	36.0
Through 22 September 1966	*Episode:* *"Where No Man Has Gone Before"*
Network/Program	*Rating*
	8:30 p.m
NBC/*Star Trek*	32.0
ABC/*Tammy Grimes Show*	21.0
CBS/*My Three Sons*	34.0
	9:00 p.m.
NBC/*Star Trek*	28.0
ABC/*Bewitched*	30.0
CBS/Movie	33.0
Through 13 October 1966	*Episode: "Mudd's Women"*
Network/Program	*Rating*
	8:30 p.m
NBC/*Star Trek*	30.0
ABC/*The Dating Game*	24.0
CBS/*My Three Sons*	35.0
	9:00 p.m.
NBC/*Star Trek*	23.0
ABC/*Bewitched*	32.0
CBS/Movie	36.0

(Source: UCLA-Special Collections)

Table 2.5

Star Trek Ratings—Selected[27]

Through 27 October 1966	Network			
Total audience	12,350			
Household %	22.5			
Average audience	8,950			

Episode: "Miri"	8:30 p.m	8:45 p.m.	9:00 p.m.	9:15 p.m.
Share of audience %	25.4	23.1	NA	27.6
Average audience by 1/4 hr.	14.9	14.9	18.0	17.2
Total audience	11,090		15,150	
Household %	20.2		27.6	
TV households using TV	64.1	65.0	64.1	63.3

Through 3 November 1966	Network			
Total audience	13,380			
Household %	24.3			
Average audience	9,940			

Episode: "Dagger of the Mind"	8:30 p.m.	8:45 p.m.	9:00 p.m.	9:15 p.m.
Share of audience %	28.6	29.3	NA	28.1
Average audience by 1/4 hr.	18.8	18.6	17.9	17.2
Total audience	NA		NA	
Household %	NA		NA	
TV households using TV	63.7	64.2	63.2	62.0

(Source: UCLA-Special Collections)

past history of performance according to dayparts, or specific times, and a program's performance record. Performance is defined as a program's ability to deliver regularly the predicted audience or better.

Although this system may have relieved the threat of tighter federal scrunity and direct supervision of broadcasting, it meant networks had to operate in a marketplace that was vulnerable to mercurial changes in public taste. The new economics of broadcasting made networks partners with independent program producers. In this new arrangement, networks partially compensated their partners' production costs. Independents used lines of credit to make up the difference between actual costs and network compensation. In turn, networks were particularly sensitive in recovering their fees paid to producers from charges to advertisers.

American networks entered the 1966 season with high expectations. CBS determined its commercial spots were worth $45,000. NBC believed its ad spots would bring $43,000 apiece and ABC planned on receiving $40,000 per spot (see table 2.6). At these rates each network could cover its own costs (labor, administrative overhead, promotion, affiliate compensation, and news) and buy programming. Therefore, any weakness in ratings translated into an inability of a network to fulfill its contracts with sponsors and pressure on corporate earnings.

CBS's spot-buy projections not only placed the network more than $1 million ahead of NBC but could have turned ABC into the bargain network for advertisers if the third-place network's programming outperformed estimates. In this kind of situation, NBC must have felt double the pressure. It is significant, then, that despite *Star Trek* decline in viewership, NBC network executives decided to bet on the series improving its performance and extended their relationship with *Star Trek* by ordering ten more episodes for a total of twenty-six episodes.[26]

NBC's schedule featured four new shows for the season in the

Table 2.6

Comparative Projected Ad Revenue per Commercial Unit 1966-67		
ABC	*The Invaders*	$44,000
	Batman	41,000
	Voyage to the Bottom of the Sea	37,500
	Time Tunnel	32,000
	The Avengers	31,000
	The Green Hornet	27,000
NBC	*Man from U.N.C.L.E.*	51,000
	T.H.E. Cat	50,000
	Girl from U.N.C.L.E.	39,000
	Star Trek	35,000
CBS	*Wild Wild West*	39,500
	Mission: Impossible	39,500

(Source: *Variety*)

science fiction/fantasy category. This was twice as many new programs in the same category as its rival CBS's order (two new shows) and one-third smaller than ABC's new entries (six new shows) in that same category. By December 1966, NBC's combined schedule showed real gains against its competition and its decisions looked positively prescient. NBC's Grant Tinker expressed confidence about the company's overall performance and believed that the network was in the ascendance.[27] Key in this response were statistics that showed NBC with solid appeal among younger, highly desirable viewers.[28]

Unfortunately, *Star Trek* never recovered in the ratings, despite the unprecedented volume of fan support for the show's continuation, and failed to meet the television industry's standards for success.[29] *Star Trek* was canceled after its third season, before the producers could accumulate enough episodes to satisfy the typical requirements of the post-network syndication market (conventionally off-network syndication requires at least 100 individual programs for daily scheduling, so-called "stripping," and only 79 episodes were produced originally).[30]

Star Trek's failure to find the kind of first-run, prime-time mass audience networks demand must have been quite a disappointment to the program's creator, Gene Roddenberry. Although he knew about the show's poor ratings, there were other indices of popularity that Roddenberry felt should be brought into the balance. Roddenberry believed the campaign could be built around several key points, including the unofficial fanzines the show generated, the show's positive reception among selected critics and television columnists, the marketing of a *U.S.S. Enterprise* model and the fact that it was already the top-selling model kit in history, the Mr. Spock character's considerable female appeal, and the Smithsonian Institution's decision to include the show among its archives and exhibits. He also cited its demographics, its first or second rating on local stations, and the interest of hospitals and medical researchers in the show's vision of future medical technology as implying a larger and more desirable audience for *Star Trek* than ratings actually revealed.[31] He believed in his creation. Nevertheless, the decision to cancel *Star Trek* was implemented based on its dismal ratings, high production costs, and poor performance in domestic commercial spot sales (NBC's fees were at least $10,000 less than its budgeted minimum) and foreign per-episode sales (in the international marketplace, *Mission: Impossible* earned $33,000, *Mannix* brought in $28,500, and *Star Trek* returned only $23,500).[32]

Charting a New Course

Television sociology, behind and in front of the camera, changed forever as a result of the civil rights movement's successes in lobbying the media industry and in prodding the nation to dismantle segregation. Before this point, African Americans appeared on television in the background of urban settings as atmospheric details, as functionaries (i.e., any of various categories of servants), or as entertainers (e.g., boxers, singers, and comedians). In the case of *Amos 'n Andy,* the roles created for radio by Jewish dialect comedians Freeman Gosden and Charles Correll presented a skewed and minstrel-derived image of African Americans for whites' viewing pleasure.

However, by the mid-1960s, American television's treatment of African Americans began to liberalize. African Americans began to appear in featured roles on westerns, as regular recurring characters in urban dramas, and as entertainers with entire shows built around them. In fact, American television networks made hiring African Americans and fair employment practices an explicit, stated policy that independent program producers were expected to follow. For example, once NBC had come to terms about *Star Trek* joining its fall 1966 broadcast schedule, Mort Werner, NBC vice president for programs and talent, advised Roddenberry that the network had a "long-standing policy of non-discrimination" and that as new members of the "network family," they were seriously expected to adopt this attitude toward minority hiring as well. Werner pointed out that one in eight U.S. citizens were nonwhites, and

> Our efforts to assure that the programs broadcast on our facilities are a natural reflection of the role of minorities in American life have met with substantial success. . . . NBC's employment policy has long dictated that there can be no discrimination because of race, creed, or religion or national origin and this applies in all our operations. . . . In addition, since we are mindful of our vast audience and the extent to which television influences taste and attitude, we are not only ancious [*sic*], but determined that members of minority groups be treated in a manner consistent with their role in society. . . . While this applies to all racial minorities, obviously the principal reference is to the casting

and depiction of Negroes. . . . Our purpose is to assure that our medium, and within permissive framework of dramatic license we present a reasonable reflection of contemporary society. . . . We urge producers to cast Negroes, subject to their availability and competence as performers, as people who are an integral segment of the population, as well as in those roles where the fact of their minority status is of significance. An earnest attempt has been made to see that their presence contributed to an honest and natural reflection of places, situations, and events and we desire to intensify and extend this effort.[33]

Werner suggested that Roddenberry refer to other NBC programs, such as *I Spy*, *The Andy Williams Show*, *The Man from U. N. C. L. E.*, and *Run for Your Life*, as exemplars of implementing network policy.[34]

Star Trek's most distinguishing feature was its willingness to reflect at the heart of the series concept the social change that the civil rights movement fostered during the 1960s and that NBC embraced.[35] It stood out among other American television programs because of its willingness to tackle the contemporary civil rights movement's controversial destabilization of segregation's prescriptive code of public behavior for whites and blacks and the realignment of relations between whites and blacks, men and women it implied.[36] The program's casting was, perhaps, the most obvious place where this self-consciousness about race was expressed.[37] Originally, the *U.S.S. Enterprise*'s executive officer, next in command in the absence of the captain, was supposed not to be another white male but a woman of color.[38] Here Roddenberry describes his original conception of the *U.S.S. Enterprise*'s executive officer:

> "Number One." The Executive Officer. Never referred to as anything but "Number One," this officer is female. Almost mysteriously female, in fact—slim and dark in a Nile Valley way, age uncertain, one of those women who will always look the same between years twenty and fifty. An extraordinarily efficient officer, "Number One" enjoys playing it expressionless, cool—is probably Robert April's [the captain's name initially] superior in detailed knowledge of the equipment, departments, and personnel aboard the vessel. When Captain April leaves the craft, "Number One" moves up to Acting Commander. [39]

Moreover, as shown in the series second pilot, "Where No Man Has Gone Before,"[40] the series' recurring cast, the ship's command staff (known as the bridge crew plus the chief engineer and chief medical officer), was formulated to reflect a new kind of television sociology, one based on multicultural diversity.[41] *Star Trek* was Roddenberry's platform for examining contemporary social ills and formulating solutions implemented by an ethnically diverse crew.[42] The *Enterprise* bridge crew in its first season included a white, male captain from America (James T. Kirk), a male Japanese navigator (Sulu), a male Russian helmsman (Chekov), a male extraterrestrial (Vulcan) science officer (Mr. Spock), a male Scottish chief engineer (Scotty), a Southern, white male American chief medical officer (McCoy), and a female African communications officer (Uhura).[43] With this kind of cast of regular characters with their various backgrounds, *Star Trek* was presenting its audience with a kind of United Nations in space.[44] And like the United Nations, the series fostered an image of cooperation among the ship's crew and an unswerving belief in utopian ideals.[45]

From conception to realization as a network series, however, the intent to break new ground on race and gender with *Star Trek's* cast met strong resistance. For example, the notion of "Number One," the ship's executive officer and the captain's confidant, as a black female never got off the page. By the time Desilu Productions/Paramount agreed to partner with Roddenberry to develop a pilot, "Number One" was rewritten as a white female. The pilot, "The Cage," piqued NBC's curiosity, but with two reservations. First, NBC asked Roddenberry to craft a second pilot, a very unusual second chance, that would put less emphasis on the "cerebral" and more emphasis on action. Second, NBC objected to two characters, the female executive officer and the Vulcan, and strongly urged Roddenberry to drop both of them in the next pilot. With the prospect of a network deal in the balance, Roddenberry compromised again. The role of the white female executive officer was eliminated, and the actress who played her, Majel Barrett, was reassigned to play a new character, Nurse Chapel, a member of the ship's medical team, in the second pilot, "Where No Man Has Gone Before." Therefore, *Star Trek* would not advance an image of female equality at the crucial command and control level. On the other point, the alien Other, Roddenberry held his ground and eventually won the network's grudging approval for this character.

The inclusion of an alien Other as a continuing cast member is both curious and laudable. On the one hand, to get NBC's approval for the series Roddenberry ceded to the network's objection and dropped the idea of having a female in a position of authority and command over male crewmates. On the other, it may be considered something of a positive development in that it brought a member of a different culture (although fictional) into a position of power and respect. Actually, the character Mr. Spock was based in part on key qualities of the earlier female Number One.[46] In justifying his choice to keep Spock, Roddenberry claimed, "Spock helps keep our broad space potential alive for us. We have found his unusual look and logical computer mind serve remarkably well as counterpoint to our very human starship captain, Bill Shatner."

Nowhere, however, was Roddenberry's sensitive approach to casting more clearly and visibly expressed than in the character of Uhura. Uhura, one of the ship's senior officers, was unmistakably featured as a competent African complement to the other officers and as a female officer whose technical expertise as communications officer functioned as the crew's lifeline to the United Federation of Planets and Starfleet. Roddenberry may have been forced to relinquish his original and untried *dramatis personae*, the African female Number One, but he preserved her defining qualities— race and intelligence—and used them to create two ethnic characters: one an alien, the other a Terran.[47]

That decision, perhaps more than any other, locked race and ethnicity in as recurring series themes. It implied the need to go beyond hackneyed, dualistic racial stereotypes and to develop treatments of these subjects that appreciated nuance and ambiguity. Roddenberry may have felt somewhat disappointed about being forced to adapt his ideas to network arguments. Nevertheless, he made sure that in any agreement to change the casting, he got out of the deal more than he gave away. That is, he may have lost out on his vision of the original cast, but (and here he had NBC's own fair employment policy on his side) he made certain that race and ethnicity were inextricably woven into the series.

However, the program's commitment to treating social issues was not limited to its casting, but extended to the series' teleplays as well. Freed from the melodramatic formulas of past science fiction television, Roddenberry steered his writers towards creating dramas that often focused on racial issues and explored their moral, political, and social consequences with dimensionality and maturity.[48]

Throughout its three network seasons, *Star Trek* focused approximately one in every three programs, at least at the level of a subplot and often for an entire episode, on ethnicity (Terran or extraterrestrial) or race relations issues (many of which felt as if they were torn from journalism's coverage of the civil rights struggle domestically and internationally). In "Balance of Terror" (airdate: 15 December 1966, episode 9), viewers are introduced to a mysterious and militarily aggressive race known as Romulans whose technology rivals the Federation's but who are regarded with suspicion and racial animus. "The Conscience of the King" (airdate: 8 December 1966, episode 13) brings Captain Kirk's tragic past alive as a series of unexplained murders revive memories of Kodos the Executioner, colony governor who during a famine divided the population into survivors and those to die, after the pattern of the Nazis camps. Kirk and Spock discover a new form of life in "The Devil in the Dark" (airdate: 9 March 1967, episode 26), establish communications, and learn that as different as life-forms seem, there is more in common that connects all life. The *Enterprise* tries to intercede between the apparently primitive Organians and the Klingon Empire in "Errand of Mercy" (airdate: 23 March 1967, episode 27), only to find out that this alien society is far from incapable of taking care of itself. While on a mission with Federation Ambassador Nancy Hedford, Kirk, Spock, and McCoy find Zefram Cochrane, inventor of warp drive, alive on a small world with an energy being that he does not know loves him deeply.

Spock, driven by an irrepressible mating instinct, returns to Vulcan and audiences get a look at alien culture, its beliefs and customs in "Amok Time," (airdate: 15 September 1967, episode 34). "Journey to Babel" (airdate: 17 November 1967, episode 44) explores the relationship between alien father and son (Sarek and Spock) and his father's biases toward Terrans. Deep in space, the *Enterprise* discovers two Earth-like planets and is drawn into an ongoing biological war between the tattered remnants of Asian and Caucasian armies. Captain Kirk falls under the biochemical "spell" of the beautiful Dohlman of Elas (played by Asian actor France Nuyen), loses his head, and risks losing his ship in "Elaan of Troyius" (airdate: 20 December 1968, episode 57).

On a mission to save an idyllic world and its inhabitants, who resemble first Americans of the Great Plains, Kirk loses his memory and begins a new life complete with a wife pregnant with his child in "The Paradise Syndrome" (airdate: 4 October 1968, episode 58). In "The *Enterprise* Incident" (airdate: 27 September 1968, episode 59), Kirk and Spock conspire to steal Romulan technology, only to have a love affair blossom between Spock and the beautiful Romulan commander, a member of a related alien species that he must betray. Kollos, ambassador from a species so horribibly ugly that looking directly at them causes insanity, and Dr. Miranda Jones, a blind Terran and Federation escort, fall in love. Klingon and Federation crews have to overcome their xenophobic attitudes about each other to defeat an invading, malevolent life-form that feeds off of racial hatred in "Day of the Dove" (airdate: 1 November 1968, episode 66).

The episode "Let That Be Your Last Battlefield" (airdate: 10 January 1969, episode 70) dealt explicitly with racism and wrestled with the means individuals and groups subjected to exploitation and discrimination could use to achieve freedom and equality.[49] "Patterns of Force" (airdate: 16 February 1968, episode 52) examined the rise of Nazism as a metaphor for what arises when one culture of technological superiority interferes with another, thereby transplanting racism and genocide into that world.[50] "Plato's Stepchildren" (airdate: 22 November 1968, episode 67) created a situation in which the bridge crew were captives of an Olympian race. While separated from the responsibilities of the *Enterprise*, Kirk and Spock are manipulated by the telekinetic powers of the planet's inhabitants into romantic tableaux. In this way, the interracial romantic potentials between several of the *Enterprise*'s officers, Captain Kirk and Lieutenant Uhura, and Mr. Spock and Nurse Chapel, are revealed.[51] "Space Seed" (airdate: 16 February 1967, episode 24) brings twenty-third century astronauts into contact with space travelers aboard a derelict spaceship who are survivors of nuclear holocaust at the end of the twentieth century. The *Enterprise* crew rescues these twentieth-century astronauts only to discover that they are the products of a eugenics program to improve humanity's physical and mental capacities and to create a superior race (this is, of course, Aryan race theory that continues to pollute much of western culture). "The Ultimate Computer" (airdate: 8 March 1968, episode 53) introduced audiences to Dr. Daystrom, the African American scientist and inventor of duotronics, the revolution in electronics that makes deep-space travel and exploration possible, and to the concept of total automation and its possible consequence for the human spirit and labor. "The Cloud Minders" (airdate: 28 February 1969, episode 74) envisioned a world where the intellectual sophistication of urbanites is bought at the price of condemning generation after generation of people to back-breaking labor as miners and where a formalized system of social codes was employed to police and maintain that relationship.[52]

With this kind of ambitious agenda of consciousness-raising about race,[53] it is small wonder that no less a public figure and leader of the post-*Brown v. Board of Education* civil rights movement than Dr. Martin Luther King, Jr., praised *Star Trek* and expressed his particular approval of Nichelle Nichols's character, Uhura. As Nichols recalled, Dr. King considered her character to be emblematic of the presence of African Americans in the future; that her character was depicted as a productive contributor to her shipboard society's well-being was not lost on him.[54]

Behind *Star Trek*'s cast and narrative treatments there is, as there is with any program's development, the intention to shape a dramatic context that resonates with social conditions and to which an audience can comfortably relate. By creating a new kind of cast for a continuing dramatic series, a kind of United Nations in space, Roddenberry hoped to add a younger audience—raised in the shadow of the U.S. space program, liberally inclined toward U.S. foreign policy overtures, such as the Peace Corps, foreign aid, and the "good neighbor policy," and who were now in college but who had grown up watching *Bonanza, The Virginian, The Rifleman, The Bounty Hunter, Branded,* and *Wagon Train*—to the older proven audience of the western. Moreover, each of the individual episodes expressed an optimism about the solubility of social problems that appealed to a youthful generation, many of whom had marched in civil rights demonstrations or who, as many more could afford to do, openly denounced segregation and advocated a new equality that allowed all individuals irrespective of race to make unfettered contributions to society and, in turn, to expect society's positive reception of African Americans.

An Ambiguous Ending

All of these efforts to craft a topical series—one that was sensitive and responsive to the decade's civil rights struggle and visualized a society that survived these problems to become utopian, once politically or economically motivated restrictions had been eliminated, a place where everyone could find fulfillment—did not go unappreciated by the series' viewers or subsequent devotees. As proof of the viability of this vision and its continuing positive reception by previous and new audiences, six feature-length motion pictures about the series characters also have been produced, earning more than $1 billion at the box office, and three more broadcast television series, called *Star Trek: The Next Generation, Star Trek: Deep Space Nine,* and *Star Trek: Voyager* have been offered directly to nonnetwork syndication, ensuring that the Star Trek franchise will be one of the most profitable in television history.[55]

Star Trek failed on network television. It was able, however, to transition to local syndication, where its popularity continued to grow and transform it into a perennial favorite.[56] Moreover, *Star Trek* left a imprint on network broadcast television. Over the next eighteen years, science fiction programs never ceased to be a key part of each of the three networks' schedules. ABC television, for example, broadcast *Land of the Giants* (1968-1970), *Journey to the Unknown* (1968-1969), *The Sixth Sense* (1972), *The Six Million Dollar Man* (1974-1978), *Kolchak: The Night Stalker* (1974-1975), *Battlestar Galactica* (1978-1980), and *Lazarus Syndrome* (1979). NBC's schedule included *Night Gallery* (1970-1973), *The Invisible Man* (1975-1976), *Man From Atlantis* (1977-1978), *Project U.F.O.* (1978-1979), *Buck Rogers in the 25th Century* (1979-1981), *V* (1984-1985), *Amazing Stories* (1985-1987), and *The Bionic Woman,* which began at ABC in 1977 and moved to NBC for 1978. CBS's network program development, notwithstanding the network's long commitment to an older, upscale demographic, brought viewers shows such as *Planet of the Apes* (1974), *The New Adventures of Wonder Woman* (1976-1979), *Incredible Hulk* (1978-1982), and *Twilight Zone* (1985-1987).

Chapter 3

Change beyond Television

Each fall when American television networks publish their broadcast schedules, they are participating in a ritual that gives an impression of stability and predictability. Regular ceremonies, like the announcement of network program slates, belie the frenetic pace of a media industry that is in constant, creative motion in so many directions: analysis of existing programs' ratings, commissioning of new pilot programs, development, production, post-production, marketing, and advertising. Not only does the ritualized fall premiere create a smooth transition from one program season to the next, but its familiarity encourages a feeling of comfort that one could never get from the fluid and often contradictory domestic and international relations of a complex society like America. Indeed, during the period between *Star Trek* and *Star Trek: The Next Generation*, the nation was rocked by domestic and international turmoil and unsettling change.

Domestically, America went through a series of social protests, legislated social reforms, assassinations, economic uncertainty, and a presidential resignation that tested the nation's resiliency and moral fiber. Divided over the war in Vietnam and the civil rights movement, at times America seemed to be the nation of youthful rebels against grown-up leaders. Under the leadership and pressure of President Lyndon Johnson, Congress passed a series of civil rights measures of historic proportions. Federal legislation guaranteeing voting rights, equal housing and accommodation, and equal opportunity in employment raised the hopes of

African Americans that a future society would include them, not treat them with suspicion and contempt. Those hopes, however, dimmed as Dr. Martin Luther King, Jr., Robert Kennedy, and Medgar Evers were assassinated.

For the next fifteen years, the nation seemed to turn away from the previous era's agenda of social reform. Three of the next four presidents were Republicans—Richard Nixon, Gerald Ford, and Ronald Reagan—and their administrations made no significant attempts to advance the cause of civil rights or equality between the races. Reagan's administration, in fact, actively supported efforts to roll back and dissipate African Americans' prospects for integration into the general society. Challenges were mounted against school busing programs; affirmative action in employment and education; and federal, state, and municipal contract set-aside programs for minorities. Under a philosophy of deregulation, African Americans watched as government enforcement of desegregation withered. Recoiling from any association with past injustice to African Americans, these administrations promoted nostalgic themes about traditional values and social policies that ignored this country's legacy of racialized customs and laws. By the mid-1980s, the nation's emphasis had been shifted away from domestic issues and toward international relations and contesting communism.

During the 1980s, the United States' principal international rival, the Union of Soviet Socialist Republics, experienced unprecedented change leading up to the collapse of its central government. The speed of change may be illustrated by the fact that between 1980 and 1985, three Soviet presidents died in office: Leonid I. Brezhnev on 10 November 1982; Yuri V. Andropov on 9 February 1984; and Konstantin U. Chernenko on 10 March 1985. However, it was the next Soviet president, Mikhail Gorbachev, who personified change by leading the nation away from a command-and-control economy based on Communist Party rule and toward decentralization and Soviet-styled democratic reforms. As important, Gorbachev met with American President Ronald Reagan in Washington on 8 December 1987, and finalized arrangements for the dismantling of all 1,752 U.S. and 859 Soviet missiles with a range between 3,000 and 4,000 miles. These kinds of initiatives began the thaw in the bilateral relations of these cold war enemies and heralded an era of greater cooperation and peaceful coexistence.

With enmity ebbing, the old adversaries retreated from the politics of confrontation and entered the early stages of the normalization of bilateral relations. The United States, without the pressure of constant criticism from and comparison with a rival economic power, was free to redefine its politics and image. U.S. politicians were quick to assert that the Soviet Union's initiative translated into a concession of ideological, economic, and technological defeat. The United States in the post-cold war era has hastened to realign its image in the international and domestic spheres as being governed by the tenets of the free-marketplace. Characterization as a free-market nation meant an emphasis on expanded opportunities for entrepreneurial activity, established businesses, and multinational enterprises. In such an atmosphere, the previous generation's interest in fairness, equal opportunity, and diversity came to be seen not only as counterproductive (adding what were considered unnecessary and expensive burdens on business and inhibiting productivity) but as undemocratic (defined as anything that challenged the existing economic and political institutions that support the financial and social organization of society).

Minority Employment in the Media Through the 1980s

The 1968 election of Richard M. Nixon as president of the United States marked the beginning of the end of the federal government's role in developing minority employment policies and pressuring, even if only gently at times, film studios, independent producers, and network and local broadcasters about affirmative action hiring. This change in attitude, however, may be traced to the series of urban riots that raged across the country from 1964 to 1968. These massive civil disturbances effectively cooled off white America's willingness to press forward with civil rights reforms. Nixon responded to this shift in the national mood toward civil rights, and the displeasure with mounting Vietnam War protests, by making a rejection of dissent central to his presidential campaign. Within the Republican Party doubt surfaced about Nixon's toughness in the face of these kinds of pressures. In fact, during the Republicans' quadrennial convention in Miami, Ronald Reagan made a nearly successful run against Nixon for the party's nomination. To solidify his position, Nixon, in a series of meetings with southern delegations, presented a go-slow approach on race matters. This became known as Nixon's "Southern strategy," and with it in place he won the presidency with the smallest percentage of African American votes in the history of the group's enfranchisement.

However, Nixon's politician's ego would not allow him to concede that the entire black electorate was forever lost to him.[1] Nevertheless, Nixon the candidate and Nixon the president exploited the public's resentment of black gains and civil rights leaders' constant rhetorical polemics to shore up his political base.[2] His administration was bookended by two policies on race: not imposing desegregation on the South and not forcing integration on the North. In short, Nixon saw no future for the politics of integration.

The liberal mood of the American establishment and the political strategies of advisors like Patrick Moynihan encouraged Nixon to make well-crafted gestures toward racial equality such as the Family Assistance Plan, continuing the Office of Economic Opportunity, programs for subsidized housing, revenue sharing and block grants for cities, increased welfare payments, and expansion of the food stamps program. In Nixon's first administration Model Cities, Southern school-desegregation cases, and numerical goals for affirmative action were all pushed forward.

In his second term, Nixon, constrained from running again by the Constitution, dropped his calculations and maneuvering among minorities and special interest groups. The impact of being freed from the political fray on racial programs was direct and fateful. For example, the Family Assistance Plan, perhaps the hallmark of his first administration, was designed to reform federal antipoverty programs. As such, it did not focus on race as the only criterion for federal assistance but rather attacked a thicket of federal income-support programs that ignored the social consequence of these race-based policies (e.g., regulating the presence of males in the homes of single mothers on assistance). In Nixon's second administration it was sharpened into a strategy to halt black migration to the cities, and as a means to shift from welfare for single mothers to federal support through the tax code for intact families. In his second term, Nixon had no cause to maintain even the semblance of a liberal stance; programs such as Model Cities, Office of Economic Opportunity, and several other Great Society programs were dumped.

Eight years of Republicans, from Nixon to Ford, had the effect of withering existing affirmative action programs and undercutting the public support that was so broadly felt little more than a decade before. Even the election to the White House of a Democrat, Jimmy Carter, in 1976 could not reverse this trend. President Carter may have personally supported affirmative action, may have even been interested in the issue of expanding minority and female hiring in the media, but no new initiatives were announced or enacted during his administration. Carter seemed to emerge onto the political landscape from nowhere and was as close as Americans are likely to come to picking a president from the phone book.

Carters' plain, rural Southern background was both an advantage and an obstacle. His political career was formed in the post-civil rights era South, where the Democratic Party dominated. The dominance of the Democrats in Georgia eliminated the contention, maneuvering, and nuance that characterize two-party races. His campaign enjoyed the luxury of focusing on moral ideology and virtually ignored political ideology. For a nation growing increasingly cynical after Nixon's crimes and Ford's pardon of Nixon, Carter's promise of a new standard of moral leadership was a welcome change. Lacking any intraparty or Republican challengers freed Carter to concentrate on his outsider message and image, but it also meant that he never built relationships among the various factions of the Democratic Party. Carter tried to turn this situation into a positive by vowing not to becoming a prisoner of pressure and special interest groups. But what it really meant was that his candidacy and administration paralleled the nation's shift in mood about race and the nation's continuing responsibilities to right past wrongs.

To put it another way, Carter's candidacy was the agent of the destruction of George Wallace and the Southern wing of the Democratic Party, and his presidency was probably the last direct political effect of the Civil War. Ironically, given this context and Carter's obviously personal ease around African Americans and lack of reluctance about appointing blacks to posts within his administration and being photographed with prominent African Americans, his moral ideology precluded him from forming alliances among urban, female, and racial groups that could have served as a foundation for embracing the nation's diversity and championing affirmative action. Instead, the success of Carter's campaign against Washington "insiders," his administration's inattention to nontechnical domestic issues, and his failure to develop a political ideology for addressing social problems led directly to the nation's shunning the hard work of building a consensus on race, gender, and the cities and to the emergence of a challenger to Carter's bid for a second term who embraced consensus-building around political ideology; rejected pro-black Constitution amendments, and federal statutes, policies, and programs that established and advocated a broad definition of equality; and posed as the ultimate "outsider": Ronald Wilson Reagan.[3]

By the 1980 presidential election, attacks on affirmative action as a federal policy and federally sponsored goal successfully challenged several specific interpretations and implementations of the policy and led the Republicans to adopt a strong antiaffirmative action position as a national party platform plank. Ronald Reagan's election as the nation's fortieth president meant that affirmative action was less universally espoused as a national value than it had been fifteen years before and that it would come under broad attack from white males who believed the policy injured their professional careers and businesses.

Without strong proddings and the constant threat of legal suits and fines from Washington, affirmative action was severely wounded. With a president whose hostility to affirmative action was open and who encouraged lawsuits to dismantle it in principle and fact, affirmative action declined throughout the 1980s. The absence of any clear supportive signals or positive guidelines for implementing policy from Washington and the nation's chief executive's denial of any race- or gender-based inequities in American society gave many leaders in the public and private sectors permission to abandon affirmative action and reduced the commitment of others to the level of timid caution.

For example, by the 1980s the media industry's affirmative action initiatives, to the extent that they existed at all, were either broadly cast or the result of an individual's commitment. For example, nearly every one of the major studios had created their own version of an in-house program for identifying and developing young talent. A studio, such as Disney, might define its program to emphasize training for screenwriters and animators. Others, with less specific needs, created more general training and development programs. While the origins of these programs date from the late 1960s when civil rights groups and trade union reformers brought the Hollywood establishment up short for their hiring practices toward minorities and women, by the mid-1980s young white males and females flocked to and overwhelmingly benefited from these programs.

Bill Cosby's efforts to bring young minority people into Columbia Pictures was exemplary of the impact of an earnest individual with professional clout. Cosby had neither the time nor inclination to mentor the trainees, nor did he possess the familiarity with the technical community that would have opened the way for new bonds of friendship and sharing to grow from the seeds he sought to plant. Perhaps the pedagogical role that he had carved out for himself was too large for one man, even a "triple-threat" superstar (recordings, television, and advertisements), to fill. Not even his famous charm and professorial manner could overcome the odds against so tremendous a project: bringing uninitiated young minority men and women into the intense personality- and relationship-driven culture of Hollywood media.

The Federal Communications Commission (FCC), which is the federal agency that oversees broadcast media public policy and technical standards, had since the 1960s repeatedly faced pressure to reshape its guidelines to foster greater minority participation in all the aspects of media business that came under its purview. Civil rights activists argued, for example, that if the federal government was going to weigh in on the side of integration and affirmatively intervene to improve the condition of minorities in American society with legislation and programs, the FCC's role should be to stimulate greater minority participation at all levels of broadcasting. However, Reagan administration officials rejected any obligation to carry on race reforms and used deregulation, the philosophy of eliminating government's legal watchdog relationship to business, to authorize backing off the FCC's licensing preference for women and minorities begun in 1974 and its other programs monitoring how minorities fared in the media industry.

The nation's economy in the 1980s did nothing to help matters. Many businesses complained that following affirmative action guidelines was an expensive employment program that carried the added burden of training and resulted in a competitive disadvantage.

In the mid-1980s, the general economic outlook was mixed: housing starts, interest rates, and the dollar were down, and unemployment edged up. After the stock market crash of 1987, confidence in the American economy was deeply depressed, and prospects for strengthening affirmative action programs in the media dimmed. Tensions between minority and sympathetic FCC commissioners and conservative commissioners grew until Zora Brown, assistant director of FCC's minority enterprise program, resigned after the agency reversed its long-standing program of giving preferential consideration to minority applicants for broadcast licenses.[4]

Evidence that affirmative racial reform was in retreat could also be found in the employment and development records of the film studios and television networks. For example, SAG surveyed its membership and reported that despite the fact that all minorities comprised more than 20 percent of the population, actors of color constituted less than 10 percent of the leading roles in film, television, and commercials. Ironically, the only area of improvement for actors of color was in roles as criminals and prostitutes.[5] The report continued to point out that "on the eight current American Federation of Television and Radio Artists (AFTRA) soaps, only 10 blacks are engaged as contract performers. . . . Statistics indicate that the employment of minority news announcers is at a virtual standstill and, in some cases, past gains are being eroded."[6] Moreover, the report noted the FCC "has proposed new rules which would relax Equal Employment Opportunity reporting requirements, hastening the erosion of past gains."[7]

Behind this change in political perspective on race and media lay another reality: media as big business. During the 1980s, the advent of high-risk, leverage bonds precipitated the systematic transfer of key elements of the broadcast industry from their original owner/operators to owner/investors. By the end of the decade, all three major television networks were bought by other parties and would be run by lawyers or professional managers, not by their founding entrepreneurs. The huge amounts of money that these sales required created staggering debts and punishing repayment schedules that forced network managements to focus relentlessly on billings, expenditures, and the television marketplace. For minorities, this fixation on the bottom line, whether corporations were desperately trying to service their debt or loading up with obligations to ward off any future hostile takeover possibility, meant that networks were no longer in the mood or perceiving themselves to be in the financial position to take chances on assisting minorities. John Oxendine, president of Broadcap, an industry capitalization fund, summarized the situation when he said, "[F]or various reasons, those who were once philosophically attuned have stopped aiding minorities."[8]

Industry Changes and
Star Trek: The Next Generation Adapts

Television program schedules can give the false impression that little changes in broadcasting because they tend not to change much from year to year. Despite the apparent consistency of network schedules, broadcast network television was facing a period of significant business and technological change as it entered its fourth decade. In the mid-1980s, something extraordinary occurred in American broadcasting. Between 1985 and 1986, the ownership of all three national broadcast television networks changed hands. ABC was bought by Capital Cities. NBC was bought by General Electric. And CBS, fending off a hostile takeover bid from Ted Turner, was bought by Lawrence Tisch, then a low-profile businessman and head of Loews hotels and theaters.

While each of these deals was struck for different reasons, they had the common effect of leaving these networks burdened with tremendous, sometimes crippling debt. One of the results of the overhanging threat of this kind of debt was to impose conservative restraint on the networks. Conservative restraint meant tightening department budgets, sloughing off unproductive operations, and keeping a tight reign on programming costs. There may have been constant rumors of the imminent return of *Star Trek* to network television, but given the poor ratings of its first network outing and the costs associated with mounting a quality science fiction series, networks in the 1980s were in no position to take another risk. Even considering the profitable and popular feature-length *Star Trek* motion pictures, which had proven that the series' audience was still loyal, a resurrection of *Star Trek* was no easy matter.

The decision to put *Star Trek: The Next Generation* into production must have been difficult given the projected budget deficits and the changing climate of television in the mid-1980s. Between 1984 and 1986, Paramount Pictures took the idea of bringing *Star Trek* back to the three networks and was turned away by each. Fox Broadcasting, which was just gearing up its plans to launch a "part-time" network, reportedly negotiated more intensely than the others.[9]

As the new television season was rolled out in October 1987, the industry still had two more shocks to absorb. First, on 19 October the New York stock market fell 500 points. The falling stock market eroded share prices across the "big board," including those of ABC, CBS, and NBC. Then, too, Hollywood and New York media professionals were bracing themselves for the impact of Rupert Murdoch's promised inauguration of a fourth broadcast network. Fox would divide the television audience further and put more pressure on broadcast networks to derive profits from advertising revenues. Fox's inauguration and the fallen stock prices must have created considerable nervousness among broadcasters who were already concerned about the impact of reduced ratings and the decreasing size of broadcast television audiences on the profitability of network broadcasting.

Over the preceding ten years, the share of audience available for networks to deliver to advertisers had diminished because of technological advances (see figures 3.1, 3.2, and 3.3). For instance, dur-

Figure 3.1

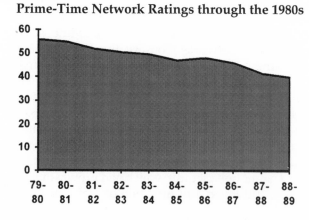

Prime-Time Network Ratings through the 1980s

(Source: *Nielsen Television Index*)

Figure 3.2

Network Prime-Time Total Shares

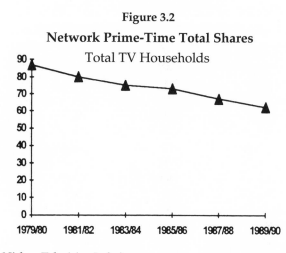

(Source: *Nielsen Television Index*)

Figure 3.3

Average Television Viewing Totals

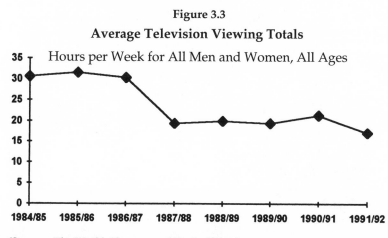

(Source: *The World Almanac and Book of Facts*)

ing this period the home video markets blossomed and matured, significantly affecting the nation's televisual habits.[10] Sales of prerecorded videos were measured at $171 million in 1980 and were projected to reach $3 billion by the end of 1987 as the ownership of home video recorders grew (table 3.1).[11] To compound matters further, while television viewing continued to grow across all categories of viewers, broadcast television lost viewers to competing forms of television (table 3.2). The proportion of households with

Table 3.1

VCR Sales

Year	Sales to Dealers (in thousands)	Factory Sales (in millions)
1977	209	180
1978	402	326
1979	475	389
1980	805	621
1981	1,361	1,127
1982	2,035	1,303
1983	4,091	2,162
1984	7,616	3,585
1985	11,853	4,738
1986	13,174	5,258
1987	13,306	5,093

(Source: *Electronic Media*)

Table 3.2

Television Viewing Trends Across Media

Year	Broadcast TV%	Independent TV%	Public TV%	Basic Cable%	Pay Cable%
1983–84	69	19	3	9	5
1985–86	66	18	3	11	5
1987–88	61	20	4	15	7
1989–90	55	20	3	21	6
1990–91	53	21	4	24	6

(Source: *Universal Almanac*)

cable increased from 22 percent in 1980 to 60 percent in 1993. Moreover, between 1984 and 1993, cable's share of television advertising expenditures more than tripled, rising to 8.2 percent; the networks' share slid from 42 percent to 34 percent. Once cable television crossed the 50 percent penetration threshold, advertising agencies on Madison Avenue adopted the attitude that cable and broadcast television were equally potent placements for their sponsors' budgets (see figure 3.4 and table 3.3).[12] Larry Gerbrandt, a consultant and analyst for Paul Kagan, noted, "As network ratings have come down, cable's have gone up. We're getting to the point where with cable, relative to some of the network's ratings, the gap is not nearly as wide as it was two or three years ago."[13]

Figure 3.4

U.S. Cable Penetration

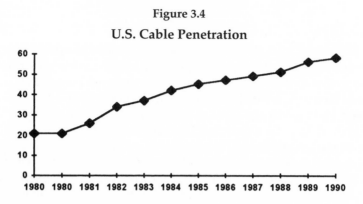

(Source: A.C. Nielsen in *Electronic Media*)

Table 3.3

Cable Television Systems: 1955-1987	
Year	Number of Systems
1955	400
1960	640
1965	1,325
1970	2,490
1975	3,506
1980	4,225
1985	6,600
1987	7,900

(Source: U.S. Bureau of Census)

This time around, Roddenberry and Paramount, the producing studio, had another kind of innovation in mind. Instead of offering *Star Trek: The Next Generation* to one of the major networks, they decided to go boldly into off-network syndication.[14] To bring this strategy to life meant that Paramount had to string together enough independent broadcast television stations to gain the necessary national coverage or potential viewership to attract advertisers. Moreover, Roddenberry and Paramount had to deliver a product that was sophisticated enough to match up against the high-tech science fiction production standards that audiences had grown accustomed to after the motion picture *Star Wars* and the television miniseries *V* (broadcast on NBC, this became the highest-rated science fiction miniseries), without seeming esoteric, so that local stations would feel confident about selling their share of commercial time to local businesses.

In summer 1987, Paramount arranged a satellite transmission of a twelve-minute sample from the premiere episode to the 181 stations it corralled together to form a syndication network covering 95 percent of the nation.[15] Following that satellite transmission (which featured Mel Harris, president of Paramount Television Group, who explained how the series would be marketed and promoted), additional stations solicited Paramount for distribution rights.[16] It would be difficult to overstate the importance of this turn of events. The entire future of *Star Trek: The Next Generation* depended on the series establishing strong, long-term relationships with independent broadcasters. Broadcasters such as Ed Trimble, vice president and general manager for KHTV-TV in Houston, Texas, were not disappointed by the initial sample. Trimble commented with pleasure, "I was very impressed. They went far beyond what I thought they would."[17]

According to Paramount's figures each episode of *Star Trek: The Next Generation* cost $1.3 million to produce. Moreover, if the series was going to have a life after its first run, Paramount would need to produce at least 100 episodes of the show. *Star Trek: The Next Generation,* then, was projected to cost at least $130 million across its first-run syndication and before it could start earning profits in subsequent, post-first-run syndication sales to local markets.[18] The series' producers must have been very happy with comments like Trimble's.

As pleased as Paramount Television Group may have been with the positive response to the sequel among syndicators, they must have derived considerable pleasure from the breaking news of how *The Cosby Show* fared in off-network syndication bidding. Bidding for the rights to broadcast this half-hour number one, prime-time network situation comedy series exceeded $300 million and was projected to reach $500 million in August 1987 alone.[19] If a half-hour comedy series could gather that kind of return, then even an expensive production such as *Star Trek: The Next Generation* might return even better results after its first-run life.[20] Beyond the moneys raised from outright licensing agreements, Viacom, distributor of *The Cosby Show,* stood to profit from the sale of barter time within each episode. In February 1988, when the bidding for barter spots opened, industry analysts estimated that Viacom could earn as much as $91 million.

The perception that syndication could be lucrative was particularly important because, using standard accounting procedures, the projected five-year cost of *Star Trek: The Next Generation* actually resulted in a much larger total figure. Simply adjusting for inflation from year to year for the projected five-year "mission" of *Star Trek: The Next Generation* produced a deficit equaling $174 million. If one considered carrying the cost of each season's production into each successive year, then the accumulated debt could have conceivably reached closer to $498.5 million.

Over the past ten years, the television industry had been buffeted by technological and business changes, too. Certainly the scale of first-run syndication that Paramount needed was risky, but it was the kind of risk that could be calculated and managed. However, there were other forces in the television business in the 1980s which could not be controlled because they transferred power to consumers: home viewing of prerecorded video cassettes and viewing of nonnetwork television sources.

Estimates of the impact of these media alternatives on broadcast television ranged as high as a viewership decline of 12 percent.[21] Softer numbers for network television translated into pressure on local affiliates to drop network shows that did not draw sufficient ratings. In that case, syndicators like Paramount stepped up their efforts to gain more prime-time affiliate clearances for their shows.[22] A key to Paramount's success with placing *Star Trek: The Next Generation* in so many markets was the series' image as a well-produced, high-production value series that was a known quantity to audiences. Network viewership erosion and vulnerability, in addition to the unprecedented, strong launch of *Star Trek: The Next Generation*, pointed the way, and soon every one of the networks with a full broadcast schedule brought on-line its version of a science fiction series. NBC television's schedule showcased *Amazing Stories, Something Is Out There,* and *Quantum Leap.* CBS's schedule boasted *Twilight Zone, The Flash,* and *E.A.R.T.H. Force.* ABC broadcast *Mission: Impossible* and *Starman.* When Fox got underway, its schedule included a high profile science fiction program *Alien Nation.* In addition, *Friday the 13th* was offered directly through syndication to local markets.

Star Trek: The Next Generation premiered across the country in a two-part opening story during the first week of October 1987. From the earliest ratings reports, Roddenberry and Paramount began to see that their new project had all the markings of a success—a big success. Nielsen's initial overnight survey of nine television markets found that the two-hour series pilot came in first in three markets, second in three others, and third in the remaining three. Significantly, six of the survey stations were UHF outlets, which regularly finished behind their higher-powered VHF counterparts. Taken together, these stations covered 99.3 percent of the nation's television viewing population.

Soon, however, the series producers were given reason to pause in their celebrations as second- and third-week ratings showed a weak performance, a drop of 17 percent, following an initially strong opening. Two-thirds of the fifteen stations' overnight metered markets actually experienced a decline in ratings from weeks 2 to 3. Only one-third saw improved ratings. One station, KHTV-TV of Houston, dropped 50 percent from a rating/share mark of

Table 3.4

Nielsen's Overnight Metered Markets Initial Ratings for *Star Trek: The Next Generation*

Station (City) Channel	Rating/Share	Market/Affiliation
WPWR (Chicago), Channel 50	11.1/17	3/Ind*
KCOP (LA), Channel 13	21.2/29	2/Ind
WTAF (Philadelphia), Channel 29	10.5/15	4/Ind
WTXX (Hartford), Channel 20	8.8/14	23/Ind
KWGN (Denver), Channel 2	17.0/28	19/Ind
WCIX (Miami), Channel 6	17.3/25	14/Ind
KBHK (San Francisco), Channel 44	11.7/18	5/Ind
KBHD (Detroit), Channel 50	15.7/23	7/Ind
KHTV (Houston), Channel 39	14.8/22	10/Ind
KTXA (Dallas), Channel 21	10.1/19	8/Ind[†]
KCPQ (Seattle), Channel 13	11.7/24	16/Ind[†]
WCVB (Boston), Channel 5	15.1/27	6/ABC[†]
WGNX (Atlanta), Channel 46	11.8/20	12/Ind[†]
WDCA (Washington), Channel 20	9.0/17	9/Ind[†]
WPIX (New York), Channel 11	15.6/23	1/Ind[†]
WVII (Bangor), Channel 7	14.0/26	154/ABC[‡]

* Ind = independent
[†] Results from October 3–5 surveys
[‡] Results from October 10–12 surveys
(Source: *Electronic Media* and *Broadcasting Yearbook*)

11.8/22 on 10 October to 5.6/11 on 17 October (table 3.4).[23] However, by the time the cumulative national ratings for the third week were posted, *Star Trek: The Next Generation* had climbed to 11.5, up from its initial average rating of 10.5. By mid-November, Nielsen reported that *Star Trek: The Next Generation* had achieved an average national rating of 10.5 through 25 October—twice the rating of the next highest first-run, nationally syndicated program, *She's the Sheriff* at 5.3 (table 3.5 and 3.6). Analysts reviewing that information pointed out that *Star Trek: The Next Generation* numbers were particularly strong among women. According to Nielsen survey results, women aged eighteen to forty-nine represented 28 percent of the audience for *Star Trek: The Next Generation*, a mere five points less than men (33 percent) in the same age group (table 3.7). Admitting surprise, Lennie Bart, an official with the New York-based station representation firm Seltel, noted, "That's an outstanding figure for young women."[24] Outstanding indeed, especially given the fact that viewership of the off-network syndication of the original show was found to be skewed heavily toward males (table 3.2).[25]

Solid ratings were only one way *Star Trek: The Next Generation* demonstrated its impact on television. By the end of 1987, this sequel had proven so popular with key audiences, such as women eighteen to forty-nine years old, that several network affiliates decided to schedule it preferentially over network developed programs. The examples of ABC affiliates WMGC-TV in Binghamton, New York, and WVII-TV of Bangor, Maine, illustrate this point. Officials at WMGC-TV chose not to telecast *Dolly*, an ABC musical-variety program, because they did not want to move *Star Trek: The Next Generation*. Management of WVII-TV decided to leave *Star Trek: The Next Generation* in its regular Saturday night slot and to tape and shift *Dolly* to the following Friday night. An additional six ABC affiliates deflected network pressure and kept the sequel series in primetime, but moved it to another night. WTLV-TV (Jacksonville, Florida), WTXL-TV (Tallahassee, Florida), and WCVB-TV (Boston, Massachusetts) moved *Star Trek: The Next Generation* to Saturday at 9 P.M., and all three stations pre-empted the ABC series *Ohara*. WHTM-TV (Harrisburg, Pennsylvania) moved *Star Trek: The Next Generation* to Friday night and pre-empted the network's offering *Mr. Belvedere* and *The Thorns*. WZZM-TV (Grand Rapids, Michigan) scheduled the series for Friday night and preempted *Mr. Belvedere* and *Full House*. WCTI-

Table 3.5

Star Trek: The Next Generation **Average National Ratings, First Season**

Week	Rating	Rank
10/4	13.4	NA*
10/11	8.6	NA*
10/18	11.5	3
11/1	8.9	5
11/8	10.5	4
11/22	12.7	3
11/29	10.5	4
12/6	11.0	5
12/13	10.3	4
12/20	7.9	8
1/3	7.7	7
1/10	8.8	6
1/17	9.0	6
1/24	11.5	3
1/31	10.3	5
2/5	11.4	4
2/21	10.9	5
2/28	10.2	5
3/6	9.0	5
3/20	9.3	5
3/27	10.1	4
4/3	11.4	3
4/10	8.5	4
4/24	10.4	4
5/1	10.8	4
5/8	9.7	3
5/15	9.7	4
5/22	9.4	5
5/29	10.2	3
6/5	7.5	4
6/12	7.4	4
6/19	8.0	4
6/26	8.6	4

*NA = not available
(Source: *Electronic Media*)

Table 3.6

Star Trek: The Next Generation **Yearly Cumulative Ratings**

1989	10.4
1990	10.5
1991	11.8
1992	12.0
1993	10.8

(Source: *The World Almanac and Book of Facts*)

Table 3.7

Star Trek: The Next Generation **Demographics**

Gender	Age	Percentage
Women	18–49	28
Men	18–49	33
Teens	+13 years	11
Pre-teens	<12 years	10

(remaining 12 percent divided between viewers under 18 and over 50 years of age)
(Source: *Electronic Media*)

TV (Greenville, North Carolina) bumped the science fiction sequel to Thursday and preempted *The Charmings* and delayed the start of *The ABC Thursday Night Movie*.

However, audience measurement in ratings was only half the success story of *Star Trek: The Next Generation*. The other half was the revenue Paramount could collect from barter sales of commercial time within each show. Barter is the swapping of programming to stations in return for advertising time to be sold nationally by the syndicator. With its strong ratings performances, Paramount sold barter spots in the sequel series for about $70,000 for each half minute. At these prices Paramount calculated it would be able to recoup $980,000 per episode.[26] Good barter sales left a deficit of $320,000 per episode or about $8 million across the first season. Against the full production costs across 100 episodes of $130 million, a deficit of $8 million per year must have looked very good—very good indeed considering that the season began with a crash of the New York stock market.

The audience reception of *Star Trek: The Next Generation* and the potential for financial return that industry analysts foresaw for it did not go unappreciated by other television executives. In spring 1988, as the new television programs in development for the upcoming fall season were revealed, network plans included six new science fiction series: *Cyberforce* from Warner Brothers for ABC; *Mars: Base One* (no production company listed) and *miCRO-NAUTS* from MGM/UA for CBS; and *The Incredible Hulk* from New World plus *Invaders* and *Out of Time* both from Tri-Star, for ABC.[27] Science fiction had proven successful at the box office; television spin-offs and clones were the next logical steps.[28]

If public acceptance of science fiction could be transferred to other high-production value, television programs similar to *Star Trek: The Next Generation*, then television programmers might have a way to rebuild television audience share. By the end of 1987, Nielsen reported that its figures confirmed a minimum 8 percent drop in the three networks' prime-time television viewing.[29] The success of syndication (e.g., *Star Trek: The Next Generation*), cable television,[30] pay television,[31] and prerecorded videocassettes added up to stiff competition for conventional broadcast television.

As television programmers looked forward to the new season, the question running through the industry was summarized by Dennis Leibowitz, vice president of Donaldson, Lufkin, and Jenrette, who said, "One of the big questions is whether we are heading into a permanent period of target marketing as opposed to the traditional mass marketing, because of improved research tools and the need to snare additional ad dollars in an increasingly competitive marketplace."[32] Thomas Murphy, Cap Cities/ABC chairman, reviewed the reports of the new season's reduction of advertising revenues for his company and the industry and confirmed that "Demand for advertising at the television network and throughout our operation has slowed, and we see no signs to indicate that this situation will improve in the immediate future."[33]

Declining network viewership should have been good news for alternative media outlets such as the ad hoc syndication network that Paramount cobbled together for *Star Trek: The Next Generation*.[34] However, as preliminary 1988–89 season schedules were being revised, syndicators wondered whether weaker network viewership would force discounting of network commercial time and undermine their "upfront" market for barter sales, too.[35]

Then, too, the accelerating trends in cable television penetration, videocassette home taping, and Fox's debut eroded the big three networks' previously unquestioned hold on advertising. Conditions jelled for high-concept, high-production-value, syndicated programs to compete in the media marketplace, if they could target audiences with the right demographics to attract sponsors' dollars.

In general, syndicators pitched their product for the upcoming season at a price level between 8 and 12 percent above the previous year. Brian Bryne, President of International Advertising Sales, felt that those levels would maintain syndication's competitive edge with advertisers and explained, "The networks will start off at 20 percent to 22 percent increases, probably wind up with 14 to 16 percent, and for us to be competitive we have to come in below them."[36] Even with this increase, syndicators stood to lose money, because the companies on average lost around 20 percent in the stock market crash of 1987.[37]

Nonetheless, as the television industry looked forward to the 1988–89 season there was residual apprehension left over from the 1987–88 season, which had been marked by the stock market crash and the writers' strike.[38] These were events that had particular significance in the media business. During early summer 1988, weeks in advance of the major efforts to sell television commercial time, national advertisers were already sizing up the previous year's ratings and evaluating new buys. Brian Byrne, IAS president, reported that his company had already sold more than 20 percent of the $150 million inventory it sells in first-run syndication shows for Orbis Communication and Paramount.[39] His company's promising start was attributed to the willingness of advertisers to pay "double digit cost-per-thousand increases on some of the better-rated returning shows, including *Star Trek: The Next Generation*."[40]

While the big question in network television was whether the ongoing WGA strike would delay the start of the fall season, syndication television confidence in science fiction/fantasy-type programs led to the preparation for the fall premiere of six new programs: *Freddy's Nightmare, Monsters, Munsters Today, Superboy, Twilight Zone,* and *War of the Worlds.*[41] The glow of good fortune so surrounded the *Star Trek* concept that Paramount Domestic Television took the unusual step of restoring the original *Star Trek* two-hour pilot episode entitled "The Cage," which had never been televised, and used it as a special on 3 October to generate interest for the sequel series' second season.[42] Notwithstanding this special event, the start of the second season of *Star Trek: The Next Generation* was delayed until 21 November because of the WGA strike.

As preparation for a second season of *Star Trek: The Next Generation* continued, several changes were introduced to the series. Whoopi Goldberg lobbied for and was cast as a new recurring character called Guinan. A new standing set, "10-Forward," was constructed to serve as the crew's lounge and socialization area presided over by Guinan. Goldberg's addition to the cast was a rather odd circumstance. First, Goldberg called the show's producers and asked them to hire her. Second, the Guinan character, a member of a distant and enigmatic race living in diaspora after their home world was savaged by a cybernetic race called the Borg, is never associated with Terran Africans or African Americans, and the obvious connection between these two races of people of color was not made part of the character's development.

The fact of Guinan's presence among the crew of *Star Trek: The Next Generation* owes little to the program's creators. As Whoopi Goldberg is quick to point out, during the hiatus between the series' first and second seasons, she contacted producers Rick Berman and Michael Pillar and expressed her interest in joining the crew. The fact that a female African American actor had to take the initiative in making contact with television producers not only reflected the industry's poor performance record of minority employment but illustrates a kind of convenient memory that ignores the fact that the original series included an African American female, Nichelle Nichols, as a member of the series' regular cast. In a further ironic twist on this successor to a series that quite consciously addressed issues of race and social reform, none of the three characters who are visibly of dark complexion, Worf, Geordi La Forge, and Guinan, are identified with, socialize among, or develop along story lines that share thematic issues in common with the history and culture of Africans and African Americans.

Launching a New TV Sequel

Star Trek: The Next Generation rocketed across American television sets in fall 1987. The new series, set seventy-five years after the original, featured a new, completely redesigned version of the starship *Enterprise,* serial number NCC-1701-D, and a new group of continuing characters. As in the earlier series, this version demonstrated a commitment to representing diversity in the *Enterprise*'s command staff. And, as in the original series, the current series associates command with a white, male authority figure, Captain Jean-Luc Picard.[43] In addition, William Riker, the new galaxy-class starship's executive officer, who assumes command in the captain's absence, like the green-skinned Mr. Spock before him, is a white male, too. Nevertheless, on *Star Trek: The Next Generation* below this executive officer level, department heads reflects more diversity than before. Now, the chief medical officer, Dr. Beverly Crusher, and ship's counselor (a combination psychic and psychologist), Deanna Troi, are females. The remaining department heads are a walking reference library. Lieutenant Commander Data is an android, but a white-gold male android; chief engineering officer Lieutenant Geordi La Forge is of African descent; chief of security Lieutenant Worf is a Klingon (see figure 3.5). Beyond these characters, who are closely related with their shipboard duties, the new series expands the cast of continuing characters with Wesley Crusher, Dr. Crusher's son and science prodigy, and, beginning with the series' second season, Guinan, an enigmatic time and space traveler who runs the crew lounge, called 10-Forward, and serves as the ship's unofficial hostess and wise "old soul."[44]

A great deal can happen in a fictional universe in nearly a century. Not only has research, colonization, and exploration of space continued, but the United Federation of Planets has expanded to include many alien civilizations discovered during the interim. And an old nemesis has turned ally, the Klingon Empire.

The scope of the Federation has been enlarged so much over that of the first series that the Federation flagship, the *Enterprise,* must have the capacity to chart the vast, uncharted realms of the galaxy. The *Enterprise,* in another change from its predecessor, was redesigned to carry a complement of more than 1,000 beings. Whereas the previous starship's crew were members of Starfleet, the sequel's *Enterprise* carries crew members' families along with Starfleet officers and enlisted personnel.

In all of these ways—an enlarged, robust federation, a bigger, faster flagship vessel of exploration, and the presence of families—

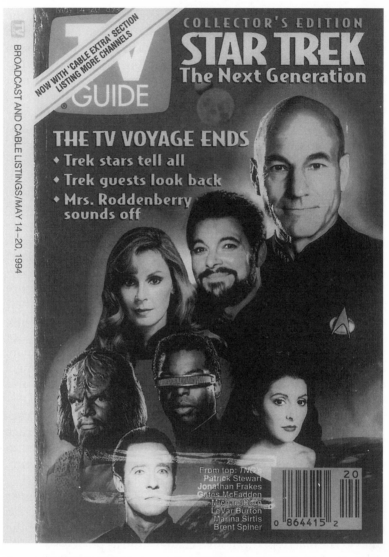

Figure 3.5: *TV Guide* bids farewell to *Star Trek: The Next Generation* (May 14–20, 1994).

the world of the sequel series is identified with stability. At first glance this may seem odd. How can a drama set against an interstellar background of travel, bizarre antagonists, and uniquely threatening phenomena be associated with a concept like stability? But this is precisely the point. The United Federation of Planets has been so successful at including aliens within its organizational ranks that, in the seventy-five years between the two series, it has grown into a bureaucracy of galactic proportions. In this organizational context, the first objective of the Federation is the maintenance and survival of the Federation. In its earlier phase, the Federation and Starfleet were in the business of expansion. The Federation and Starfleet of the sequel series are dedicated to order. Swashbuckling has become passé, and personalities and leadership styles like Captain Kirk's are inappropriate, even dangerous. Instead, seventy-five years after his voyages, the Federation and Starfleet need captains who exhibit the qualities of diplomats and managers.

In this fantasy future, the hero is no longer characterized by a willingness to risk personal safety, the ship, and crew—everything—to make contact with "new life, new civilizations." In *Star Trek: The Next Generation*, Captain Picard, the central character, is first and foremost a manager. As a manager, Picard's first duty is to protect and preserve his crew and other assets, not place them in jeopardy or at risk. Picard is depicted as much more patient and cerebral, a problem solver who relies on his department heads rather than flashes of inspiration.

Star Trek: The Next Generation completed seven seasons, and, with more than one hundred and fifty episodes "in the can," this version is marked by a strong commitment to dealing with this sociology in its stories.[45] However, throughout its first five seasons, only 22 of 126 episodes, 17 percent, dealt overtly with ethnicity at least at the level of a subplot or as the focus of the entire episode. This represents an erosion of more than 16 percent from the ratio of the previous series.[46] Consequently, the current series increased its development of dramas among species of the multiethnic Federation, as well as other alien civilizations encountered in space.[47]

During its first year, in "Code of Honor" (episode 4), the *Enterprise* gets entangled with a planet whose culture is similar to Earth's Chinese, whose inhabitants physically resemble Africans. *Enterprise* Chief of Security Tasha Yar, a white female, is thrust into a deadly matrimonial conflict, when a calculating husband decides to use her combat skills to defeat and kill his wife so that he may inherit her wealth. "The Battle" (airdate: 14 November 1987, episode 10) introduces the Ferengi, a species of sniveling, short, sharp-toothed, brown-skinned race space traders whose misogynist culture is solely dedicated to turning a profit.

The second year, in "The Measure of a Man" (airdate: 11 February 1989, episode 35), Picard, at Guinan's prompting, successfully argues that Starfleet's plan to seize the android Data and make a robot race based on his design amounts to nothing less than reintroducing slavery.

In the third year, when the Chrysalians in "The Price" (airdate: 11 November 1989, episode 56) open negotiations for navigation rights to a wormhole that they control, the Federation, represented by the *Enterprise*, and Ferengi cultures clash. Near the end of that year, DaiMon Tog, a Ferengi delegate to a trade conference, kidnaps Will Riker, Lwaxana Troi, and her daughter, Deanna, in "Menage à Troi" (airdate: 12 May 1990, episode 72) to use the Betazoid women's telepathy in business negotiations.

With "Heart of Glory" (airdate: 19 March 1988, episode 20), "A Matter of Honor" (airdate: 4 February 1989, episode 34), "The Emissary" (airdate: 24 June 1989, episode 46), "Sins of the Father" (airdate: 17 March 1990, episode 65), "Reunion" (airdate: 3 November 1990, episode 80), "The Mind's Eye" (airdate: 25 May 1991, episode 98), and "Redemption" Parts 1 and 2 (airdates: 15 June and 21 September 1991, episodes 100 and 101), the series reestablishes the Klingon race from the previous series, as members of the Federation, and develops that plotline through personal feuds (between Worf and Duras), the assassination of K'Mpec, and a Klingon civil war. Klingon family dynamics take center stage in "Family" (airdate: 29 September 1990, episode 76) and "New Ground" (airdate: 4 January 1992, episode 110) as Worf has to adjust his self-image when first his parents and then his son enter his professional world.

The *Enterprise* rescues a young boy in "Suddenly Human" (airdate: 13 October 1990, episode 78) from a wrecked Talarian ship and tries to reunite him with his Terran relatives, but fails when he chooses the love for his adopted Talarian father over his genetic heritage.

Captain Picard is kidnapped and held with three members of different and incompatible alien species as part of an unidentified alien scientist's behavioral experiments in "Allegiance" (airdate: 24

March 1990, episode 66). The *Enterprise* becomes embroiled in a situation that could wreck a recently negotiated peace with a new, reptilian, and Machiavellian race known as the Cardassians in "The Wounded" (airdate: 26 January 1991, episode 86). In "Darmok" (airdate: 28 September 1991, episode 102), Picard and the captain of a new dark-skinned race, the Tamarians, must develop trust, learn to communicate, and face a life-and-death battle together.

There are four episodes that figure prominently in the way *Star Trek: The Next Generation* conceptualizes ethnicity. For convenience, here they will be grouped into two pairs focusing on Worf as an alien Other and Geordi La Forge as an Africanist Other.[48] In the sequel series' second season "The Emissary" (airdate: 24 June 1989, episode 46), the romantic attraction between Security Chief Lieutenant Worf, who was orphaned when Romulans destroyed his Klingon colony on Khitomer,[49] rescued by Starfleet, and raised by Terran foster parents, and Federation ambassador K'Ehleyr, "the half-human/half-Klingon hybrid he once loved,"[50] is rekindled. The two are reunited when an ancient Klingon ship, from the era when Klingons and the Federation were antagonists, is discovered about to emerge from cryogenic suspension and threatens devastation for unsuspecting Federation ships and colonies. In the series' third season, "Reunion" (airdate: 5 November 1990, episode 72) brings Worf and K'Ehleyr together again, after a two-year separation, and he learns from her that they have a son.[51] Peace between the Federation and the Klingon Empire, and the integrity of Worf's new family, hang on Picard's decision between Gowron and Duras (who accused Worf's father of treason at Khitomer) of who should succeed K'Mpec as leader of the Klingon Empire's Ruling High Council and which of the two pretenders to the Klingon throne murdered K'Mpec.

In the first episode of the second pair, the *Enterprise*'s chief engineer, Geordi La Forge, must use his skills to extricate the ship when it stumbles into a power-draining mine field. In "Booby Trap" (airdate: 28 October 1989, episode 54), La Forge saves the situation by creating a three-dimensional simulation of both the *Enterprise*'s original engines, as designed at Utopia Planitia Fleet Yards at the Mars colony, and Dr. Leah Brahms, a junior member of Galaxy-Class Starship Development Project. His computer engine model serves as a baseline for comparisons with his modifications and as a testbed for possible solutions. His simulation of Brahms functions as an ideal expert consultant and female partner for the bachelor engineer. When Dr. Brahms, in the flesh, visits the *Enterprise*, in "Galaxy's Child" (airdate: 9 March 1991, episode 81) to inspect La Forge's changes to "her engines," he has to work out a real-life relationship with "the woman of his dreams." Together they wean a strange infant interstellar life form that has imprinted on the Enterprise, as its mother, and suckles energy from its engines.

Each of these four episodes centers on some of the effects of contact with different cultures. "The Emissary" and "Reunion" focus on the personal agonies of two Klingons (one orphaned and raised on Earth, the other half-human and half-Klingon) to reconcile their backgrounds with Klingon traditions. "Booby Trap" and "Galaxy's Child" deal with the difficulties an individual who is embedded in technical culture has in dealing with people.

Star Trek: The Next Generation continued its parent series' interest in demonstrating that a multicultural society can flourish. However, where the earlier series used a broad canvas, the current one seems to shift the examination of the consequences of interaction among cultures to a more personal level. Nonetheless, both sets of programs maintain the image of Starfleet as a utopia where cultural differences are combined productively. Perhaps this shift relates to the general society's retreat from commitment to or faith in broad scale movements and government programs that characterized the Johnson period of the earlier series and the rise of fierce individualism that colored the Reagan–Bush era, during which the latter series was formulated. Or perhaps the swashbuckling bravado of *Star Trek* reflected the environment and spirit of its era of owners/entrepreneurs who ran broadcasting. Likewise, the management and administrative inclination of *Star Trek: The Next Generation* might reflect the situation in which lawyers, agents, and professional investors not only control the day-to-day operations of contemporary broadcasting but received regular validation in the nation's symbolic and institutional life in America in the 1980s.

To Go Boldly Beyond into International Markets

The postnetwork history of *Star Trek* and the potency of the series as a mass media commodity is indicated by the fact that it has been playing somewhere in the United States, not to mention its international broadcast licensing, continuously since it was canceled by NBC-TV in 1969; by *Star Trek*'s genesis of a minor "industry" of a least a dozen annual *Star Trek* conventions (featuring memorabilia or collectibles from Paramount Studios, guest appearances by cast members of the original series, and participants who dress in their own versions of Starfleet uniforms or as series characters); and by its parent company's (Paramount Pictures) negotiations with three companies that produce and market interactive computer games based on *Star Trek, Star Trek: The Next Generation,* and *Star Trek: Deep Space Nine.*[52] The continuing popularity of the *Star Trek* concept is further demonstrated by the fact that the Hilton Hotels Corporation and Paramount Parks, a division of Viacom Incorporated, entered into a joint venture to construct a new $50 million Las Vegas hotel with a family-oriented entertainment complex based on the 325 hours of *Star Trek* programming.

Star Trek programming is available in the United States and several other countries both as syndicated television programming and as videocassette versions of individual episodes for sale to collectors. However, *Star Trek: The Next Generation,* now concluding in first-run syndication in the United States, is similarly distributed by contract to domestic and international television syndication markets and is available as individual episodes on videotape, although the complete schedule of more than 180 programs is not yet a complete retail catalogue. A survey of television listings from around the world demonstrates the globe-spanning popularity of Roddenberry's vision of the future and shows either *Star Trek* or *Star Trek: The Next Generation* playing in at least fourteen countries around the world, representing eight languages and international cultures (table 3.8).[53]

The largest group of international subscribers are English speakers. Among English-speaking international television broadcasting systems, Channel 9 in Australia distributes the fourth season of *Star Trek: The Next Generation* to Melbourne, Perth, Brisbane, and other regional centers; the BBC in the United Kingdom currently holds a contract for *Star Trek: The Next Generation* through the series' third season and in August 1993 began to show seasons 4 through 6; Britain's SKY One acquired the rights to program *Star Trek: The Next Generation* beginning in August 1992; Ireland's RTE's schedule for the same show parallels that of

Table 3.8

Star Trek's **Regeneration outside North America**

English outlets	1.	Australia	Sydney, Channel 9
	2.	Ireland	RTE
	3.	New Zealand	TV3
	4.	United Kingdom	BBC & Sky One
	5.	Armed Forces Network	
French outlets	6.	Belgium	VTM
	7.	Switzerland	TSR
Swedish outlets	8.	Sweden	TV/5 Nordic
	9.	Finland	TV2
Dutch outlets	10.	The Netherlands	KRO TV
Italian outlet	11.	Italy	Italia 1
German outlet	12.	Germany	SAT1
Japanese outlet	13.	Japan	Sendai TV
Spanish outlet	14.	Spain	Telemadrid

(Source: The Star Tek FTP Archive, administered by D. Joseph Creighton at ftp://ftp.cc.umanitoba.ca/startrek/lol/lol.tos and ftp://ftp.cc.umanitoba.ca/startrek/lol/lol.tng)

the United Kingdom; TV3 in New Zealand carries season 4 of *Star Trek: The Next Generation;* and Armed Forces Network distributes the sequel series through season 4 to U.S. military personnel on bases throughout Europe.

The next largest language groups are French (Belgium and Switzerland) and Swedish (Sweden and Finland) viewers. Belgium's VTM airs the third season of *Star Trek: The Next Generation.* Swiss TSR television has begun to carry *Star Trek,* and Finnish Channel 3 (MTV3) airs *Star Trek: The Next Generation* on an irregular, noncontinuous basis (because its 200,000 viewership is too small an audience to make support economical), but there are plans to shift the series to Finnish cable TV2 where its potential audience could reach one-half million. In Sweden, TV5/Nordic carries the second season of *Star Trek.*

On the next tier of international broadcasters there are five countries representing five distinct languages. The Netherlands shows *Star Trek: The Next Generation* (in English with Dutch subtitles) during the summers through season 2. The same series is carried in Italy over Italia 1. In Japan season 3 of the show is aired by Sendai television. German viewers can see *Star Trek* in its third run on SAT1 (with strong inclination to contracting for *Star Trek: The Next Generation* and *Star Trek: Deep Space Nine* as soon as they become available). In 1991, Spain's Telemadrid aired the first and second season of *Star Trek: The Next Generation* (table 3.8).

It is clear that Star Trek™ and its vision of the future has grown into a global phenomenon. Despite the cancellation of *Star Trek*, its mythology, mix of characters and their relationships, and universe of wonders to explore has never ceased to attract audiences. Soon it may well be the case that some version of Star Trek™ will be playing before television audiences somewhere in the world every night.

Chapter 4

Casting into the Future:
Ladies and Gentlemen, Officers All

One of most commented-on aspects of *Star Trek* and *Star Trek: The Next Generation* is Roddenberry's conception of the starships' crews and the relationships among each series' recurring characters. *Star Trek* stood out from contemporary programs because it represented the work of interstellar exploration and scientific research as being accomplished by multiethnic, multinational crews of highly trained professionals that even featured an alien. When Roddenberry got the chance to bring *Star Trek: The Next Generation* to television, he insisted on preserving this key concept and expanding the definition of ethnic diversity among the cast to include additional places for extraterrestrial personnel. As American society struggles with redefining the workplace as inclusive of the nation's diversity, both *Star Trek* series modeled a workplace where men and women, whites and blacks, and aliens functioned together as professional equals.

The recurring cast of *Star Trek* largely centered on the *Enterprise*'s command staff, known as the bridge crew, plus the chief engineer and chief medical officer. The series' regular cast of characters included a white male captain from America (James T. Kirk), a male Japanese navigator (Sulu), a male Russian helmsman (Chekov), a green-skinned, male extraterrestrial (Vulcan) science officer (Mr. Spock), a male Scottish engineer (Scotty), a white male, American medical officer (McCoy), and a female, African communications officer (Uhura).

Each of these officers is depicted as a thoroughly trained professional whose responsibilities require that they master complex technology, face danger with unflappable courage, and answer the unknown with creativity. In addition, Roddenberry was very careful to specify that these officers were not mere automatons but in the long tradition of sailors have become friends with their crewmates. Friendship and a sense of camaraderie among shipmates are at the center of *Star Trek* and *Star Trek: The Next Generation,* demonstrated by the ways these officers relate to and depend on one another and grow from those experiences.

At the core of *Star Trek* are the three characters Kirk, Spock, and McCoy and the nature of the relationships they forge. As captain of the *Enterprise,* Kirk sets an extremely high standard of performance that tends to isolate him from those he commands. He occupies the top of a pyramidal command structure and relates to his crew through their functions and the information and advice he solicits from them. Relating to command staff and subordinates through their functions exaggerates his loneliness. However, Kirk, a veteran space explorer, has developed two important friendships that serve as a balm and ease the responsibilities of command. Kirk's closest friends are Mr. Spock, the Vulcan science officer, and Dr. McCoy, chief medical officer.

Spock, writers and directors are told, would attribute his strong friendship with Kirk to the captain's superior command expertise and would deny any intimation of affection. Because he is a Vulcan, an extraterrestrial species renowned for its imperturbable logic and steadfast loyalty, Mr. Spock offers Kirk a bedrock friendship. Spock's adherence to the Vulcan philosophy of logic and his training in computer sciences gives him an affinity for technology over the confusion of emotions. Spock was allowed one conventional-type friend, Yeoman Janice Rand. The Writer/Director Guide states:

> About the only person on the ship who can joke with Mr. Spock at all is the Captain's Yeoman, Janice Rand. Perhaps beneath her swinging exterior is a motherly instinct for lonely men—at any rate, Yeoman Janice [*sic*] can mention things few others would dare say to Spock's face. And in return, guessing logically at some of her secrets, Spock will give (if you will excuse the expression) tat to tit. . . . They have an unspoken agreement that the joke will only be carried so far.[1]

Rand's relationship with Kirk is, however, limited to her job and is kept totally professional. After a few appearances, this character was dropped.

An American Southerner by birth and temperament, McCoy's friendship with Kirk grows from the fact that both men must know the rest of the crew and their strengths and weaknesses in intimate detail. McCoy is informal, distrustful of advanced technologies, and compassionate, sometimes to the extreme. Between Spock and McCoy there is a strong strain of distrust. This cuts both ways. McCoy distrusts Spock because the science officer suppresses emotions and rejects his human sensibilities. As a doctor, McCoy recognizes these as symptoms of possible pathology, and he persists in chiding his crewmate to "loosen up," lest Spock's behavior compromise McCoy's medical evaluation of his proficiency. On the other hand, Spock regards McCoy as an almost hopeless mess of emotions. McCoy's hair-trigger temper and chivalrous womanizing are contradictions to Spock that undercut McCoy's image as a medical scientist. Spock never hesitates to point to these as "primitive" qualities that must detract from McCoy's efficacy as a diagnostician and surgeon. At the base, the strength and strain in their friendship comes from the fact that they are both men of science and cannot understand how the other can do his job effectively with the psychological burdens they each carry.

As they serve together and outside their duties, Spock and McCoy offer Kirk friendships in which he can let his guard down and relax. Both men are his trusted confidants. These are also the most clearly defined and developed *Star Trek* characters.

The relationships among the other recurring *Star Trek* characters are not nearly as well delineated. Chief Engineer Scott, for example, relates well with Spock because of their mutual preoccupation with machines. He is clearly an overachiever who regards Kirk's demands for instant engineering solutions as an opportunity to display his formidable understanding of technology. Therefore, he and Kirk have a relationship based on their professional roles. Scotty, however, is closest to McCoy, with whom he can relax and enjoy a few "medicinal" drinks.

As for the characters Uhura, Chekov, Nurse Chapel, and Sulu, virtually no evidence establishes any strong friendships among them or the other recurring characters. The series producers' attention to these characters stopped after their character portraits were defined by outlining their backgrounds, education, and official duties aboard ship.

The naming of *Star Trek*'s continuing cast is one of the series' most intriguing aspects. Examination of the names that were selected for these characters may provide additional insights into their essential qualities and how their friendships relate to the central concept and themes of the series.

Throughout the series, Kirk identified himself to strangers as "Captain James T. Kirk." It turns out, for instance, that the *Enterprise* captain's name is actually "James Tiberius Kirk." Upon closer examination, each of these three names carries meanings that imbue this character with personality traits, historical dimension, and cultural resonances that relate him to some of the deepest conceptual levels of Roddenberry's series.

The captain's first name, James, refers to James I (King of England). James I is, of course, responsible for convening the greatest scholars of his time together in England to translate the Holy Bible into English. James I, son of Mary Stuart who was beheaded following her unsuccessful assassination plot against Elizabeth I, first united England and Scotland under his regency. His royal project, this translation of religious scriptures, provided James I not only with the image of divine authority but gave him a practical tool for establishing his rule over the diverse people who occupied the British Isles. This English version of the Holy Bible serves the king as shield and sword. So, James I is combination warrior and politician whose enemy is whatever threatens the integrity of the empire.

The captain's second name, Tiberius, resonates with historical meaning, too. Tiberius, of course, refers to the Roman emperor who lived from 42 B.C. to 37 A.D. During Tiberius's life span, Christianity emerged to challenge the Roman Empire's paganism. During his life, the known world and the most powerful state in that world were transformed by the emergence of a new philosophy that revealed a completely new way of seeing existence, the nature of the universe, and humanity's destiny. This new philosophy, which was based on transcending individual difference through love and faith, represented a fundamental change from the xenophobic, martial domination of Imperial Roman society. Tiberius, then, is a leader whose life bridges two worlds: one secular and exclusive, the other sacred and inclusive. So, this name signifies a man whose personality embraces two radically different modes of behavior and worldviews. He lives at the dawn of a new age when the definitions and limitations of life are completely rewritten. His name evokes a social situation in which the violent confrontations may erupt at any time but may be thwarted by understanding, compassion, and brotherly love.

The captain's third name, Kirk, bears closer examination. Kirk is Scottish for *church*. This choice for the lead character's last name evokes religion and faith. This man's identity as commander—his relationship to diplomatic duties, his fellow crewmates, and his twin missions as researcher and galactic garrison officer—is founded on a strong element of belief in the moral right of his position. Also, *church* carries the added signification of sanctuary from the perils of mortal existence and the focal point of the community of believers. In this sense, it is one of the most important cultural institutional (nodes) within the community through which individual lives are threaded and their worth reaffirmed. Kirk is the lens through which all of the diverse functions of the crew are focused, related to each other, and reinforced.

Together these three names signify the series' central concept and principal themes. *Star Trek* offers viewers an adventurous journey from a familiar, old world into the dawn of a new one full of mystery and awe. Our surrogate voyagers not only regularly hone their abilities but champion a doctrine that tests their conviction and willingness to sacrifice themselves to it. Their reward includes the knowledge that they are building a future beyond earthly limitations.

Star Trek characters below the command level are identified by names that use this technique to add signification and reinforce the series' main ideas, too. Next in the ship's chain of command is Leonard H. McCoy, M.D. In fact, in circumstances of medical emergency McCoy's authority actually supersedes the captain's. This character's personality and his name form a tight knot. As ship's physician, McCoy is inextricably bound to the body. He, of course, must often function under extreme stress with life-and-death pressures weighing on him. But the body is more than chemical processes and functions; at base, the irreducible fact is that emotions define human life. As a doctor McCoy may serve the body, but as a man he is ruled by emotions. Leo, the diminutive form of this character's first name, brings to mind "Leo the lion" and associates him with ferocity. As much as he is forceful and demanding, he is also a tempestuous hothead. In the American vernacular, a McCoy is one-half of that pair of perpetually feuding Southern families, the Hatfields and the McCoys. Therefore, he represents the two essential aspects of humanity: the compassionate individual and the romantic ruled by his emotions. As a symbol for humanity, he's "the real McCoy," a genuine token of the type.

The *Enterprise*'s executive officer (whom Roddenberry referred to as "Number One") doubles as the ship's science officer and is Spock, the Vulcan. "Spock" is the only name ever associated with this character.[2] In contemporary America, the name Spock is most readily identified with Dr. Benjamin Spock, the pediatrician. *Star Trek*'s Spock holds an advanced degree in computer science and so is a doctor, too. Benjamin Spock is perhaps most famous in American society for bringing scientific knowledge and logic to the nerve-racking tasks of childrearing. *Star Trek*'s Spock, obviously, trades on this identification. Moreover, the name "Spock" is almost less a name than a sound. By reducing a character's name to the quality of an onomatopoeic approximation of a sound, identification is founded at the physical level, the most basic fact. By linking this character with a basic physical fact, the audience is prepared for Spock as computer expert/science officer who is drained of emotion and relates to everything as cold, discernible facts.

The ship's communication officer is the lone female of command rank on the bridge and is called by the Swahili word for *freedom:* Uhura. Both by featuring a black actor as a regular member of the series' cast and by giving this character a name that is unmistakably associated with the civil rights movement sweeping over and transforming America, Roddenberry intended to identify his program with the evolution of humanity beyond racial discrimination and skin-color discrimination.

As we turn from this examination of the naming of *Star Trek* characters, it is clear that much of the original concept behind the series was being carried or reflected at this level. Revisiting these names, at the level of their cultural connotations, it is possible to regard them as threads of meaning that are consistent with and act as part of the fabric for the larger tapestry of values Roddenberry wove with *Star Trek*. Each contributes some vital element where the lack of any one would render his vision of the future too formulaic, without subtlety and closure.

Star Trek's characters reveal, in part, the way drama and conflict were factored in at this minute level. Overarching the series are the twin questions of humanity's destiny and surviving the unknown terrors of space. In other words, what is the human response to the life-and-death challenges? Spock, the cold, unmoving, logical scientist, as his name implies, reduces matters with computer-like precision to choices between yes or no. Dr. McCoy, "the real McCoy," reacts to situations with an outpouring of emotions that represent humanity at its most basic. Captain James T. Kirk leads by synthesis, that is, he receives the contradictory information, reactions, and attitudes from Spock and McCoy and finds a solution that combines their perspectives from a fresh, idiosyncratic point of view that saves the day. Completing this process, Uhura confirms (as the vital link to both Starfleet and the audience) the success of the captain, senior staff, and crew to solve problems and their ability to travel at will.

Drawing back from these specifics of character development, the question arises as to whether there is any further evidence of this pattern of relationships among these characters. Clearly, these characters represent a multiethnic and multinational microcosm of humanoid life. Moreover, the adventures and conflicts that arise in each episode are reconciled as the members of this crew bring their talents to bear on solving the problem at hand. The narrative trajectory of *Star Trek,* the way the series' narratives center on the question of identity through discovery, revolves around the ability to distill various points of view. But was this conception of these relationships and values confirmed at any other level of the *Star Trek* production? This central concept is rather neatly captured in the series publicity photograph (figure 4.1).

Across the background of the photograph are all the computer displays and station consoles that identify the *Enterprise*'s technology: its technological tentacles that stretch into space collecting data. Standing immediately in front of these computer consoles are, from left to right, Scott, Chekov, Uhura, and Sulu—in other words, a Scot, a Russian, an African, and a Japanese. This back row symbolizes the multinational, multiethnic nature of a crew that includes males and females. Next, Chapel is positioned one step in

Figure 4.1: The original crew of the Starship *Enterprise*, from left: James Doohan as Scotty, Walter Koenig as Chekov, DeForest Kelley as Dr. Mc-Coy, Majel Barrett as Nurse Chapel, William Shatner as Captain Kirk, Nichelle Nichols as Uhura, George Takei (rear) as Sulu, and Leonard Nimoy as Mr. Spock.

front of and below the rear grouping and determines a straight line from Chekov to Kirk. Chapel's pose between the row of department head and the senior staff indicates that the command is not so much a matter of pure machismo as it is a modulation of male and female perspectives: the ability to see the other person's perspective, bridge the various professional experts, and synthesize their information into a plan of action. This idea that command is at its core the synthesis of various points of view is represented by the way that McCoy, Kirk, and Spock are arranged in the midground of the picture. That is, the tempestuous McCoy and the cool, logical Spock bracket Kirk, who sits forward forming the apex of a triangle. Also, the ethnic Others (Mr. Spock, Mr. Sulu, and Lt. Uhura) are blocked or situated together on the right side of the photograph.

Supporting promotional materials, even when they were not developed by Paramount or Desilu, reflected the centrality of the white male character. For example, the first *TV Guide* cover (figure 2.1) shows Captain Kirk in the foreground of the frame and in larger scale than Mr. Spock. Kirk is also costumed in a lighter-color tunic (yellow). Behind Kirk, a pattern of lights surrounding his head creates a halo-type effect. In these ways, Kirk is identified as more important, a trusted and almost sanctified character. Mr. Spock, who is paired with his captain in this cover, is positioned behind Kirk, wears a darker-color tunic (blue), and has no patterns of lights completely surrounding his head. In this way, Spock is depicted as having less importance than Kirk, who is depicted as being a "heavier" or more complex character and morally ambiguous.

When *Star Trek: The Next Generation* was in development at Paramount, Roddenberry built on and amplified the kind of earlier character development he had used in *Star Trek*. Prospective series writers, whose approach to episodic television relied on formula plots and conventional characters were cautioned by Gene Roddenberry, the series executive producer, that melodramas were unacceptable because they do not "require believable people" and that "believable people are at the heart of good *Star Trek* scripts."[3]

These "believable" characters are at the core of the series along with the idea of relationships of trust and friendship among the commanding officers of the new *Enterprise*. When developing the recurring characters for *Star Trek: The Next Generation*, Roddenberry returned to the pattern of focusing on the same operational departments that he used in the previous series. In the sequel series, the number of recurring characters, again the command staff plus key department heads, is expanded to include the son of one of the ship's officers. The regular cast of *Star Trek: The Next Generation* consisted of an older, male European captain (Jean-Luc Picard), a young, white male American executive officer (William T. Riker), a Scottish female chief medical officer (Dr. Beverly Crusher), an African-descended male chief of engineering (Geordi La Forge), a Klingon male chief of security (Mr. Worf), a white-gold-tinted male android (Mr. Data), a half-Betazoid, half-Terran female ship counselor (Deanna Troi), and a white, teenage male science prodigy and ensign (Wesley Crusher).

As before, each of these characters is depicted as a thoroughly trained professional or, in the case of Wesley Crusher, as a child prodigy. These Starfleet personnel share qualities that include the mastery over complex technology and the willingness to face danger with unflappable courage and answer the unknown with creativity. Also as before, these characters form strong bonds of friendship with their crewmates that reveal even more about these characters.[4]

Starting at the top of the command hierarchy, Captain Picard is described as having four important shipboard relationships. The four characters with whom Picard has close bonds are Riker, Troi, Data, and Guinan. Between Picard and Riker there is essentially a professional relationship. These two men must depend on each other for the safety of the ship and crew, but Picard regards Riker as more than a professional colleague and thinks of him as a trusted friend. The relationship between Picard and Troi is more unusual, because her Betazoid abilities give her access to Picard's innermost feelings whether invited or not. As captain, Picard dearly guards his privacy, so he keeps Troi at a distinct professional distance. There is no intimation of intimacy between them. Ironically, Picard's relationship with Data is the one that comes closest to actual friendship. At first it might seem odd that Picard would feel close friendship with an artificial life-form. But Data provides Picard with the daily opportunity to reexperience the way learning and discovery stimulate the individual's growth and shape his outlook. Picard sees Data's purity of logic and insatiable appetite for knowledge as an opportunity for mentoring about the dimensionality of human experience. His immaturity reinforces Picard's stature as a wise older male, mature adult, and leader.

Next, Commander William T. Riker is described as having three relationships. His closest mates aboard the *Enterprise* are Troi, La Forge, and Wesley Crusher. Before joining the *Enterprise* as "Number One," Riker and Troi were a romantic couple. However close they may have been to becoming engaged or married, their Starfleet careers intervened and forced them to separate. To their credit, they still regard each other as friends. Serving together on the *Enterprise* has meant that they have had to put their past relationship in perspective and see each other as individuals. They manage to be warm and comfortable with each other yet give one another the freedom to develop new intimate relationships.

Riker's best male friendship is with Geordi La Forge. Riker, who is a young, vital man and something of a ladies' man, regards La Forge's blindness as an interference with his romantic experiences. Riker is determined to help La Forge make up for lost time. Riker regards Wesley as the younger brother he never had, and Wesley reciprocates with hero worship for Riker as "the perfect Starfleet officer."

Data, the artificial life-form fabricated by Dr. Soong, is the next in the *Enterprise*'s chain of command. As described earlier, Data's closest relationship is with Picard. His other relationship is with Geordi La Forge. The tie that binds these two characters is engineering: Data the mechanical man, La Forge the master mechanic.

Roddenberry hints at the possibility of Dr. Crusher and Picard "developing a strong mutual attraction." However, he provided no more information regarding that possibility beyond that vague intimation, nor are other relationships with Dr. Crusher described.[5] Troi's relationships with Picard and Riker have already been described, as have Geordi La Forge's relationships with Riker and Data. Worf, the only Klingon serving aboard a Starfleet vessel, was conceived as serving without the comfort of friendship.[6] The youngest member of the recurring cast, Wesley Crusher, enjoys the friendship of three officers: Picard, Riker, and La Forge. Picard and Wesley have a stern father-and-son relationship that is a bit shaky because of the older man's unfamiliarity with the parental role. Wesley's relationship with Riker is a big brother-little-brother relationship described earlier. His friendship with Geordi logically follows from their common interest in technology, mathematics, and engineering. Guinan is the most enigmatic and the last recurring character to join the ship's crew. There is the suggestion that Guinan and Picard have a special friendship. However, Roddenberry's guide for writers and directors provides no further information about Guinan's friendship with Picard or any other crewmate.[7]

Some of the names of the continuing characters of *Star Trek: The Next Generation* seem at least as interesting as those found in the original series. A closer look at the new *Enterprise*'s bridge officers' names might provide a basis for comparison with the earlier series' continuing cast of shipboard command officers.

Here the *Enterprise*'s captain is Jean-Luc Picard, a proud scion of ancient France. In examining the symbolism of this character's name we must, then, be sensitive to French culture. His first name Jean evokes Ste. Jean, or St. John, also known as John the Baptist. St. John is associated with Midsummer's Day and the midpoint of summer. This double symbolism is particularly engaging. St. John, of course, traveled far and wide with an unorthodox message of brotherhood and redemption through faith in a power that surpassed the authority of all earthly governments. He has been described as a man of wisdom, patience, and humility. These are the key qualities of Captain Picard, too. Moreover, his tenure as the *Enterprise*'s captain coincides with a middle phase in this fictionalized evolution of humanoid exploration of space. The first phase, of swashbuckling adventure and captains like Kirk, is long past. The Federation's successes means it has grown, more and more civilizations have been absorbed within its hierarchy, and space exploration has turned into largely an administrative problem. Picard, as an older, middle-aged man, is the dutiful keeper of the flame—a kind of manager—until the humans enter their third phase of space tenure and transform themselves beyond the limitation of the physical universe.

Jean, spelled *Jeanne*, naturally evokes associations with Jeanne d'Arc. This historical French figure is synonymous with brilliant military leadership and passionate dedication to religious conviction to the point of personal, physical endangerment. Jeanne d'Arc is equally a towering example of integrity, even unto torture and death. Her legacy is the triumph of spirit so committed to an idea that she drew others—by the authority of her faith—to join her and to advance the reach of Christianity through the force of arms. As captain of Starfleet's flagship, Picard must face the very real prospect of capture and mistreatment at the hand of forces hostile to the Federation. Also, as a quasimilitary leader, one of his main responsibilities is contact with "new life and new civilizations" with an offer of Federation membership, a commitment to something greater. In this way, these two figures, one historical and the other fictional, are linked.

His second name, Luc, is French for Luke. Luke was one of Jesus' twelve apostles and one of the four evangelists who wrote about Jesus' life and times. Before meeting Jesus, Luke was a physician and therefore well educated about the physical world. Also, he was a gentile. Luke was one of Jesus' inner retinue who switched both occupation and religion to accept a vocation as a disciple. The point here is that Luke's witness changed his world-view, transformed him from being dedicated to the empirical to explicating and sharing the ineffable "good news" about redemptive spiritual love. Picard has himself experienced an analogous conversion. His Starfleet Academy training was supposed to lead to a career as an archeologist, but the spiritual quest for affirmation of the power of life among the stars won out over uncovering dead civilizations and unlocking their secrets.

There are three possibilities for the surname Picard, two French, one Swiss. It might equally refer to Jean Picard, or Émile Picard, or Auguste Piccard. The first was the first French astronomer after whom a crater in the first quadrant of Earth's moon is named. The second was a mathematician. Astronomy and mathematics are, of course, the keys to modern astrophysics. Astrophysics is the science that will be the main preoccupation of the research voyages of the starship *Enterprise* and her crew. The third historical figure with this surname, Auguste Piccard, was a physicist who investigated radioactivity and atmospheric electricity. Additionally, he was the first to make an ascent into the stratosphere to an altitude of 57,793 feet in an airtight gondola of his own construction and was a deep-sea explorer and designer of bathyscapes.[8]

The executive officer of the new *Enterprise* is William Thomas Riker. His first name quite possibly refers to a character, William T. (Tiberius) Rice, from Roddenberry's earlier failed series, *The Lieutenant*.[9] Moreover, the name William comes from the Old German "Willahelm" that, in turn, is composed of *Wilja*, meaning will or leader, and *helma*, which may be translated as helmet. Taken together, we might say that William stands for someone whose role is to protect his captain or leader. This is indeed an appropriate first name for the first officer of the *Enterprise*.

Throughout most of this series, Riker's middle name is undisclosed; in formal introductions he is referred to as "William T. Riker." This formulation, of course, echoes back to the way the first series' captain referred to himself and was announced formally to others, that is, "This is Captain James T. Kirk of the *Enterprise*," or "This is Captain Jean-Luc Picard of the *Enterprise*." This anomalous situation was resolved in a recent episode that revealed the discovery of a duplicate "Riker" (created in a transporter accident that occurred before Riker accepted assignment aboard the *Enterprise*). In this episode, for the first time, Riker's middle name is given as Thomas. Thomas comes into English from the Hebrew word for *twin*. It may well be that the series producers and story editors used the fact that the character Riker's middle name had not been fully specified as an opportunity to craft an episode that would resolve this gap.

This character's last name is much more elusive.[10] Some evidence indicates that Riker may be either a corruption of Rickert, which is an Anglicization of the Dutch Rijkert, or a corruption of Ricker (Rickerson, descendent of Richere). Rijkert is a variation on Richard, which is associated with the concepts of rule and tenacity, and Ricker may be thought to mean might or force of arms.

The choice of the *Enterprise*'s executive officer's names match and announce his essential, Starfleet-defined functions: strong, military-style protector of the group leader; a second in command who follows the book even though it may require him to seem harsh.

Among the recurring characters in the sequel series is the *Enterprise*'s chief medical officer Beverly Crusher. Her first name, Beverly, is a British place name meaning beaver stream. Following the public's reception of G. B. McCutcheon's novel *Beverly of Graustark,* with its heroine a beautiful Southern woman named Beverly, this name became popular. It is interesting to note that here, with this character's first name, an association is made with American Southern culture and with one of the original series' most colorful characters, the emotionally overflowing Dr. McCoy, also a Southerner. Her last name, Crusher, derives from a verb that means to overpower. The combination of these names yields "a powerful or determined and beautiful woman." The casting of this character seems to bear out this interpretation.

As with the inaugural series, its successor includes a recurring cast member who is of African descent. This character is the ship's chief engineer, Geordi La Forge. If we follow the step-by-step strategy in approaching this character's names, we can see how they combine to form the definition of this character. First, Geordi may be thought of as either a corruption of Georgi, the Bulgarian form for George, or a fairly common British (Scots) nickname for George. Second, George is a Britishism for the automatic pilot used in airplanes, another form of servant ("Let George do it!"). And as a British colloquialism, it may also refer to Geordi as the nickname for anyone from the Newcastle area (coal mining) of northeast

England.[11] At this point, then, our interpretation of this first name yields "a subordinate whose work involves developing sources of energy and whose countenance carries the mark of that work" (e. g., darkened skin).

La Forge, this character's second name, is literally translated as "the forge." It is a name associated with smiths and anyone who works with forges. *Forge* is used for both the place where metals are tempered and shaped and the techniques used for this work. In the *Star Trek: The Next Generation* context, *forge* refers more generally to the fabrication of technology or the use of advanced techniques to maintain the integrity and security of the ship and its missions.

Taken together, these names describe a character whose role is subordinate to others' command authority, who understands and manipulates sources of energy and physically bears the symbols of his intimate contact with energy (darkened skin) and technology (high-tech prosthetic artificial eye sensors).[12]

On this version of the *Enterprise*, there is a psychologist/counselor named Deanna Troi. Deanna is another form of Diana. Diana, from Roman mythology, was the goddess identified with Earth's celestial satellite and designated protector of women. As the ship's sole female bridge officer, Deanna represents all women: projection and protector of womankind. Troi, her last name, is a variation on the spelling of the Greek city Troy, which evokes the story of Helen, whose beauty drove men of the ancient world to war to win her love.[13] Here, as with the Beverly Crusher character, a female character is associated with the quality of disarming physical beauty. Moreover, Troi's principal attribute involves her ability to read others' emotions; she is a kind of humanoid emotional radio receiver. Rather than her colleagues who display command, technical, scientific, or medical expertise based on empirical data, Troi deals in the insubstantial.

The android officer named Data is the final expression of what was only alluded to in the earlier series' character, Mr. Spock. The fact that he has only one name places additional stress on this single name: Data. Throughout *Star Trek: The Next Generation*, crewmates address this android as "Mr. Data," echoing the earlier series' science officer who was defined by logic. Moreover, in attaching a name to a character that is synonymous with facts, information, and statistics, this series reduces experience of reality to empirical confirmation (that which can be observed, confirmed experimental, or calculated). That earlier character's penchant for logic and order and his desire to escape human emotions come to completion in Lieutenant Data.[14]

Threading through the names of this crew, one can recognize several of the major themes around which this successor series was centered. Tradition and order in this series replace the brash and adventurous spirit of its parent program. This emphasis on tradition is supported by parallel developments that place a high value on personal integrity and near-religious faith in science. In this brave, future world, where the Starfleet/Federation bureaucracy manages the scientific exploration of space, the presence of female characters indicates that the biases that block individuals from rising to challenge no longer obtain. Race and gender have been embraced by Starfleet and the Federation, and females and ethnic Others (Terran and non-Terran) are seen in every Starfleet/Federation context. Indeed, one of the important related issues in *Star Trek: The Next Generation* is the extension of humanity to cybernetic lifeforms. Unfortunately, their names indicate that the point of identification for audiences with these characters has less to do with twenty-fourth century opportunities for female, ethnic, alien, and cybernetic Others and more to do with contemporary attitudes about work, sex, and race.

Much of the consistency between the two series doubtless stems from the fact that Roddenberry wrote the guidelines for both and guided production, including selection of line producers and early script approval, with a firm hand.[15] An example of the series' self-conscious attention to detail is demonstrated in the rigorous guidelines that writers and directors were required to adhere to so that consistency was maintained from episode to episode and with known scientific facts and characters' traits.[16] In fact, Roddenberry's guidelines spend considerable time drawing character traits and creating logical relationships among continuing characters.[17] From these guidelines for the series, it is clear that, as with *Star Trek*, this one would be based on exploring the ways ethnic diversity combines to meet new challenges at the frontiers of human experience and knowledge.

Unfortunately, the character names in *Star Trek: The Next Generation* do not self-consciously reference the kinds of pivotal personages and moments in history that represented changes in philosophical perspectives and marked advances in Western humanist traditions in civil and human rights or heroic human qualities. That is, the recurring character names of *Star Trek: The Next Generation* reveal a shift of emphasis to the level of personal valor, commitment, and accomplishment. Beyond this, the values expressed with these characters' names include security, technical craft, physical appeal, strength, and the intimation that humans are in essence empirical observation machines plus ineffable emotions. Overall, the sequel displays a rather antiseptic quality that is perhaps due to the fact that at no point do these character names or their connotations indicate larger social issues that plague American society, as was seen with the recurring characters' names from *Star Trek*. Instead, the naming of the recurring characters in *Star Trek: The Next Generation* and the acting reflect a shift from the contemporary social landscape to issues of personal fulfillment in service to the administrative needs of Starfleet and the United Federation of Planets.

If we step back from considering the individual members of the crew of *Star Trek: The Next Generation*, it may be possible to discern other patterns of association among these recurring cast members. Regarding the group as a whole, it appears that the recurring characters of the series form a family group: Picard as father; Crusher as surrogate mother figure; Troi as daughter; Riker as older brother; Worf as the second oldest male sibling (and a kind of mirror image of Riker); as younger brothers Data, Geordi, and Wesley Crusher, the doctor's adolescent son, respectively; and Guinan as the eccentric visiting relative.[18]

Although Picard functions as the patriarchical head of this family, he is definitely presented as a bachelor father figure, alone, stern, and slightly somber. Crusher is not associated with him as his wife or mate. Instead, Crusher should be thought of as the eldest daughter who assumes the responsibilities of a mother but none of the functions of the wife, in the absence of the mother/wife figure. Riker and Worf are very similar: both are extremely dedicated, anxious for command, and are physically robust specimens of mature males. One explanation for the fact that Riker and Troi never rekindle their romance may lie in this family metaphor: it is taboo for siblings to be sexually intimate in this society. The fact that Data, Geordi, and Wesley form only fleeting relationships with females that never really develop beyond the first blush of flirtation is a strong association with youth and sexual immaturity. Guinan is depicted without any romantic partner or indication of sexuality. Moreover, her character exhibits liberal doses of whimsy that suggest the kind of free play allowed when distant relations visit and interact with younger members of the extended family.

The characters in *Star Trek: The Next Generation* reveal, in part, the way drama and conflict were factored in at this level of detail, too. Together they comprise a surrogate family with which audiences may identify. There is in these relationships no sense, as we saw in the earlier series, of these characters forming a larger, organic quality that permits the synthesis of information and ultimately success.

Again drawing back from these particulars of character development, we return to the question raised earlier: is there any further evidence of this pattern among these characters? As before, they represent a broad definition of humanoid life, including many different ethnic and national identities and expanded to embrace artificial life. However, in *Star Trek: The Next Generation* the adventures and conflicts that arise in each episode are reconciled as the individual members of this crew bring their talents to bear on solving the problem at hand in isolation or within their specific department. The narrative trajectory of *Star Trek: The Next Generation*, the way the series' narratives are presented in each episode and across each season, tends to validate the individual over the collaborative process among equals. A reference to the standard publicity photograph for the series will illuminate this point (see figure 4.2).

The publicity photograph for *Star Trek: The Next Generation* is rather self-consciously modeled after the ones for *Star Trek* (see figure 4.1). As with the earlier photograph, across the background are the computer displays and station consoles that identify the *Enterprise*'s technology. Standing immediately in front of these computer consoles and stations are, from left to right, Riker, Data, Guinan, Geordi, and Worf. As before, this array of personnel represents a mix of male, female, white, black, physically challenged, and artificial life. Troi, Picard, and Crusher are standing near the foreground.

This image may bear similarity to the earlier bridge crew photograph, but there are differences. First, this photograph does not

Figure 4.2: The crew of *Star Trek: The Next Generation,* from left: (back row) Jonathan Frakes as William Riker, Brent Spiner as Data, Whoopi Goldberg as Guinan, LeVar Burton as Geordi La Forge, Michael Dorn as Worf; (front row) Marina Sirtis as Deanna Troi, Patrick Stewart as Captain Picard, and Gates MacFadden as Dr. Crusher.

have the subtle blocking that we found in the earlier example, blocking that links the characters arrayed across the background and the qualities they represent with the command staff in the front. Second, as discussed earlier, these recurring characters form a new kind of television family group with an older, European man as patriarch and two extraterrestrials and an android. A third point of difference emerges, however, as we examine the details of the way the individual characters are represented. Each of the recurring characters that are female, extraterrestrial, ethnic, or biracial are depicted in other than the standard Starfleet uniform. Crusher wears a powder-blue lab coat, Troi is shown wearing a skin-tight jump suit with a plunging neckline, Worf wears a Klingon sash, La Forge's eyes are covered by his visual instrument and sensory organ replacement (VISOR), and Guinan is dressed in decidedly civilian clothing and is the only character who wears a hat. By making these costuming choices, the creators of the series are using subtle symbols to mark them as different, create a distance between them and their shipmates, and establish the category of Other.

The blocking of the characters, where they are positioned, reveals a fourth difference from the earlier photograph. This picture is divided by the curving arc of a balustrade into two distinct groups. The key point here is that Picard stands in the foreground with the aristocratic Troi and the statuesque Crusher. In other words, the patriarchal head, Picard, is bracketed by beautiful, single women. This blocking strategy underscores that privilege of patriarchal authority that grants the white male leader access to women. Picard, with a lovely lady on each arm, is marked as the most important and powerful male in the grouping. Despite the plotlines that link Picard with Guinan in a special relationship of trust and intimacy, this single and presumably available female was not selected to stand by his side. Instead, Picard is flanked by two white female actors. Obviously, this blocking strategy privileges the white females over the African American and underscores them as more desirable by virtue of their proximity to the patriarchal leader, Picard.

Across the background, from left to right, are Riker, Data, Guinan, La Forge, and Worf. Their relative position marks them as having less importance than Picard. Riker and Worf, who bookend this grouping, are possible competitors for Picard's authority. But by positioning them behind a bar, they are represented as effectively blocked from challenging the leader. Moreover, Riker's and Worf's relegation to secondary importance is further marked by their proximity to Terran and extraterrestrial Others.

According to this analysis of the publicity photographs command on *Star Trek* was represented as the combination of the specific training and personalities of the recurring characters focused through Captain Kirk. However, the publicity photograph for *Star Trek: The Next Generation* represents command much more as a privilege associated with white male maturity. The photo's image of recurring characters of *Star Trek* seems consistent with the prior discussion of how the crew functions together and the way success was defined: the expertise of officers and crew is synthesized through Kirk. However, the image of the recurring characters of *Star Trek: The Next Generation,* as shown in its publicity photograph, seems consistent with the earlier discussion of how the crew members function and relate to each other and the way command was defined: Picard stands alone, aloof as captain and supported by his steadfast association with the Starfleet/Federation hierarchy. As if to underline the privilege and prerogatives of white male authority, Picard is surrounded by available women (Troi, Crusher, and Guinan) who form a triangle with him at the center.

Supporting promotional materials, even when they were not developed by Paramount, continued to reflect the centrality and importance of the white male captain. For example, the *TV Guide* cover that commemorated the end of *Star Trek: The Next Generation's* first-run syndication (figure 3.5) depicted the show's entire continuing cast. We can see striking similarities in the way this publication depicts these characters and characterized Kirk and Spock years before and the way its symbolization is consistent with both the series' portrayal of character relations and the Federation's hegemony over member worlds. For example, Picard is represented in the background and in a larger scale than the other characters. Leading down from him on a diagonal line to the left are Riker and Crusher. Across the bottom third of the cover are Worf, Geordi, Data, and Troi. The two white Terran officers, Riker and Crusher, are represented on a smaller scale than Picard. However, the lower-ranked officers are represented on the smallest scale. Moreover, all of the ethnic others are grouped together at the bottom of the cover. Furthermore, Worf and Geordi, two dark-skinned ethnic Others, are next to each other. The Betazoid Troi is depicted in a way that her black hair forms a barrier between her and the dark-skinned males. And, Data, the android Other, occupies the very bottom of the frame. This mode of representation clearly recapitulates the white male privilege and hierarchical organization of the Federation and its attitudes toward ethnics, aliens, and Others.

Cultural products, such as television series, reflect in their aesthetic qualities and choices the periods of their development. *Star Trek* and *Star Trek: The Next Generation* are not exempt from comparisons with their times. The first series was created and produced during the 1960s, a decade that encouraged collectivist political and social approaches to social issues. Individuals who were not part of the ruling elites and their representatives in government and business came together to overcome some of their disadvantages and gain a voice in determining the social agenda. From this analysis of some of the key elements of *Star Trek*, it seems clear that the series in a very fundamental way reflects the spirit that the success for its space-bound society depended on the integration of individuals into a purposeful collective.

The sequel series was produced during the "greed is good" era of the 1980s, a decade that encouraged a go-it-alone, highly individualistic, even self-indulgent approach to life and social interaction. Social and political activities were discounted and viewed within the context of business or currying business advantage from increasingly powerful national and international corporations. In this view, the individual's effort received validation to the extent that it benefited corporate, not social, objectives. From this perspective, society is considered a function of business development; public good and culture, a by-product of commerce.

Chapter 5

Selected Logs

> Quit yelling and listen to me. I'm letting you in on a trade se-
> cret: Really bad media can exorcise your semiotic ghosts. If it
> keeps the saucer people off my back, it can keep these Art
> Deco futuroids off yours. Try it. What have you got to lose?[1]

As a reader of science fiction; a regular viewer of both *Star Trek* series; a confirmed consumer of science fiction mass media products
such as comic books, short stories and novels, radio and television
programs; and someone who studies and teaches about media representations of ethnicity, I am drawn to examine the ways
ethnicity is handled semiotically by a media product that is so popular and globally disseminated. Ethnic and Africanist representations in any broadcast or cable television program are in and of
themselves worth study, as part of the continuing analytical project to examine the relationship between society and race. Also, because the country's television marketplace requires producers to
develop programming that audiences of millions of viewers will
appreciate and engage, the sheer size of the audiences for these series and their costs of production make them noteworthy as cultural products. Moreover, when a series becomes an export product, it brings American attitudes and values to an international
television market that includes Eastern and Western Europe, the
Far East, Central and South America, and ultimately a world environment predominantly composed of people whose ethnic, religious, and cultural identification does not originate with the West.

The interest of researchers engaged in the study of ethnic images in mass media is thus redoubled.

I do not intend to assert an ad hominem "politically correct" argument about these programs nor frankly to celebrate their intention to develop characters, situations, and themes sensitive to the general social pressure to ameliorate society's treatment and mass media images of African Americans. Rather, to avoid reduction,[2] this analysis will be limited to the television series *Star Trek* and *Star Trek: The Next Generation* and will use extracts from selected episodes or programs that feature at least a plot line or an entire episode centering on ethnicity.[3] The goals of this analysis will be to determine the specific semiotic codes that are associated with ethnicity, compare the meanings of those codes, at the denotative and connotative levels, and determine whether any change occurs from one series to the other. The results of such a comparison should reveal the extent to which ethnicity can be accommodated to the mythopoetic impulse to create social fantasies about the future and the extent to which representations of ethnicity demonstrated in these programs break from the one-dimensional stereotypes associated with American media's uses of ethnicity.[4]

Rather than constructing another review of *Star Trek* and *Star Trek: The Next Generation* or evaluating their aesthetic elements, I am interested in exploring the complexity of televisual communication. Ambiguous and subtle meanings will be teased from these televisual texts to construct alternative readings—that is, readings other than those that advance the specific plots.

This project proposes to draw attention to spectatorship as an active process of reception and to highlight how a television viewer's identity and relationship with various categories of viewers, such as general audience and dedicated viewers of *Star Trek* series, may be supported by the active process of constructing or inscribing a place for viewers as a part of the ongoing reading of televisual texts. Another point here is to resist the dominating effect of production categories, genres, and interpretations associated with other aspects of the mass media process, such as advertising, celebrity interviews, and behind-the-scenes documentaries.

Limiting criticism to aesthetic categories, chronological treatments, or thematic discussions only generates more rules about structure and form and prohibits examination of how writers' and directors' choices of symbols set meanings in motion.[5] Instead of deducing normative rules that are then applied to determine whether a series or episode successfully executes a particular formula, this study endeavors to understand how a text functions and may support more than one reading.[6] Television writers and directors could hardly be interested in redoing what has been done before only to render it perfect according to some normative and prescriptive rules of form. Such a position constitutes another reduction of creativity that reverses the relationship between writers and directors and their critics, making the latter's work more important.

Star Trek and *Star Trek: The Next Generation* episodes will be deconstructed here to articulate narrative content that may otherwise remain inaccessible. This study renounces the temptation to develop new structures or readings based on interpretations of those aesthetic categories. More than promoting free play, deconstruction—especially when combined with a gradual, systematic reading—produces a reading of a televisual text that goes beyond mediating on "the indeterminacy of meaning."[7] Instead, by breaking the text's narrative unity—shifting from encouraging interaction (readerly) to appreciating production (writerly) choices—its central voice is excised, and suppressed cultural and political meanings resurface.[8] Accordingly, this analysis shuttles back and forth through the selected episode extracts to produce a commentative text[9] as substitute for a simple representative explanation or review and to reveal the possibilities of symbolic richness and levels of ideological content so far obscured.[10]

An additional dimension of this study may be found in its intention to examine two distinct television series, separated by twenty-five years but related by having the same origin (Roddenberry) and by expressing the same, central utopian concept (i.e., the future as multiethnic and full of adventure and challenge).[11] It follows, then, that the semiotic meanings obtained in the initial phase of this analysis, which identify the episodes or portions thereof that center on ethnicity, would be subjected to further examination to relate them to this future mythology.

This project will first identify from the specific selected extracts the symbolic codes associated with the representation of an Other, here limited to recurring ethnic Starfleet officers or featured ethnic characters. Next, these selected extracts, where issues about ethnicity are the central focus, will be subjected to narratological and semiotic analyses[12] to release the specific content from their dramatic contexts and then be compared to produce a more fluid reading that relates these symbols to the larger televisual context.[13] Third, this study will evaluate the extent to which, in the face of the changing economic context of television and social change, producers adhered to a formulaic representation of ethnicity or, in fact, boldly went where few have gone before. Finally, the characters, actions, and values represented in both series will be evaluated against the background of changing American cultural, business, and race relations.

Thus, this examination has three phases: syntagmatic, paradigmatic, and synchronic. In the syntagmatic phase, the audiovisual content of the selected episodes and extracts from *Star Trek* and *Star Trek: The Next Generation* will be examined as they unfold, to cull from the episodes and the extracts the major categories through which ethnic themes are developed. In the paradigmatic phase, the audiovisual content of the two series will be examined to reveal any recurrent symbolic information (e.g., physical appearance, actions, sociological relationships among characters, and characters' habitats) that is associated with the representation of ethnicity across all selected episodes. The synchronic phase involves determining and explicating any patterns or relationships between the codes of representation (e.g., the physical appearance of an ethnic character and his or her ability to form personal relationships) that articulate—or obdurate—a utopian social vision on ethnicity.[14]

Selected *Star Trek* Episodes

Three episodes from *Star Trek*—"Space Seed," "The Ultimate Computer," and "Plato's Stepchildren"—and four from *Star Trek: The Next Generation*—"The Emissary," "Reunion," "Booby Trap," and "Galaxy's Child"—were identified for analysis on the basis of their treatment of racial or ethnic themes at least at the level of subplot. The three episodes from *Star Trek* coincidentally were spread across the series' three seasons. "Space Seed" was picked from the series' first year, "The Ultimate Computer" in the second year, and "Plato's Stepchildren" in the third season.

There are six examples (numbered 1.1 through 1.6 here) from

"Space Seed" in which ethnicity emerges explicitly and becomes central to the narrative. (1.1) The first occurs immediately after the *Enterprise* finds a small, old, derelict spaceship adrift in deep space. An *Enterprise* team beams over to the ancient ship to investigate and discovers its passengers in suspended animation. Chief Engineer Scott surveys the ship's condition and cryogenic equipment and, turning to the sleeping passengers, describes them by referring disparagingly to their racial heritage: "They're all mixed types, Western, mid-European, Latin, Oriental."

(1.2) Back aboard the *Enterprise*, Kirk revives one of these mysterious travelers and wonders about the origins of the ship and its passengers. He asks Spock whether he thinks they could be criminals. Spock reassures Kirk that they are not likely to be criminals because deep-space exile was too expensive and too great a technological challenge to be used to exile criminals.[15]

(1.3) The next instance takes place in the *Enterprise*'s sickbay where Khan Noonian Singh (identified as a northern Indian Sikh), the first "sleeper" brought to the *Enterprise* from the crippled *S.S. Botany Bay*,[16] attacks Dr. McCoy immediately following his resuscitation. While Dr. McCoy makes a medical log entry, Khan surveys the surroundings, discovers a wall-mounted display of ancient surgical instruments, moves from his bed to the display, takes down a scalpel, and returns to his bed. Moments later, when McCoy comes in to check on his patient, Khan, who pretends to sleep, suddenly reaches up, grabs McCoy, puts the scalpel to the doctor's throat, and demands to know what has happened to him.

(1.4) The fourth occurs in the context of a dinner given by Kirk to honor Khan. Khan arrives at the quarters of Lieutenant Mc-Givers, an *Enterprise* historian, to escort her to dinner and, noticing her paintings of some of Earth's most dynamic and romanticized leaders, says to her, "All bold men of the past: Richard the Lion-Hearted, Leif Erikson, Napoleon. A hobby of yours, such men of the past. I am honored. Thank you. But I caution you, such men take what they want." After the dinner, McGivers goes to Khan's quarters to apologize for Spock's and Kirk's rude behavior at dinner and to pursue her infatuation. Alone again, McGivers succumbs to Khan's magnetism; an amorous embrace leads to passionate kissing. However, matters turn more serious as Khan confides to McGivers his plan to take over the *Enterprise*. She balks at the idea but succumbs to her emotions and agrees to help.

(1.5) The fifth example occurs as Kirk reveals to Khan that they have figured out his identity and he interviews Khan to find out about the reasons behind his starflight. Khan replies that their purpose was "a new life, a chance to build a new world, other things I doubt that you would understand." Kirk probes further: "Why? Because I'm not a product of controlled genetics?" Khan blurts back, "Captain, although your abilities intrigue me, you are quite honestly inferior. Mentally. Physically. In fact I am surprised about how little improvement there has been in human evolution. Oh, there has been technical advancement. But how little man himself has changed. No, it appears we will do quite well in your century." This exchange highlights Khan's personality in conflict with Kirk's and points out Khan's vulnerability, his psychological flaw: self-defeating hubris about his genetic constitution.

(1.6) Near the end of the episode, after Khan has captured the bridge crew and incapacitated the *Enterprise,* the sixth instance occurs. Khan berates the command staff, sans Kirk, because they are unaugmented humanoids: "Nothing ever changes, except man. Your technical accomplishments. Improve a technical device and you may double productivity, but improve man and you gain a thousandfold. I am such a man. Join me. I need your technical skills to operate a starship. Join me and I will treat you well." And later in that scene, Khan directs one of his renegades to force Uhura to engage the ship's monitoring screen and tune it to observe Kirk being tortured in the medical department's decompression chamber. Uhura's initial refusal to cooperate causes her captor to slap her face, and Khan comments ironically, "I should have known that suffocating together on the bridge would create heroic camaraderie among you. But it is quite a different thing to sit by and watch it happening to someone else." After he forces Uhura to activate the screen, the crew is forced to watch Kirk in the chamber suffering as its atmosphere is withdrawn.

The episode "The Ultimate Computer" introduces the character of scientist Dr. Richard Daystrom (whose research expertise includes physics, electronics, and computer science). It contains five examples (here 2.1 through 2.5) of content that bear on ethnicity. Dr. Daystrom, an African-American inventor and developer of duotronics (the technology that enables devices throughout spaceships to function), joins the *Enterprise* to install and test his latest breakthrough in computer technology: multitronics, the basis for the M5 computer as the *Enterprise's* new coordinating brain for a series of war games designed to test its command and control capacities. Daystrom is understandably anxious to prove that his technology is truly revolutionary and that he is still capable of the scientific creativity and innovative applications of the theories that marked his youth. Unfortunately, Daystrom's research project perturbs the *Enterprise's* smooth veneer of familiar relationships and expectations.

(2.1) The first indication that Daystrom's work is not welcome occurs as the scientist is making the final installation of M5. In engineering, deep within the ship's bowels, Daystrom and Kirk have a sharp confrontation. Daystrom reports, "M5 is ready to take control of the ship." Kirk questions, "Total control?" Daystrom asserts, "That is what it is designed for, Captain." Kirk protests, "There are certain things that men must do to remain men. Your computer would take that away." "There are other things that a man like you might do," Daystrom argues. "Or, perhaps you object to the possible loss of the prestige and the ceremony accorded the starship captain. The computer could do your job and without all that."

(2.2) The next instance transpires as Spock and Kirk evaluate M5's performance. Kirk, troubled over M5's formidable capabilities, relents, "Machine over man, Spock? It was impressive. It might even be practical." Spock, however, says "Practical, Captain? Perhaps, but not desirable. Computers make excellent and efficient servants, but I have no wish to serve under them. Captain, a starship also runs on loyalty . . . to one man and nothing can replace it or him."

(2.3) Later, after the M5 unit attacks and destroys a robot ore-ship, Kirk orders the unit disengaged, the trials halted, and the *Enterprise* returned to a nearby starbase for a formal investigation. In engineering, McCoy confronts Daystrom over M5's performance and challenges him to find a way to disconnect the errant machine. McCoy demands, "Have you found a solution? A way to shut that thing off?" Daystrom shoots back, "You don't shut a child off when it makes a mistake. M5 is growing, learning." McCoy flashes back, "Learning to kill!" Correcting McCoy, Daystrom lectures that M5 is learning "to defend itself . . . quite a different thing. When a child is taught it is programmed with simple instructions and, at some point, if its mind develops properly, it exceeds the sum of what it

was taught. Thinks independently." Still worried, McCoy counters, "That thing is a danger to all of us. Now find some way to shut
it off." Daystrom tries one last time to convince McCoy, "You can't
understand. Frightened because you can't understand it. I'm going
to show you, I'm going to show all of you. It takes 430 people to
man a starship. With this you don't need anyone. One machine can
do all those things they send men out to do now. Men no longer
need die in space or on some alien world. Men can live and go on
to achieve greater things than fact finding and dying for galactic
space which is neither ours to give or to take."

(2.4) The fourth instance follows an unsuccessful attempt to
neutralize M5. Kirk and Spock confront Daystrom and learn about
the secret at the heart of the multitronics revolution. Spock queries
Daystrom about the unit's performance: "It is not performing in a
logical manner." Kirk joins in, demanding, "Dr. Daystrom, Dr.
Daystrom, I want an answer right now. I'm tired of hearing about
the M5's new approach. What is it exactly? What is it?" Spock,
softening Kirk's impatience, says, "I don't mean to offend, sir. But
it behaves with an almost human pattern." Daystrom boastfully
answers, "Yes, quite right Mr. Spock. You see, one of the arguments against computers controlling ships was that they could not
think like men." Kirk, still impatient, spits out, "Your new approach?" Daystrom answers, "Exactly! I've developed a method
of impressing human engrams upon the computer circuits, the re-
lays are not unlike the synapse of the brain. M5 thinks, Captain."
Then later, Kirk and Spock learn that the human engrams that
Daystrom used as his model for computer circuits were his own
(and falls, therefore, into that category of notorious fictional scientists whose self-experimentation leads to disaster). Also, according to this formula, Daystrom's (Frankenstein) creation is his
progeny and a monster (as people fear out-of-control science).

(2.5) The fifth instance occurs in the *Enterprise's* sick bay after
Kirk successfully forces M5 to disconnect itself by using the logic
of M5's program prohibitions against harming humanoids to convince it that it has broken its own prime directive by committing
murder. The machine responds by disengaging all systems, and
Kirk regains command. Moments later in sick bay, Kirk, Spock,
and McCoy stand over the unconscious body of Daystrom. McCoy
offers his prognosis on Daystrom's condition: "He'll have to be
committed to a total rehabilitation center. Right now he's under

sedation and heavy restraints." Full of irony, Spock remarks, "I would say that his Multitronics unit is in the same condition," and Kirk says, "That's exactly the situation I was hoping for."

The episode "Plato's Stepchildren" contains two further illustrative examples (3.1 and 3.2). On a shielded planet deep in space, the *Enterprise* encounters a small community of thirty-eight aliens (the products of a eugenic program that renders each thousands of years old but vulnerable to infection) who lived on Earth at the time of the Greek civilization and pattern themselves after Plato's vision of a utopia. Kirk, McCoy, and Spock respond to a medical emergency distress call from the planet's inhabitants, beam down to the surface, and treat and cure the leader of the alien community. Immediately upon regaining his health and control over his formidable telekinetic powers, the leader orders the *Enterprise* officers captured and tells them that they can never leave.

(3.1) To make this sentence more acceptable, Nurse Chapel and Lieutenant Uhura are forced into the ship's transporter and beamed to the planet as mates for the human males. Uhura reports, "We were forced into the transporter and forced to beam down. It was like becoming someone's puppet." Chapel confirms her report: "I thought I was sleepwalking, and I couldn't stop myself." The women's observations indicate that they are not in control of their actions and are being manipulated against their wills.

(3.2) Later, the women are forced to participate in romantic tableaux vivant created by the leader of the Platonians for the amusement of his people. During this scene Chapel is compelled to embrace and kiss Spock, while Uhura is propelled into Kirk's arms. Both women speak their unspoken desire for their superior officers and their shame at being manipulated.

Selected Episodes from *Star Trek: The Next Generation*

Four episodes were selected from *Star Trek: The Next Generation* for this portion of the study: "The Emissary" was picked from the series' second year, "Booby Trap" from the third, and "Galaxy's Child" and "Reunion" from the fourth season.

"Booby Trap" explores the more subtle aspects of Geordi La Forge, *Enterprise* chief engineering officer. In terms of this analysis, five moments (here numbered 4.1 to 4.5) from this episode draw our attention.

(4.1) In the first of these scenes, La Forge is found on the ship's holodeck where he has programmed a romantic beach setting (complete with a strolling gypsy violinist), a picnic meal, and a female shipmate whom he hopes to woo. He is awkward with the young woman (hurriedly presses his intentions upon her), and his attempt at high-tech seduction fails completely.

(4.2) Following his disastrous date, La Forge retreats to 10-Forward to "salve his wounds" with a libation or two. He encounters the enigmatic Guinan there and asks her advice on the subject of women. La Forge asks weakly, "Tell me something, Guinan—you're a woman right?" Guinan replies wryly, "Yes, I can tell you I'm a woman." Still puzzled, La Forge asks, "What is it that you want in a man?" Guinan asks, "Me personally?" La Forge: "As a woman. What's the first thing you look at?" Guinan says flatly, "His head." La Forge interprets her answer to mean "His mind, of course." Correcting him, Guinan says, "No. His head. I'm attracted to bald men." A surprised La Forge asks, "Seriously?" "Seriously." La Forge wonders, "Why?" Guinan explains, "Maybe it's because a bald man was kind to me once, when I was hurting. Took care of me." La Forge muses aloud, "I'd like to do that." Guinan points out, "Well, I take care of myself these days." La Forge clarifies himself, "I mean, take care of somebody. I just don't get it. I can field-strip a fusion reactor. I can realign a power-transfer tunnel. Why can't I make anything work with a woman like Christy? It's like I don't know what to do. I don't know what to say." Guinan reassures him, "You're doing fine with me." La Forge answers, "You're different," and Guinan says, "No, you're different." La Forge tells her, "But, I'm not trying now." "That's my point," says Guinan.

This is one of the rare instances in both series in which two ethnic characters (Others) are depicted as comrades, not adversaries. Furthermore, Guinan reassures La Forge about his ability to attract a romantic partner and gives him advice to act naturally around females. The normally shy La Forge seems to take her point provisionally.

(4.3) In the next example, the *Enterprise* is trapped in an energy-draining minefield, and La Forge re-creates a virtual mockup of the *Enterprise's* engines, as designed at Utopia Planitia in Drafting

Room 5 of the Theoretical Propulsion Group on Mars Colony, with the ship's holodeck (his version of a ship in a bottle), to test his theories for restoring power against the engines' original baseline specifications. To access information files from the original design team, La Forge instructs the computer to use Starfleet records to re-create the voice of its prolific junior member, Leah Brahms. La Forge speaks to the computer, "Damn. Right back where it all started. Oh, this is incredible! Leah did you design this?" A coldly efficient mechanical voice (Brahms) says, "The dilithium chamber was designed at outpost designated Saran D-l. Some of the Federation's best engineering minds participated in its development." La Forge argues, "That's the visiting dignitary talk. What's the inside story. Off the record." The computer replies, "Access denied. Personal logs are restricted." La Forge, despairing, comments, "Great. Another woman who won't get personal with me on the holodeck." The dialogue in this sequence reveals that La Forge still feels sorry for himself over his failures as a ladies' man. Moreover, his remarks on the computer denying him access to Dr. Brahms' personal diaries foreshadow not only La Forge's creation of a simulation of Brahms but are also an ironic comment on the quality of any relationship between humans and holographic humanoid simulations, too.

(4.4) Later in the episode, La Forge continues to work to free the Enterprise from its trap, a dilemma in which *Enterprise* power provides the energy necessary for the alien minefield to ensnare the ship. Using information from Starfleet records, La Forge instructs the computer to construct a simulation of Brahms, complete with personality factors, and he, as engineer, and designer-simulacrum Brahms work together on the holodeck mockup engines and argue about refit strategies. Both are very capable and opinionated engineers. Moreover, they explain to each other their thought processes and show all the signs of a good team. La Forge protests firmly, "No! No! No!" Brahms answers, "Will you listen to me!" La Forge lectures, "You can't boost the warp power that way!" and Brahms explains, "We can just increase the speed of the parallel subspace field processors to gain a quicker response time. . . ." La Forge outlines his plan: "I want to give us enough power to strengthen the shields and barrel out of here, not blow us up!" to which Brahms replies, "This is my design we're talking about. I did the calculations myself." La Forge forcefully warns, "I don't care if you built yourself out of an old Ferengi cargo ship. It's going to go [whistles] 'boom' and we're going to go with it." Brahms, getting irritated, warns, "I am not used to having people question my judgment." La Forge snaps back, "And I'm not used to dying! [Pause] OK, look. You worked in a lab on a static model. This is a working machine. It's got tens of thousands of light years on it." Brahms, listening, answers, "True." La Forge presses his point, "Damn right! [sighs] Listen, we could never be sure that the circuit paths are sealed." "You're good," Brahms relents. "You're very good." La Forge boasts, "I know my ship, inside and out." Brahms appreciatively comments, "Well, then, you must know me inside and out. 'Cause a lot of me is in here." La Forge responds to her warmth: "You know I always wished that a chief engineer could be present when a ship is being built." Brahms agrees, saying, "That's what's wrong with designers. . . . we never get out in space." La Forge points out, "Well, you're there now."

This scene moves through at least two distinct topics. Across this dialogue a relationship between equals is being drawn; both La Forge and Brahms are represented as proud and brilliant, but each appreciates the other's point of view. Clearly a team relationship is growing. In the middle of their work, the nature of the relations develops from purely technical to personal as the Brahms hologram confides a cherished wish.

(4.5) Later, after La Forge has developed a radical tactic of manually maneuvering out of the ancient minefield on thruster jets, the *Enterprise* gains complete freedom from the trap and La Forge returns to the holodeck. La Forge confesses to Brahms, "You know, I always thought technology could solve almost any problem. It enhances the quality of our lives, lets us travel across the galaxy, even gave me my vision. But sometimes you have to turn it all off, even the gypsy violins." Not understanding the reference, Brahms asks, "Violins?" La Forge laughs, "Different program." Brahms beams, "We made a good team." La Forge shrugs, "Umm." Brahms insists, "Yeah, we did." "Maybe we can do it again some time," La Forge suggests. Brahms invitingly points out, "I'm with you every day, Geordi. Every time you look at this engine, you're looking at me. Every time you touch it, it's me."

Here again, the dialogue takes up two distinct topics. First, La Forge expresses his realization that technology, his area of mastery, is not always the solution to problems. Second, La Forge and the Brahms-simulacrum share very personal admissions that sound like what one would overhear between two people at the end of a date. As if to make this point crystal clear, the engineer and his creation kiss "good-bye" (at the door to reality, as it were).

The episode "Galaxy's Child" is a companion to the earlier "The Booby Trap" and is the occasion for the return of Dr. Brahms. In it are four examples (5.1 through 5.4) of content that fall within the parameters of this investigation.

On a routine equipment resupply mission, the *Enterprise* receives a special dignitary, Dr. Leah Brahms, now senior design engineer of the Theoretical Propulsion Group of the Daystrom Institution for Advanced Physics. Captain Picard assigns Chief Engineer La Forge the duty of welcoming their special guest aboard and making sure she gets every opportunity to inspect the *Enterprise* engines. La Forge finally gets his chance to meet Leah Brahms in the flesh.

(5.1) La Forge answers Picard's summons, "You wanted to see me, Captain?" "Yes, Mr. La Forge," says Picard. "It seems that the exemplary nature of your work has caught the attention of Starfleet Command. In fact, someone is coming onboard just to see the engine modifications you've made." La Forge asks, "Who, Captain?" Picard gives the details, "The senior design engineer of the Theoretical Propulsion Group, Dr. Leah Brahms." La Forge continues to show his disbelief: "Leah? Is coming here? This is terrific." Picard queries, "It is?" La Forge tries to explain away his enthusiastic interest by saying, "Well, I mean I've studied her schematics for years. She was responsible for a lot of the engine design on the *Enterprise*." Picard concludes the interview with, "Well, this should be a rather enjoyable visit then. She'll be transporting aboard as soon as we reach the starbase. Would you like to greet her on our behalf?" La Forge, agreeing, says, "I would love to, Captain. Thank you."

La Forge's enthusiastic response to news of Dr. Brahms's tour of inspection signifies his residual feelings of attraction for her simulacrum and his continuing obsession with the idea of a personal and professional relationship with a woman who shares his understanding and appreciation of technology.

(5.2) Later in 10-Forward, La Forge nervously awaits Dr. Brahms's arrival. Guinan recognizes La Forge's symptoms and tries to draw him out. Guinan warns, "You keep picking at that uniform and you're going to wear it out." La Forge admits, "I guess I am a little nervous. It's not every day that a man comes face-to-face with his dream." Guinan asks, "What?" La Forge elaborates, "OK, do you remember about a year ago when we were caught in that booby trap that the Menthar set?" Guinan indicates agreement: "Um-hmm." La Forge retells the crucial facts, "OK, while we were trying to get out of it, I went down to the holodeck to study an engine prototype that was made when the *Enterprise* was first designed and the computer, well, it gave me an image of the engines, but it also gave me this hologram of the designer, Dr. Leah Brahms." Guinan retorts, "So you met a computer-simulated female." La Forge agrees, "Yeah, but not an ordinary computer-simulated female. I mean, she was brilliant, of course, but warm, friendly. And it was like we worked as one. I would start a sentence, and she would finish it. What I didn't think of, she did. It was just so comfortable. Hey, I know it was just a holographic image, but the computer was able to incorporate personality traits from her Starfleet record." Guinan cautions, "Geordi, you know, everybody falls in love with a fantasy every now and then. . . ." "No. No. Guinan," La Forge asserts. "See, you've got it all wrong. I'm not necessarily expecting anything romantic here. I just know whatever, Leah Brahms and I are going to be good friends."

La Forge's use of the phrase "her schematics" is an obvious double entendre that betrays his real feelings toward the designer of the *Enterprise's* engines. Despite his protestations to the contrary, La Forge is "in love" with his creation or fantasy of Leah Brahms. However, when the two meet, sparks fly as the talented engineers argue over La Forge's modifications to engine design specifications. The exchanges between La Forge and the real Dr. Brahms have all the markings of a "high-tech" lovers' quarrel.

(5.3) Following La Forge's official reception of Dr. Brahms, he quickly discovers her contempt for his modifications of her engine designs. La Forge, chided by Brahms's criticisms of his efforts, decides to patch things over by inviting her to an informal dinner in his bachelor quarters. La Forge welcomes her, "Come on in." Brahms, surprised, remarks, "You've changed." La Forge admits, "Yeah. Uniforms are so formal." Brahms observes, "You're less formal than any Starfleet officer that I've ever met, Commander." La Forge asks, "Am I? Really, I just wanted to make you feel more comfortable." Brahms bristles, "I'm fine, thank you." "I'm sorry, come in and have a seat," La Forge says. "Can I get you a drink?" Brahms still resists, "Ah, no. Thank you." La Forge asks, "You sure?" Brahms answers, "Um-hmm." La Forge comments, "Your hair, you know it's different." Brahms, puzzled, asks, "Different than few hours ago?" La Forge quickly answers, "No, I mean it's different from what I expected. Different from your Starfleet records." Brahms recalls, "Oh, yes, I used to wear it up." "Yeah," Brahms wonders, "Why would you need to see my personnel files?" La Forge covers by saying, "Standard procedure when guests come on board. Protocol. I mean, it was nothing specific, actually just. . . ." Brahms apologizes, "Commander La Forge, if I seem to be somewhat unyielding in my views its because I care so very much about my work." La Forge agrees, "Oh, I know." Brahms continues to explain, "To be honest, people find me cold, cerebral, lacking in humor." Extending friendship, La Forge says, "But they are wrong, I assure you." "Well, I try not to be that way," Brahms states. "But when it comes to my designs, my engines, especially the ones on the *Enterprise*, it's. . . ." La Forge finishes her thought: "It's like they are your children." Brahms, surprised, says "Yes, exactly. . . ." La Forge continues to express her thoughts, "So naturally you're a little possessive about them." Brahms responds with amazement, "You understand that?" La Forge asserts his feelings, "Yes, I do. You see, I feel the same way." Not quite believing, Brahms says, "That's amazing. I don't think that anyone has ever . . . sometimes I feel more comfortable with engine schematics than with people." La Forge suggests, "Well, maybe you just haven't met the right people."

On one level, this scene relates that Brahms's attitude toward La Forge lacks the deference and respect that someone like La Forge, who attained command rank, should expect. On another level, what is going on here is a failed courtship. La Forge has made a nest and invited a healthy female into it. Brahms seems receptive at first; there may be a subtext of marital problems that indicates vulnerability. La Forge begins the scene intending a romantic conquest, switches to befriending and empathizing with her, only to be rejected by Brahms.

(5.4) The next morning La Forge and Brahms meet to inspect the *Enterprise's* engines and his modifications. Brahms sets the agenda for the inspection by pointing out, "The first thing I'd like to do is inspect the power-transfer conduits." Inside the power-transfer conduit, Brahms points out, "The acoustic signature doesn't sound right." La Forge compliments her, saying, "You're probably the only other person in the galaxy who could pick that up." Brahms asks, "What's causing it?" La Forge, pointing ahead, says, "It's right up here. . . . It's a mid-range phase adjuster. Puts the plasma back into phase after inertial distortion." Brahms, acknowledging the innovation, praises La Forge: "This has never been done before. I don't even think this has ever been conceived of before. You should write a scientific paper." La Forge is embarrassed and, laughing, deflects the compliment: "Unh-unh, doctor. No. Writing is not exactly one of my strong suits." Brahms persists, "But this kind of refinement should be shared. And you deserve the credit for it." La Forge demurs, "Well, maybe we could collaborate. Writing is one of your strong points." Brahms registers discomfort, saying, "Commander La Forge, ever since I came onboard there's seemed to be something a little peculiar about your attitude. You seem to know things about me even though we've never met." La Forge bends the truth and tells her, "Well, er, to tell you the truth, I've studied you. Your writings, your Starfleet file. I've admired you. You know, your work." Brahms admits, "Well, I'm flattered, but. . . ." La Forge begins to confess, "And I, er, well I really wanted to meet you for a long time and I'd like to think we could become friends, maybe good friends." Brahms tells La Forge, "I thought you knew . . . I mean, you know everything else about me. But Commander, if I'm hearing what I think I'm hearing, then you should know I'm married."

The episode "The Emissary" contains two instances (6.1 and 6.2) that characterize Klingon culture and values and contributes to the developing portrait of extraterrestrial ethnicity. Moreover, K'Ehlyer, a beautiful half-Klingon, half-Terran female, is introduced in this episode and returns in the episode "Reunion."

(6.1) As the episode begins, K'Ehleyr, a Federation ambassador, arrives aboard the *Enterprise* with a secret mission. She has been charged by Starfleet with the task of intercepting and pacifying a ship filled with Klingon warriors who are about to emerge from seventy-five years of cryogenic sleep to face a Federation they know only as an enemy. Once aboard the *Enterprise*, K'Ehleyr reveals that she believes it is hopeless to try to mollify the Klingons and suggests that the *Enterprise* prepare to destroy the ancient warriors.

She also reveals that she and Worf are previously acquainted. First, the ship's chief medical officer, Dr. Pulaski, and, later, the ship's counselor, Deanna Troi, comment on K'Ehleyr's mixed racial heritage. Troi, in a passageway conducting K'Ehleyr to her quarters, tries to establish a rapport by referring to her own transspecies heritage. However, Troi's opening remark reveals a surprising lack of sensitivity and intelligence on her part. Troi says, "I didn't know that it was possible for a human and a Klingon to produce a child." K'Ehleyr points out, "Actually, the DNA is compatible with a fair amount of help. Rather like my parents." Troi sympathizes, "I know exactly what you mean. My father was human and my mother is a Betazoid." K'Ehleyr comments, "Really? It was the other way round for me. My mother was human. You must have grown up like I did trapped between two cultures." Troi makes the saccharine comment, "I never felt trapped. I tried to experience the richness and diversity of the two worlds." "Well, perhaps you got the best of each?" K'Ehleyr jokes, "Myself, I think I got the worst of each." Troi corrects her, "Oh, I doubt that." K'Ehleyr insists, "Having my mother's sense of humor is bad enough. It's gotten me into plenty of trouble." Troi asks, "And your Klingon side?" K'Ehleyr confesses, "That I keep under tight control. It's like a terrible temper. It's not something I want people to see." Troi argues, "Everyone has a temper." K'Ehleyr points out, "Not like mine. Sometimes I feel there is a monster inside of me fighting to get out." Troi realizes, "And it frightens you?" K'Ehleyr admits, "Of course it does. The Klingon side can be terrifying. Even to me." Troi points out, "It gives you strength. It's a part of you." "It doesn't mean I have to like it," K'Ehleyr insists.

(6.2) The second instance in this episode returns viewers to the ship's holodeck where they are treated to presentations of Klingon aerobics and mating practices. The scene centers on two past lovers, K'Ehleyr and Worf, whose strong feelings toward each other are in conflict and compounded by their being required to solve what appears to be an intractable problem. K'Ehleyr heeds Troi's advice and seeks out holodeck recreation to relieve her stress. Worf, on orders from Picard to relax, independently turns to the holodeck where he has stored his personal calisthenics program.

Upon entering the holodeck, Worf discovers that K'Ehleyr is already inside and has accessed his calisthenics program, which uses "virtual combat" as a paradigm for exercise. First, Worf

watches K'Ehleyr, then he joins her in an more advanced com-
bat/exercise routine. Fighting together against virtual opponents
forces them closer together; they drop their aloofness towards
each other, and they renew their extremely passionate feelings for
each other.

The episode "Reunion" includes four sequences 7.1 through 7.4
that concern this study. The *Enterprise's* deep-space mission to
study a maverick sun is interrupted by the sudden appearance of
a Klingon battle cruiser and the reappearance of Federation Ambassador K'Ehleyr. K'Ehleyr beams aboard the *Enterprise* accom-
panied by a Klingon child to convey two secrets. The first is an ur-
gent request from K'Mpec that Picard personally officiate at the
ceremonies to determine whether Duras or Gowron will succeed
him to head the Klingon High Counsel. K'Ehleyr's other secret is
deeply personal; the child who beamed over with her is hers and
Worf's son conceived during her previous voyage aboard the *Enterprise*. Matters are further complicated by Worf's recent acceptance of official Klingon discommendation, a judgment of personal and familial dishonor for his father's alleged treason in
conspiring with the Romulans to invade the Klingon outpost at
Khitomer. Worf's acceptance of his son and any commitment to
K'Ehleyr is overshadowed by his desire to protect them from censure and shame.

So Worf has a family, ready-made, but no less a family. One
level of conflict in this episode involves the impact of Worf's discommendation on K'Ehleyr and Alexander, their child. In other
words, Worf is uncertain; he dares not accept his family, because
accepting them will subject them to public sanction and dishonor.

(7.1) The first instance that bears on ethnicity occurs following a
fatal explosion on K'Mpec's ship; it kills two Klingons. Worf and
K'Ehleyr let down their defenses and confess their love for each
other. Worf tells K'Ehleyr that if she had told him that she was
pregnant by him, he would have insisted they marry, not because
tradition demands it but because he loves her. K'Ehleyr, in turn,
lets down her guard and admits that she needs him and that he is
a part of her. Unfortunately, Worf has accepted discommendation
from the Klingon High Council, and he refuses to subject K'Ehleyr
and Alexander to that censure.

These scenes revisit a romantic relationship between Worf and
K'Ehleyr that was first presented in "The Emissary." Moreover,

they provide a glimpse into the heart of fantasy culture by giving a brief sample of Klingon attitudes toward gender, mating, marriage, and the ways male and female Klingons express their romantic feelings toward each other.

(7.2) Unfortunately, tragedy strikes. The next example follows K'Ehleyr's attempts to find out more about the circumstances surrounding the Khitomer massacre. Duras's treachery accelerates as he acts to silence all who know about his father's collaboration with the Romulan's sneak attack on Khitomer. When he discovers that K'Ehleyr is in communication with the Klingon Imperial Information Network, he flies into a rage that results in his killing K'Ehleyr. In deep rage, Worf seeks out Duras, who has since fled to his ship, challenges him to combat and kills him.

(7.3) Worf's killing Duras is such a breach of Federation law and Starfleet regulation that Picard calls Worf before him for his judgment. The exchange between Picard and Worf in the captain's ready room forms the third instance in this episode that relates to ethnicity. A stern Picard observes, "The *Enterprise* crew currently includes representatives from thirteen planets. They each have their own individual beliefs and values, and I respect them all. But they all have chosen to serve Starfleet. If anyone cannot perform his or her duty because of the demands of their society, they should resign. Do you wish to resign?" Worf answers soberly, "No, sir!" Picard continues, "I had hoped you would not throw away a promising career. I understand your loss. We all admired K'Ehleyr. A reprimand will appear on your record."

(7.4) The sequence ends with the fourth example that provides further insights into Klingon culture, customs, and psychology. After K'Ehleyr's death, Worf must again decide whether to acknowledge the son he initially rejected. First, Worf comforts Alexander and admits that he is his father. However, Worf goes on to inform Alexander that his foster parents will soon arrive and take Alexander to Earth to Russia to live with them.

There is great irony in this scene, for at the same time that Worf embraces his son in a very real and emotionally troubling sense, he pushes him away. We see a circle made complete: Worf was orphaned through the attack on Khitomer, Duras's father's fault, and Alexander is orphaned by Duras. Moreover, both orphans get raised on Earth by foster parents who are white.

Summary

The *Star Trek* episodes examined here—"Space Seed," "Ultimate Computer," and "Plato's Stepchildren"—resulted in seventeen extracts that centered on ethnicity or race. The four episodes of *Star Trek: The Next Generation* identified in this chapter—"Booby Trap," "Galaxy's Child," "The Emissary," and "Reunion"—led to fifteen extracts focusing on race.

A wide variety of social situations are depicted in these thirty-two extracts. In these scenes, as part of setting the social context between characters, a number of subjects or topics of conversation emerge. In four instances—two from "Space Seed," one from "The Emissary," and one from "The Reunion"—the social interaction involves an act of violence on the part of the ethnic male toward women, other ethnics, and members of Starfleet. "Space Seed" also contains two instances in which characters, the passengers aboard the sleeper ship, are referred to with derogatory comments that focus on ethnicity. The mental capacity of ethnic characters is questioned once in "Space Seed," twice in "Ultimate Computer" and "Galaxy's Child." The loyalty of ethnic characters is an issue under discussion once in "Space Seed," twice in "Ultimate Computer," and once in "Reunion." In "Space Seed" and "The Emissary," there is one example of a discussion in which miscegenation is presented negatively. "Ultimate Computer" has two instances of ethnic characters' actions causing danger to the entire ship. There were two instances in "Booby Trap" and one each in "Galaxy's Child," "Reunion," and "Space Seed" in which the ability of ethnic characters to form relationships is raised. "Plato's Stepchildren" presents an instance of ethnic characters being stripped of their free will and an instance of them being forced into a romantic situation with their white colleagues. In "Booby Trap" and "Galaxy's Child," there are instances of professional rivalry that involve an ethnic character. Both "Ultimate Computer" and "Reunion" depict instances in which ethnic characters display false pride.

In the next chapter, these instances will be analyzed in more detail to develop both their fuller context and the ways their content relates to the representation of ethnicity in *Star Trek* and *Star Trek: The Next Generation*.

Chapter 6

Mission Debriefings

Like the best science fiction, "Star Trek" doesn't really show other worlds so well as it shows us our own.[1]

The relations among members of the United Federation of Planets, Starfleet officers and their missions, and nonaligned alien civilizations represented in each series provides insights into the deeper and more subtle levels of meaning and cultural connotations in *Star Trek*'s vision of the future. At the syntagmatic level, denotative meaning is developed from those aspects of episodes that are associated with characters as they occur in the individual narratives. The paradigmatic level develops the connotative meaning of these symbolic codes of representation, in a later section, and compares recurrent conceptualizations, ideas, and elements to glean from them the fuller dimensions of *Star Trek*'s future for ethnic characters. In a summary section, the implications of these analyses will be addressed to better understand the creative limits of the genre and may reveal the relation between the origins of fictional creativity and events in our world.[2]

Syntagmatic Analysis

The syntagmatic axis of this analysis emerges from four distinct types or categories of symbolic codes: the environment or social setting in which the scene occurs; the sociological relationship among characters; character's actions, including gestures, postures, and

133

attitudes toward others; and characters' physical appearance expressed through anatomy and vestments. The object here is to determine whether any systematic relationship exists among these symbolic codes and, if so, to offer an explanation that accounts for them. In this way a meaningful system based on heterogeneous scenes emerges and reveals the various ways producers of *Star Trek* and *Star Trek: The Next Generation* think about and visualize ethnicity in the future.

Environment and Social Setting

For both series, the primary locus of activity is the starship *Enterprise,* whose mission is an extended exploration of space. The *Enterprise* and its crew clearly represent humanoid life in microcosm. Moreover, the *Enterprise* represents technological advance as the basis for freedom and the possible perfectibility of humans. Both *Enterprise NCC-1701,* of *Star Trek,* and *Enterprise NCC-1701-D,* of *Star Trek: The Next Generation,* function as a means of transportation and a limitation on the amount of contact between their crew and alien civilizations. These starships are so large that their sheer size means that only individuals and small "away team" groups can visit planetside. Both series employ a voice-over prologue that introduces viewers to this space "home" and its purpose, differing only slightly from the original to its progeny.

In *Star Trek* each episode is separated from the preceding program by a momentarily totally black screen.[3] This void dissolves into a prologue or "teaser" during which the dramatic situation of the episode is introduced. In the teaser a small, distant image of the *Enterprise* zooms forward into full view, and the theme music swells. As the prologue continues, the scene shifts to an interior shot of the ship's command bridge, and its ethnic bridge officers are regularly shown in this shot. Immediately our perspective shifts to match what Kirk and his bridge crew are monitoring through the ship's forward screen: a mysterious planet, enigmatic interstellar phenomenon, or alien spacecraft. A second blackout dissolves into a shot of a starfield that reveals the *Enterprise* orbiting an unidentified planet. Accompanying this image there is a voice-over by Captain Kirk, who introduces the series premise: "Space, the final frontier . . . where no man has gone before" and the specific mission of the episode.[4] The voice-over ends, and, as a third blackout dissolves, the *Enterprise* zooms forward and streaks screen right. A fourth starfield fills the screen and the graphic credit title *Star Trek* is superimposed over it. This graphic title is replaced first by a credit graphic for "William Shatner," with no role listed, and, then, by a credit title for "Leonard Nimoy as Mr. Spock."

Star Trek: The Next Generation begins immediately following a momentary black screen that separates it from the preceding commercial. This leads to a prologue, or teaser, during which the dramatic situation of the episode is introduced. In the teaser a small, distant image of the *Enterprise D* zooms forward into full view and streaks screen right across the screen. Accompanying this image, Captain Picard, in a voice-over, makes an entry into his official log indicating the ship's location and immediate mission. Next, the scene changes to the interior of the *Enterprise D* and its bridge crew and ethnic officers as they encounter the episode's basic conflict/drama. The prologue continues after another blackout with views of interstellar planets and phenomena, including a superstring, floating in space, and a screen-filling starfield as the series' theme music swells. In a voice-over narration, once again Captain Picard formally introduces the episode by declaring the familiar, though slightly altered from the original *Star Trek,* motto: "Space, the final frontier . . . where no *one* has gone before." Once again the *Enterprise D* emerges from the distance in the starfield, sweeps screen-right, engages its warp engines, and blasts off. This return of the starship marks the beginning of the third part of the introductory sequence, the credit titles. A title graphic declaring "Star Trek" nearly fills the screen only a moment later to be joined by "The Next Generation." Next, there are graphic titles for "Patrick Stewart as Captain Picard," followed by an image of the *Enterprise D* streaking across the screen and a graphic title for "Jonathan Frakes as Commander Riker" that is also followed by an image of the *Enterprise* streaking across the screen in the opposite direction. At this point, the graphic titles for the actors' credits for the characters La Forge, Worf, Data, Dr. Crusher, and Counselor Troi are displayed against a black background and starfield.[5]

Moreover, in the sample of episodes examined here, other environments or settings were found that directly contribute to the symbol system associated with ethnicity. In "Plato's Stepchildren," "Booby Trap," and "The Emissary," the trope of the "desert island," as in *The Tempest, Robinson Crusoe, Lord of the Flies, Forbidden Planet,* and *E.T.: The Extraterrestrial,* is employed. This desert island device is used here, as it has been in other instances, to isolate characters and to portray them, supposedly, "as they really are." Following Aristotle, this device assumes that human nature as it really is will only be revealed when people are removed from the normal network of social relations and restricted to a lonely laboratory.[6] This metaphor is evoked in "Plato's Stepchildren" when first Kirk, McCoy, and Spock and then Lieutenant Uhura and Nurse Chapel beam down to a hidden planet's utopian community. In "Booby Trap" and "The Emissary," the normal setting of the *Enterprise D* and the command context of the ship's bridge are displaced by a significant number of scenes that take place in the ship's holodeck. Another version of this metaphor occurs in "The Ultimate Computer" when Starfleet assigns the *Enterprise* as the test bed for Dr. Daystrom's new computer technology, all nonessential ship's personnel disembark and the ship is thereby effectively rendered a desert island in space.

Ethnic characters were associated with several other settings shown in the episodes covered in this investigation. They include sick bay, captain's mess, interior of a derelict space ship, individual crewmember's quarters, engineering, the holodeck, and the bridge. Most of these settings are part of the standing sets of each series and, as such, reflect the designers' visions of functional and private areas of a future spaceship. They also reflect the producers' interest in matching narrative development with existing production assets to use the allocated budget to maximum effect. Generally, the complex technological base that supports these ships is kept well hidden. The areas shown, however, feature individual computer consoles, display monitors, research stations, and communications controls, and each ship's bridge area is composed of individual computer-based work stations with large monitor displays. Ethnic characters are regularly shown in these areas working and relaxing. Moreover, when they are associated with the high-technology equipment that is characteristic of these settings, they are clearly depicted as sophisticated users.

Sociological Relations Among Characters

In both *Star Trek* series, the principal continuing characters are members of Starfleet, a paramilitary organization with science research, diplomacy, and defense missions, who form a tight-knit unit of shipmates who are also friends. Series stories revolve around these characters, their personal and professional crises, the dangers they face, and their creative solutions to unique problems. This group's membership reflects a variety of humanoid species, and the safety and security of the ship depends on crew members being respected for their skills. Considerable attention is devoted to developing the relationships between members of both *Enterprises*. Moreover, both series tend to limit character development to those characters that are command rank.

In the original program, the continuing characters who receive the majority of attention and whose relationships are stressed are Captain Kirk, Dr. McCoy, Mr. Scott, and Mr. Spock—two American white males, a European white male, and an alien male Other. Kirk regards Spock, Scott, and McCoy as experts within their disciplines and as trusted aides whose different ways of looking at situations provide a corrective balance for his own military (read "buccaneering") attitude. This is particularly true of Spock and McCoy. In fact, if we take McCoy at face value from the American South, then Spock's alien Otherness functions as not only a necessary guide, qua Chingachgook, into dangerous otherness of space but as a psychological ballast, even tonic, to McCoy's extremism.

Although other continuing characters are highlighted, during the run of the program only Sulu and Chekov, who are depicted as sharing the skin-color privilege of the ship's white, male commanders, develop the kind of camaraderie that even borders on that which is depicted among the ship's command staff. Still, their relationship never goes beyond a kind of joshing stage, never functions at the plot level or to shape a narrative. The series' only character who is visibly a person of color, Uhura, develops no off-duty relationships with any of the ship's crew. Significantly, the single instance of Uhura relaxing shows her among enlisted personnel in a lounge area and entertaining them with song ("The Conscience of the King," episode 11).[7]

Star Trek: The Next Generation devotes considerable effort to mapping out the relationships among continuing characters.[8] Captain Picard, unlike his predecessor, is a mature man who stands apart from his command staff and observes the strict rule of military decorum to maintain that distance. If Picard has a friend onboard, Guinan, the alien female, comes closest. Interestingly, she is clearly outside the hierarchical structure of Starfleet, and Picard seems able to relax with her in ways he will not permit himself with his crew. Therefore, the relationships of camaraderie that are explored tend to be among the ship's command personnel serving immediately under Picard. The "bible" for the series makes this clear.[9] Among these characters, the relationships between Riker and Troi, on one hand, and Data and La Forge, on the other, are most clearly articulated.[10] Before joining the *Enterprise D* crew, Riker and Troi were lovers, and they maintain a strong bond of friendship while serving together. Data and La Forge are linked and a friendship develops from their common association with electronics. Dr. Crusher, Worf, and Wesley Crusher, the remaining continuing characters, do not have strong, primary friendships with other shipmates and seem consumed and isolated by their duty functions.

Roles and Actions

The original *Star Trek* cast of continuing characters included Communications Officer Lieutenant Uhura. Although the impact of seeing, week after week, during the late 1960s an attractive, ethnic female character functioning with competence and reliability in a position of considerable responsibility should not be underappreciated, it is the case that Uhura is clearly a subordinate. Her activities are simply supportive, even servant-like, and never demonstrate any initiative on her part. The fact that the character receives and conveys other people's messages is consistent with this view. In other words, this character is limited to being a comely fixture of the ship's bridge crew and someone who provides a service for others.

Between the second and third season of *Star Trek: The Next Generation*, a new character, Guinan, appears as an infrequently appearing regular cast member. Guinan is an ethnic female survivor of a planetary civilization that was destroyed by a cybernetic race, the Borg, and, as such, wanders the galaxy as a member of that world's diaspora. Interestingly, Guinan presides over a new set, called 10-Forward, that was added to the original standing sets for the series and functions as an off-duty lounge for command staff and crew. Although any member of the ship's complement may enter and take advantage of the hospitality of the lounge, 10-Forward is another example of a circumscribed space. The character of Guinan operates this lounge as a kind of galactic bartender and, as such, is a second example of an ethnic character who functions in a service capacity.

In *Star Trek: The Next Generation*, the chief engineer of the *Enterprise D* is an ethnic character, Geordi La Forge. La Forge, as originally conceived, was thought of as being a native of Jamaica.[11] As chief engineer, La Forge is most often depicted within those below-deck areas of the *Enterprise D* where the ship's warp reactors, dilithium crystal chamber, and main engine control stations are located. This ethnic character is associated with technology; in support of this, Data considers La Forge his best friend. Some effort is devoted to representing him as inept with women. La Forge is more comfortable around machines, understands technology, and "lives" technology. When he does succeed with a woman, she is a computer simulation, thus his own fantasy, that he has programmed using the ship's holodeck. La Forge infrequently appears on the bridge with the ship's other command officers (or command staff), even though there is an engineering station located there, and is most often found far away from command areas working on the ship's engines. The La Forge character is nothing more than a glorified mechanic, a category of worker that is associated with physical effort rather than mind work.

This point is underscored when La Forge tells the actual Dr. Brahms that writing "is not my strong suit." He is capable of building machines but apparently unable to explain his devices to others. Indeed, when La Forge finally meets his counterpart from the *Enterprise,* Chief Engineer Scott boasts about the fact that he wrote the manual for Starfleet's engineering specifications. Why is what was considered a fundamental aspect of a character from a generation past not carried over and made a point of commonality between these characters who should have so much in common? Perhaps the answer can be inferred by examining the way another Africanist character functions within *Star Trek*'s mythology.

Dr. Daystrom, who was a featured character in the first series, is linked with La Forge, through their common interest in technology, and poses an interesting paradox. Initially, that earlier character embodies the highest values of scientific research and increasing personal freedom based on technological sophistication. However, as we have seen, this character's research activity leads to a direct confrontation with Starfleet in which the *Enterprise* is transformed into an engine of destruction and many lives are lost in pointless combat. The character of Daystrom demonstrates the limitations in the scope of activities allowed ethnic characters. In the context of this analysis, Daystrom seems to have committed a fatal transgression; his reach exceeded his grasp.

In other words, *Star Trek* shows, through the roles it associates with characters, that it is appropriate for ethnic characters to be employed in support of machines and in the service of technology, but conceptualizing inventions and developing technology constitute an overreaching, a hubris, that is clearly off-limits for them. Therefore, the role of the scientific pioneer is a "glass ceiling" for ethnic characters.

Security Chief Worf is distinguished as the only Klingon serving on a Starfleet vessel. Although this is something of an honor, it is also something less than it appears. As security chief, Worf is little more than a glorified police officer. This is a role that is dependent on upholding the values of the dominant culture. For producers, this situation may contain internal conflicts that support further character development; it also places the ethnic character in the position analogous to being an ethnic soldier in an occupying army. Once again, we have a role in which the character does not initiate any activity but answers to the orders of superiors. Worf, in this role as security chief, is little more than "muscle," his Klingon culture is a considerable liability, and he has little opportunity to apply Klingon values and attitudes to solve problems.[12]

Troi's role as the *Enterprise*'s counselor allows her bridge-staff status but no command responsibilities.[13] However, as ship's counselor, her role is to use her half-Betazoid telepathy and psychological training to help her crewmates adjust to long-term space travel and related problems. Like Uhura from *Star Trek*, Troi's role circumscribes any initiative, reduces her to being a medium for other's thoughts, and supports unquestioningly the dominant ideology of Starfleet. Troi's status as counselor places her within the category of personnel who provide a service rather than command.

K'Ehleyr is a recurring female Klingon character who is identified as a Federation ambassador. As impressive as that may sound, K'Ehleyr clearly descends from Uhura of the original series. Both are representatives of ethnic females who are very attractive but take no initiative. K'Ehleyr responds to the will of others and, like Uhura, delivers messages, albeit from the highest level of the Federation. She is, like Uhura, an exotic, beautiful vessel for messages.

As far as Guinan is concerned, the series' infrequently appearing ethnic female, this role is clearly limited to serving others and is essentially a bartender. In this way, this character's role revisits the Issac character from *The Love Boat*.[14]

In sum, across the several different episodes examined here, ethnic characters are found repeatedly involved in a narrow range of activities. Instead of reflecting the wide range of possible occupations and activities in a future that stretches across the known galaxy, science fiction producers have kept the modes of ethnic representations limited. In the context of a vision of the future that from its origins purported to offer audiences a more ethnically diverse continuing cast of characters, the range of actions associated with ethnic characters is surprisingly narrow.

There seem to be three distinct roles among the ethnic females in these programs. Lieutenant Uhura is a communications officer, Counselor Troi is a psychologist, and K'Ehleyr is an ambassador. Lieutenant Uhura is clearly cast in the role of the devoted servant. This character never originates an action or initiates a message; rather she is the vessel for carrying information about the actions of others to those in command. In other words, this character is limited to being a comely fixture of the ship's crew and someone who provides a service for others. She has no romantic liaisons on board. Counselor Troi also provides a service and is involved with communications, albeit of a personal nature. Like Uhura, she receives information from others and is, according to accepted professional standards, prohibited from telling her clients what to do. So she, too, initiates no actions. Moreover, the possibility of any romantic involvement seems to have been obviated by the fact that Riker dissolved their relationship to pursue a Starfleet career. She has no other lovers or mates. Ambassador K'Ehleyr's character expresses herself in two roles as a Klingon female and a Federation ambassador. Like Uhura and Troi, K'Ehleyr as Federation ambassador is a conduit for messages and initiates nothing of an official nature. And, like Troi, K'Ehleyr fell in love before she joined the *Enterprise*'s sagas, and the object of her affection is an *Enterprise* officer. Unlike her sister characters, K'Ehleyr does initiate a sexual liaison, in her case with Worf, while aboard the *Enterprise*. Unfortunately, her relationship with Worf ends with her murder. Ethnic females seem rather one-dimensional and as lovers to fare rather badly.

Five ethnic males in this study were: Lieutenant La Forge, Lieutenant Worf, Dr. Daystrom, Spock, and Khan. They may be divided in two different ways: three are Starfleet officers and two are not. Second, the Starfleet officers' actions support and protect the integrity of the *Enterprise* and Starfleet, but Daystrom's and Khan's actions put the ship in jeopardy and even threaten Starfleet's very existence.

Like their female counterparts, Starfleet's ethnic males are assigned duties that are essentially service jobs. Mr. Spock makes a point of honor of his rejection of privilege to command that his rank, service, and superior intellect clearly entitle him to. Instead, he is content to serve Kirk and Starfleet. He endeavors to prove, through acts of self-sacrifice and effacement that, as an ethnic Other and biracial extraterrestrial, he is nonetheless trustworthy. La Forge is a glorified mechanic, and Worf is essentially a policeman.

In other words, their work separates them from others and imposes limits on their contacts to those that are almost exclusively functional: La Forge relates to other mechanics and machinery, Worf with his commander and criminal types. Neither originates actions but takes action in response to orders. Khan and Daystrom, because they exist outside the control of Starfleet's command structure, are clearly renegades and must be "neutralized."

Vestments and Anatomy

One of most praised aspects of *Star Trek* is the expense and effort expended to make its vision seem possible. Nowhere is this more apparent than in the time and talent that go into costuming and make-up. Going beyond superior makeup and mechanical effects, however, ethnic characters have been defined by the series in ways that certainly make them visually distinct from others. That is, our attention is drawn to the ways in which their physical representation establishes each as a distinct type of the ethnic Other category, or marks them.

The character Khan Noonian Singh from *Star Trek* favors plunging V-neck tunics that accent his genetically enhanced barrel chest and sexual magnetism, here coded as ethnically exotic: forbidden and tantalizing. Khan also sports a ponytail that, particularly in the late 1960s, identifies him with rebelliousness and banditry. Interestingly, Worf, in *Star Trek: The Next Generation,* favors a longer hairstyle and even wears his hair in a ponytail. This hairstyle choice clearly links him with the earlier ethnic Other, Khan. Also, Worf wears a metallic sash that draws attention to his broad shoulders and full chest. The fact that this sash was first seen worn by Kang in "Day of the Dove" both links him to the earlier series and marks Kang as one of Worf's ancestors and one of the first Klingons at least provisionally to observe a truce with the Federation. Among the crew of the *Enterprise D,* Worf is the only continuing character whose skin coloring marks him as different and whose facial anatomy is grossly dissimilar from the rest of the crew.

Mr. Spock, from *Star Trek,* of course, is noted as having green blood; in fact, both Dr. McCoy and Captain Kirk revert to insulting Spock on the basis of the fact that his green blood makes him look greenish. In so doing, they use an unalterable aspect of difference, a sign of his ethnicity, as a point of ridicule. Spock is the only alien aboard the *Enterprise* and is regularly referred to in ways that highlight his extraterrestrial origin: green-tinted skin, pointed ears, and superhuman strength. This synecdochical shorthand marks him as alien, different, Other. It matters little whether the comment masquerades as a joke from Kirk or McCoy; its intent is to mark Spock's ethnic difference and to remind him that even his closest colleague are aware of it. No less than any other ethnic character, Spock is in constant jeopardy of being cast out as a traitor based on the fact that he violates the skin-privilege system that organizes Starfleet and the United Federation of Planet's ideologies. This is another way of saying that Mr. Spock's space within Starfleet is not secure. In his case, Spock's physical appearance links him to one of the Federation's continuing threats, the Romulans. This, of course, is one of the major plotlines in "Balance of Terror" (episode 7). Spock is perceived as tainted by this genetic heritage, and his loyalty to Starfleet, despite all his awards and commendations, is always open to question. Suspicion always lurks in the background of his interactions with others. Spock's heritage is a point of contention that threatens his career in "The Galileo Seven" (episode 12), "The Menagerie, Part I" (episode 14), and "The Menagerie, Part II" (episode 15).

Conversely, neither Dr. Daystrom's nor Lieutenant Uhura's characters bear any signs of special clothing or extraordinary physical treatment to accompany their ethnicity beyond their dark skins. It appears that these choices are not necessary for developing Terran ethnic characters; any signs of their ethnicity or folk traditions are effaced. In other words, Daystrom and Uhura are defined by virtue of their primary-level identification with Starfleet, and their identification as ethnic Terrans, marked by their dark skin color, is kept at the secondary level. Daystrom wears a jumpsuit devoid of the usual Starfleet markings. Uhura wears the standard uniform miniskirt with official emblems. Daystrom as an ethnic male who challenges the status quo is, therefore, a danger. Uhura as an ethnic female who supports the Federation's hegemony is no danger at all. Daystrom's neutral, even nondescript clothing and his dangerous attitude toward Starfleet's ideology and value structure combine to render him a wolf in sheep's clothing among the Starfleet fold.

The characters Geordi La Forge and Guinan in *Star Trek: The Next Generation* deserve a mention here, too. La Forge, blind from birth, sees by virtue of a special prosthetic device, called VISOR, that fits over his eyes and converts the electromagnetic spectrum into data that are fed directly into his brain. Guinan, after "hitching" a ride onboard the *Enterprise D*, is always seen wearing huge hats and flowing dresses that completely conceal her body, even when taking target practice with Worf. Troi, in turn, is dressed rather provocatively in outfits with plunging necklines that accent her sex and infer sexual availability.[15] In these ways, ethnic characters on *Star Trek* and *Star Trek: The Next Generation* are marked by their clothing and makeup as exotic and distinct from others.

Paradigmatic Level

The introductory sequence of these programs functions as a boundary marker that separates and announces each individual episode and serves as a trademark for referring to various subsequent promotions and other marketplace activities. The image of the starship *Enterprise* is a key element in this boundary marker sequence. The *Enterprise* and its crew move between worlds, orbit above alien civilizations, and are prohibited from enmeshment in local politics by virtue of the starship's sheer size, not to mention the prohibition of the "prime directive."[16] That is, the starship itself as the context of the series effectively eliminates a large number of sociopolitical variables that one should expect to encounter in an extended dramatic series that uses the galaxy as its backdrop.

In the both series, this strategy helps maintain the focus of the narratives at the level of personal and interpersonal conflicts. It follows from this strategy that encounters with other worlds and aliens can be subsumed within narratives where the emphasis is on character development. Conceptually, the *Enterprise* functions both as a means of transportation and a limitation on the amount of contact between her crew and any alien civilization. Doubtless, this kind of economy must have appealed to budget-conscious producers of both series. It follows from this strategy that encounters with other worlds and aliens can be subsumed within narratives that emphasize the exploration of characters with whom the audience already has a relationship in a familiar context.

The *Enterprise*'s role is reiterated with each episode. The beginning of each episode is separated from the preceding program by a momentarily totally black screen. This void dissolves into the *Enterprise* floating alone in space against a starfield. As the prologue continues, the scene shifts to an interior shot of the ship's command bridge and its duty officers. Immediately our perspective shifts to match what the ship's captain and bridge crew are monitoring through the ship's forward screen, such as a mysterious planet, enigmatic interstellar phenomenon, or alien spacecraft.

In this way, the *Enterprise* is introduced as a visual sign that functions at several levels. First, it appears as an island of technology in a hostile, cold, and threatening emptiness. Second, it is filled with humanoid life that depends upon it for survival and that must protect its "home" against the dangers of this inhospitable environment. Third, as the point of view shifts from objective to subjective, the audience is brought aboard and merged with the bridge crew.

This prologue sequence establishes the *Enterprise* as the boundary among the rest of the television program schedule, the network/station's program schedule, and the audience's regular viewing fare, normal life as a mediated televisual experience, and the special televisual experiences of *Star Trek*. The *Enterprise* marks a border that, when crossed, offers viewers order and routine, familiar characters and relations, and the "Unknown" that could overpower the ship's technology, challenge Starfleet's hegemony, and potentially destabilize audience rapport with the program and its characters. At the same time, the ship and its command center function, literally and symbolically, as a bridge to encounters with mystery, wonder, and surprise.

In this formula, the audience's position shifts from outside to correspond to that of Starfleet Command with the enunciation of the captain's log, which is addressed to Starfleet in the past tense. This technique brings viewers aboard and allows them to share the perspective of the ship's crew changing the "tense" of the series as it changes to the present. By moving the series' articulation to the present tense, audience's experience of *Star Trek* and *Star Trek: The Next Generation* is both personal and given the sense of unfolding as the viewer watches. This moves the audience into synchronization with each episode. This shift in perspective and tense is marked by a brief blackout. Inasmuch as viewers are already "aboard," the vistas of space that fill the ship's monitor screen, and television screen, are represented as seen by viewers, qua crew.

Next, the recitation of the ship's mission statements functions as a common creed that links the disparate audience members of both series. In the case of *Star Trek: The Next Generation*, the series title is displayed in two parts. The words "Star Trek" descend from the top of the screen over a black field. Then, the words "The Next Generation" appear directly beneath the first set. The series title thus functions simultaneously as a trademark and a visual confirmation that this program is a true descendent of the original series. As a further difference in the development of this introduction, it is worth noting that the development of the cast credit sequence of the title privileges white male authority by locating such characters' credits immediately following the sign of the *Enterprise,* while the ethnic and female characters are grouped together and positioned at the tail of the sequence some distance removed from semiotic association of identification with the series other than that of the typography of title itself. Rather than the order of this listing of characters designating the chain of command, it probably reflects negotiations between actors' agents and producers. What is significant is that LeVar Burton, whose TvQ, or popularity among television audiences (owing to his starring role on the all-time highest-ranked television miniseries, *Roots*), must certainly be at least as high as that of Patrick Stewart and Jonathan Frakes, nonetheless received less than star or top billing.

This strategy helps maintain the focus of the series at the level of continuing characters and interpersonal conflicts. Moreover, it establishes (reestablishes) the series' setting, creating a means for viewers to "beam up" to each week's adventure. In both series, these opening moments announce each week's episode and create a problematic formula. Is every possible viewer being invited to "beam up" to participate equally in interstellar drama and travel, or are some members of the audience more welcome, more sought after as viewers, and more privileged by the series than others?

Patterns of Ethnic Representation: Social Relations Among Characters

The social context of the *Enterprise* reflects both the hierarchical command structure of a paramilitary organization and an environment of multiethnic diversity. However, from *Star Trek* to *Star Trek: The Next Generation*, the overall tone or precept of the series changed. Whereas *Star Trek* swashbuckles and leaps into adventure, *Star Trek: The Next Generation* adopts a managerial, almost bureaucratic attitude toward space exploration. Perhaps this change is a sign of the maturation of *Star Trek*'s idea of space exploration: the period of dangerous, personal heroism followed by a period of careful administration. In addition, among continuing characters, four levels of social interaction among members of the *Enterprise* will be culled from the episodes and examined here: between ethnic males and ethnic females, between members of different ethnicity but the same gender, between ethnic parent and child, and between commander and subordinate. Upon close inspection these relationships fell short of embodying the principles of egalitarianism.

The mechanical efficiency of Starfleet's social order breaks down when the additional factor of ethnicity is added. This problem is illustrated in "Space Seed" and "Reunion." Early in "Space Seed," *Enterprise* Chief Engineer Scott surveys a derelict spaceship, its cryogenic equipment, and sleeping passengers. He volunteers a characterization of the ship's passengers that focuses disparagingly on their racial heritages when he says, "They're all mixed types, Western, mid-European, Latin, Oriental." This dialogue reveals that the individuals found aboard the ship are of mixed racial heritage and that miscegenation is something of an anomaly in the future. Moreover, in a later scene from "Space Seed," ethnicity is associated with criminality when Spock refers to the sleeping space travelers as "Napoleons"; after all, Napoleon was convicted by a French tribunal—under Imperial British pressure—and exiled twice. By combining the dialogue in these scenes, Spock implies, without actually making an accusation, that the ancient ship's passengers are under suspicion of violating natural and civil laws.

When Troi questions K'Ehleyr about her adjustment to being "mixed up" (the product of miscegenation between Klingon and Terran), this theme is being repeated with the same negative inferences. Nowhere is the sociology of Starfleet, its attitude toward other races and aliens, better or more succinctly put than in Picard's reprimand of Worf for killing Duras. Picard's speech succinctly summarizes Federation ideology on ethnicity. The United Federation of Planets and Starfleet demands that constituent societies submit their separate individual systems of beliefs and values to its ethos and the prime directive as paramount. Regardless of the progress of a society's relative technological development or an individual's social status within his or her society, membership within the Federation and service with Starfleet hinge on willingness to define each's identity in terms of these quasimilitaristic organizations. More than this, however, Starfleet and the Federation are definitively identified as originating from Earth. Picard's identification with the Federation is revealed in the fact that he is captain of its flagship. Nevertheless, this commanding officer, so dedicated to and so firmly identified with the Federation, finds no inconsistency in flaunting his French cultural heritage and childhood experiences. Apparently, among the privileges of membership in the dominant culture is the ability to express that cultural tradition and to force one's subordinates to suppress their cultural difference (see the episode "Half a Life").

The consequences of challenging the institution of Starfleet are at the heart of "The Ultimate Computer." Daystrom comes onboard the *Enterprise* as an outsider to Starfleet and upsets *Enterprise* social order and command structure. Initially, Daystrom's testing games for his computer invention disrupt Captain Kirk's schedule of exploration. Soon, however, M5 threatens the captain's very power and authority. Therefore, Daystrom is a personal threat and a threat to the hierarchical nature of the Starfleet command. Their dialogue also raises the question of what a man is—what defines masculinity. If a man is synonymous with what he does, Daystrom's work poses, in an ironic twist, the possibility of undermining Kirk's manhood, because it obsolesces the very idea of privileged white male authority.

Later in the episode, Spock expresses his attitude toward automation and, in the process, reinforces a social order that privileges white male authority as natural. In describing computers, Spock refers to them with the term "servant," which bears noting. The word simultaneously invokes a hierarchical social order and indicates that Spock willingly submits himself, despite his superior intelligence, strength, and aristocratic family background, to Starfleet and Kirk's command. Spock's family background and their esteem on Vulcan, his superior intellect, and dedication to and commendations from Starfleet should have led to commanding his own Federation starship. However, as an alien Other, Spock cannot call attention to himself, for fear of drawing unwanted attention and raising reprisal for intruding into an area reserved for Terrans. In addition, he must deny even to himself that he has earned command of a starship and would excel at it. Vulcans may command a Vulcan ship but not ships that are identified with the central authority of the Federation. Likewise, no Starfleet personnel serve on Klingon, Cardassian, or Bajoran ships. And the only Klingon that does serve on a Federation ship is constantly in the throes of identity crises, torn between his identification with Federation and Klingon culture. Is there embedded in *Star Trek*'s future a version of "separate, but equal" or "tokenism"?

In this episode, the challenge of Spock's superior intellect is metaphorically represented as the M5 computer, born of a Terran Other. The idea here is that the interruption (or, rather, inversion) of class/command relationships that M5 augurs should be avoided at all costs. The inference is that such an inversion would produce circumstances that would be intolerable, even if the trade-off is efficiency. *Star Trek* views innovation in the future as suspicious when change originates outside a very narrow definition of acceptable developments and inventors. The key to Federation cohesion and Starfleet command authority is its members' willingness to accept these institutional values unilaterally. That is, Federation and Starfleet membership requires that they repress their cultural differences and pledge complete loyalty. Even when Mr. Spock, a green-blooded male, commands, he does so under the aegis of Kirk, who in turn stands for the white male-dominated, hierarchical command structure of the Federation and Starfleet.

The trade-off for this kind of loyalty is adventure, prestige, and recognition. Daystrom's new computer and his very presence onboard the *Enterprise* undercut the philosophy of space exploration and every Starfleet member's raison d'être. Daystrom and his M5 computer are a clear danger to Starfleet's mission because they threaten to make manned space travel obsolete. In its place, he offers a blend of utopian idealism and protectionism, through the agency of all-powerful, sentient computers, that would result in every space explorer's retirement.

Relations Between Ethnic Males and Ethnic Females

Examples of the representation of ethnic males and ethnic females may be found in "The Emissary," "Reunion," and "Booby Trap." In "The Emissary," both Lieutenant Worf and Ambassador K'Ehleyr are depicted as hostile toward each other and uncooperative because something in their past remains unresolved. These tensions build to a climax when they meet on the holodeck where K'Ehleyr is already running one of Worf's calisthenics programs. These characters not only share Klingon and Terran cultural heritages, but both have chosen careers that take them away from the Klingon Empire and thrust them into positions where they represent the dominant force in the galaxy, the United Federation of Planets.

A constant theme in the development of these characters is the notion that they cannot truly be free around non-Klingons because their essence is too intense, too overpowering. Similarly, they are uncomfortable with their Klingon halves. This dilemma is, of course, familiar to anyone who has studied the literature of American racial stereotypes and goes by the term "tragic mulatto." According to this view of miscegenation, mulattos are tragic because they understand that they do not fit into either racial category and are subject to chronic depression and self-destructive behavior.

Together on the holodeck, isolated from the rest of the crew, Worf and K'Ehleyr combat the fierce virtual creatures of the exercise program. When the foes have been destroyed, they give in to their real, deeper passions for each other, and Worf takes K'Ehleyr's hand in his and slowly closes his around hers until her fingernails pierce her palm and blood streams out. As Worf and K'Ehleyr become lovers again, their tryst is characterized by snarling, pain, and personal injury. Following a formula that seems lifted straight out of Lévi-Strauss, love between Klingons, two alien Others, is characterized as violent, savage, and driven by sexual domination.

In this way, Klingon culture and psychology are portrayed as exotic and exciting precisely because they are conceptualized as outside the bounds of "normal." It clearly expresses the kind of dangerous risk many find a sexual stimulant. Representing romantic seduction through images of commingled blood and violent sex conjures with popular myths about vampires, sadomasochism, and AIDS transmission among minorities.

In fact, the violence between lovers that is depicted in these scenes resonates all the way back to "Space Seed," in which Khan seduces McGivers in precisely the same violent manner. In other words, at the same time that viewers may express revulsion, they may also be attracted to this representation of exotic sexual behavior as strangely titillating. Removing this scene to the holodeck ensures that this form of behavior will be contained, as well as allowing viewers a voyeuristic moment in narrative context that is the equivalent of "a safe distance," so that there is no fear of discovery. After all, it is a fantasy within a fantasy program, and pleasure may be derived from this interaction.

At the beginning of "Booby Trap," La Forge is featured in a vignette that takes place in the ship's holodeck on a date with a female Africanist shipmate. Despite the fact that La Forge has covered all the angles in creating a scene for romance, including a tropical beach, a picnic lunch, and strolling violinist, his intentions are rejected by this young woman. Regardless of La Forge's ability to program holodeck technology, it seems that the holodeck's capacity to produce fanciful settings is insufficient to ignite a romance with a real woman. Moreover, this scene is nothing less than another return of the desert island metaphor. La Forge's failure within its context marks him as incompetent with women, doomed to bachelorhood, and not able to found a family (i.e., to project his DNA into the future).

However, there are examples of adult sexual feelings among nonethnic characters on *Star Trek: The Next Generation.* For example, Picard and Crusher admit that they have loved each for a long time but never allow the matter to go further than being verbally acknowledged and felt. Riker and Troi were lovers, but Riker sacrificed the relationship to pursue his Starfleet career. And despite both being assigned to the *Enterprise,* neither chooses to rekindle their romance. These characters are represented as sexual and capable of establishing romantic unions, even if they chose not to for whatever reason. In contrast, the scene described earlier implies that when it comes to romance, the ethnic male is incapable of establishing a meaningful relationship of love and affection even when the object of the seduction is an ethnic female.

Relations Between Members of Different Ethnic Groups

In "Plato's Stepchildren," first Kirk, McCoy, and Spock and then Lieutenant Uhura and Nurse Chapel beam down to a hidden planet's utopian community. The *Enterprise* team is thoroughly disoriented by being displaced to an exotic planet with strange flora and fauna and surrounded by beings of supernatural powers (another version of a desert island, this time "The Tempest"). Away from the *Enterprise,* their crewmates, and familiar settings, these crew members are depicted as vulnerable to manipulation. As the scenario unfolds, both Uhura and Spock, two of the series' continuing ethnic characters, are forced into romantic tableaux.

In other words, under the normal circumstances of Starfleet rules, regulations, and decorum, and its system of white, male authority, romantic liaisons between races and species—between

Terran ethnic groups, Terrans and extraterrestrials, and Vulcans and alien Other—are not appreciated. Although affection and desire may be there, there are strong prohibitions against expressing them. In *Star Trek*'s vision of the future, males and females are no more able to acknowledge love in the workplace than contemporary mythology about love and work would indicate of humans today. Therefore, in the episodes examined, the true feelings of normal attraction between individuals who serve together when those individuals are different (white male and black female, white female and male Vulcan) can only be expressed when the authority under which they all serve has been obviated and control taken out from under the collective authority of Starfleet.

One might say that to give in to their feelings means that they have to step out of their place, and act "out of their minds," under the total control of some other agency. These scenes illustrate and thereby reinforce the strong social/formal prohibitions against transracial, interethnic, interspecies romance. Moreover, these scenes limit the audience's appreciation of alien mating customs and practices to brief voyeuristic moments in which difference is represented as exotic, titillating, and aberrant.[17] This kind of lapse can only happen outside the white male-centered hierarchical command structure of the *Enterprise*'s bridge. Moreover, once this rupture is sealed and Kirk, Uhura, Spock, and Chapel return to the *Enterprise*, the topic of their attraction for each other is never broached again.[18]

A second example occurs in "Booby Trap." During a conversation about love in 10-Forward, Guinan hints rather strongly that she holds a special fondness for Captain Picard. Her explanation is enigmatic, but in a subsequent episode we learn that Picard has traveled to Earth's past where he found Guinan injured and nursed her until help arrived. By putting this instance of contact and caring between two different species in the past, the possibility of this encounter contaminating command authority is circumvented. Moreover, this comment reinforces the idea that sexual bonding between white males and ethnic females is permitted, especially when the white male is in a position of authority.[19] In contrast, La Forge is attractive to Guinan only when he presents himself as weak and without self-confidence about romance. In this way, ethnic males are marked as less psychologically robust and less sexually attractive than white males.

An unusual twist on this theme occurs in "Booby Trap" when, later in the episode, La Forge uses the holodeck to create a simulacrum of Dr. Brahms. The holodeck, yet another version of the island metaphor, becomes the center of the main narrative as La Forge works with his simulation on a prototype of the engines. As they work together a bond based on professional competence forms. The trajectory of this interaction results in La Forge falling in love with the woman he created (as in *Pygmalion, My Fair Lady,* and *Metropolis*). In the scenes between La Forge and Brahms, not only are all traces of the *Enterprise*—that is, its network of social interactions—effaced, but the holodeck produces a perfect "world" based on technological challenge and equipped with a technological helpmate. This formulation appears to effectively counter the problem encountered in the earlier scene by replacing the flesh-and-blood female with a software illusion. Taken together, La Forge is allowed a romance (or, more accurately, here it takes on the quality of mental masturbation) only when nothing about it could possibly disrupt the ship's routine and command protocols at the time or in future; that is, romance and family life clearly threaten to complicate command personnel's lives beyond their ability to reconcile duties and set priorities.

Additionally, in the scenes, first on the holodeck, then in 10-Forward, and returning to the holodeck, there is a recursive pattern regarding the females La Forge meets: an ethnic Terran female, an extraterrestrial ethnic female, and a holographic white female. Each is one more step removed from his ethnic identity. From this pattern arise the inferences that an ethnic male cannot relate to a real female who looks like him and that when it comes to romance, the ethnic male is capable of establishing a meaningful relationship of love and affection only when the object of the seduction is his fantasy woman. In the context of *Star Trek: The Next Generation,* La Forge's fantasy female is a woman whose mental and physical attributes are flawless and who is unattainable: a technoid copy of a white female physicist. Although La Forge is depicted as capable, even intuitively ingenious when it comes to technology, when it comes to mastering the finer nuances of courtship and navigating the tricky cross-currents of romantic relationship, he is cast as naive, pitiful, and unattractive to females. In contrast, both Picard and Riker are depicted as successfully consummating romantic relations with noncrew females, though for various reasons each of these relationships does not last.

This scene gives us another insight into the conception of the La Forge character. He may be a brilliant field engineer. He may be able to anticipate innovations and implement them. He may even have occasional flashes of genius. But this exchange shows that he is not a real intellect. He is never represented in terms of sharing qualities like those of a research scientist. The fact that he says he cannot write a scientific paper discounts his abilities to levels of those of a talented craftsman. Instead of meeting Dr. Brahms on her terms, La Forge deflects her compliment and tries again to approach her from the point of view of friendship. He does not evaluate himself as her intellectual equal. He obviously does not know how to use the higher-level resources of the ship's computer, or he would never have made the mistake of not including her marital status in the parameters of the psychological profile from which the holodeck-Brahms was configured. Moreover, her married status effectively closes off any possibility of a romantic connection.

Another example of inappropriate contact between members of different ethnic groups, a Terran and a Klingon, occurs when Dr. Pulaski drinks a fatal poison to enjoy the full effect of Klingon love poetry, but not before injecting herself with the antidote. It should be noted in this context that Dr. Pulaski was replaced after less than a full season when Dr. Crusher returns as the *Enterprise's* chief medical officer. Dropping such a spirited and adventurous female character so abruptly seems odd, but it may be related to the ways her behavior transgressed Starfleet norms by going to such extremes to experience the depths of Klingon poetry and feeling. Her behavior legitimizes Klingon culture as worth risking the life of an unadulterated white female.

Relations Between Members of the Same Gender

Shortly after Ambassador K'Ehleyr arrives onboard the *Enterprise,* in "The Emissary," she has a conversation with ship's counselor Troi. Troi, who is half-Betazoid and half-Terran, reaches out to K'Ehlyer, half-Klingon and half-Terran, in friendship, and the two females discuss their biracial heritages. Ironically, Troi seems to be unaware what problems the issues of being biracial may have caused

K'Ehlyer. There should be a bridge of sympathy and understanding between these two females because they share a common status as alien Others and biracial females. Instead, they seem oblivious to the emotions and situations that being doubly marked must have raised in each female's life.

Surprisingly, their conversation turns to Troi's ignorance about the compatibility of Klingon and Terran DNA. Obviously Klingon and Terran DNA are compatible, or else K'Ehleyr would not exist. Troi's ignorance about Klingon and Terran compatibility is quite insulting, and her attempt at bonding is all the more spurious because she is the product of a Terran and Betazoid union and biracial, too. The women's conversation shifts from a discussion of the biological parameters of transspecies mating to consideration of the psychological consequences of being raised by parents with different ethnic backgrounds. Here, too, there is friction. Troi, who is openly antagonistic toward her mother's constant interference in her life, presents a symptom of denial when she insists that her childhood was a happy exploration of difference. K'Ehlyer recounts, with humor, her youthful difficulty with merging two cultural outlooks. By the end of their exchange, it is not clear whether these two women, who outwardly share so many points in common, can ever become friends.

Underlying this exchange is a subtext about miscegenation. This subject is introduced by the terms "blood" and "DNA." The undeniable inference is that ethnic blood is bad, because it is associated with attitudes, values, and customs that permit expression through extreme emotions and violence. This is the meaning that underlies K'Ehleyr's attitude toward her biracial nature. It is interesting to note that Troi, who does not share this negative feeling about being biracial, is the product of a union between two white races. She not only bears no trace of racial mixing, but the two "bloods" that flow in her are untainted by the negative qualities that upset and mark K'Ehleyr.

Another thing that stands out in these scenes is Troi's lack of information and sensitivity about K'Ehleyr's background. For a space-traveling psychologist, this gap is nothing less than staggering. Her attitude of security is consistent with someone whose primary identification is with the dominant culture of Starfleet and the Federation. This attitude illustrates the fact that members of superior cultures do not have to learn about "lesser races." Troi is so immersed in her identification with the Federation that she does not bother to learn anything about Worf's Klingon culture, despite the fact that his sense of separation from his roots informs his personality and effectiveness as an officer. Nor does she display any of the normal curiosity that would have led her to examine her analogous counterparts as they arise from other interspecies matings. Troi's attitude is rather supercilious; she claims that her childhood was well balanced. However, we have met her mother, Lwaxana Troi, and know that her mother's obsessive personality has overshadowed her since childhood.

K'Ehleyr's disdain for her own temper displays a kind of self-hate that is not appropriate to a Federation official of her accomplishment. In scenes with K'Ehleyr and Deanna Troi and in scenes that feature Klingons, Klingon biology and culture are described in negative terms: aggressive, threatening, and hostile; uncontrollably emotional and self-destructive; sadomasochistic and violent—something to be suppressed and hidden from others. In these relationships, we see none of the subtlety, compassion, and romance that Worf, for example, claims came into full expression in Klingon culture. Are these aspects of the Klingon soul that may not be shared with less than full-blooded Klingons? No, they remain unexplored territory here, possibly because to explore it would destabilize Federation and audience values about these activities.

Among the relationships between crew of the same gender in *Star Trek: The Next Generation*, the friendship of La Forge and Data, the android, deserves some attention. That La Forge is at home around machines is, of course, an important characteristic of his role as the ship's chief engineer. However, instead of human companionship, La Forge's closest confidant is the machine man, Data. The reason for making La Forge's best friend Data is at first obscure.

Why do the series producers represent the engineer as a personality that is *more* comfortable around and devoted to machines than people? Surely engineers fall in love and have babies. Where else do little engineers come from? Again, the producers present a rationale as the logic behind this pairing: who would be better able to understand and relate to an android than an engineer? But does this bear scrutiny? Is La Forge cast in this relationship to Data as a sign that he, too, is not quite human? (My question: Why does an android need friends? And if one did, is it not equally logical for a computer programmer, or the ship's doctor, to be Data's friend?

Each would surely find in Data an intriguing associate. Why not the chief medical officer, or the ship's counselor?) Just as the android is fully functional but sterile, La Forge is introduced here as a tragically pitiful creature who is incapable of entering into a relationship that could lead to children. He, as well as Data, are set up to leave behind no progeny and are most at home separated from others (even Picard has to return to his native soil and family to reaffirm his identity following his abduction and transformation by the Borg).

"The Ultimate Computer" gives us an example of a situation in which a white male ship's captain and an ethnic scientist must contend with a life-threatening crisis. The result of this crisis situation is that the scientist's invention and the efforts of his mature life lie in ruin, and his reputation hangs by a frayed thread. At the episode's conclusion, Kirk stands over the sedated body of Dr. Daystrom and boasts about the fact that both maker and machine are in the same condition. In other words, when there is a competition between an ethnic male and a white male representing the dominant culture, who represents that culture's command and control structure, the ethnic male will not prevail and indeed must be utterly neutralized.

Moreover, in this situation we have two males whose competition is essentially mental. In a mental contest between a white male and an ethnic male, the white male, who represents the values and beliefs of the dominant culture, must, as demonstrated, defeat the ethnic challenger and reassert through his victory the right of the dominant culture to its privileges. In the process, the ethnic male must also be found to be inferior. The parallels between Khan and Daystrom continue. In "Space Seed," Kirk neutralized Khan by exiling him to an uninhabited world; in "The Ultimate Computer," Daystrom is consigned to a rehabilitation colony, marginalized to the sidelines of galactic affairs.

This lesson is, of course, the main narrative thrust of "Space Seed," too. For all of Khan's boasts about genetic enhancement rendering him superior and invulnerable, he is defeated in the end because Kirk, in a flash of insight, uses his knowledge of the ship to literally bludgeon his rival into submission. Kirk, even under life-and-death pressure, is able to outthink the ethnic male Khan.

Relations Between Ethnic Parents and Their Children

Throughout the episodes examined in this study are several instances in which characters, by their conduct or behavior, comment on relations between ethnic parents and their children. As we have already seen, interspecies liaisons and their resultant offspring are viewed askance in *Star Trek*'s mythology. In "The Emissary," Troi's comments can be taken to question the very idea of attempting such a union for fear that the blending of biochemical compounds might produce a freak or deformity, an attitude about her own situation that Troi's banter with K'Ehleyr only thinly disguises. At the heart of this attitude is the notion that anything outside the bounds of one's own cultural experience is not normal, but is foreign and suspicious, if not outright distasteful.

This attitude is quite familiar to anyone who has followed the public discourse on television talk shows about interracial dating and marriage. In that discussion, attitudes are quite often displaced to the question of children. Although many claim that they have no prejudice about an ethnic male or female being involved with a member of the dominant group, there is the countervailing refrain, "What about the children?" Progeny of these relations are considered marked in some way that makes them less than human, certainly no longer eligible for membership within the dominant group, doomed to be identified with the "other" group, and vulnerable to retaliatory attacks, even murder—as are their parents.

The idea of an intact ethnic, multiracial, or multispecies family as a continuing part of the *Star Trek*'s starship mythology has yet to be embraced and explored. To examine the relation between family life and space service, Miles O'Brien, Keiko, his wife, and Molly, their child, are removed to a Bajoran space station that is only loosely associated with the Federation and, therefore, outside these Federation narratives. Indeed, Benjamin Sisko, an African American Starfleet commander, moves to this space station with his son Jake and assumes command after his wife has been killed at Wolf 359 in the Federation's war with the Borg. Both of these ethnic or multiracial families exist outside Federation space and outside its primary objectives of space exploration, research, and colonization. Significantly, the Africanist males struggle to maintain a family life without the nurturing presence of a woman. The image of a complete ethnic family seems reserved for those families headed by a white male and whose maternal center is occupied by a member of a racial group whose light complexion allows her to be taken as an "honorary" white.

An example of *Star Trek*'s conception of ethnic children and their families is demonstrated in the episodes "Reunion" and "Family." When Ambassador K'Ehleyr returns to the *Enterprise* in "Reunion," she brings with her Alexander, a male child who is her and Worf's son. When Worf discovers that Alexander is his son, rather than accept him and plan a way with K'Ehleyr that will keep them both near him, even if it would mean that their relationship could not be disclosed because of Worf's discommendation from the Klingon Empire, Worf rejects his son and his responsibility. This decision momentarily protects his mate and son, but the fallacy in this choice lies in the fact that it ultimately leaves K'Ehlyer vulnerable, because she does not understand the lengths to which Duras will go to maintain the illusion of his father's honor. Worf's decision results in K'Ehleyr's murder and Alexander being shipped off to Earth to be raised by Worf's Russian foster parents.

Of course, some will point out that this narrative arc merely follows a principle of economy to which producers adhere that rules out carrying any unnecessary characters beyond the cast of continuing characters and occasional featured players. However, in a series such as *Star Trek: The Next Generation* this precept is more than a little hard to justify because it is always possible to plan stories in advance, to limit the recurrence of family members, and to explain absences in terms of assignments and activities on other decks on the *Enterprise*. Alexander might be enrolled in a Federation school while K'Ehleyr went about her ambassadorial duties. Then plots might have featured Worf, K'Ehleyr, and Alexander being reunited for holidays and so forth. Moreover, in the current series, a good deal is made of the fact that the Galaxy-class *Enterprise* carries families. Therefore, the failure to provide models of ethnic families is all the more striking when the setting is a starship specifically designed to include families, and presumably there would be family gatherings for birthdays, holiday celebrations, and Starfleet and non-Starfleet ceremonies aboard ship that would allow for family participation.

In "Family," Worf's foster parents bring Alexander back to his father as the *Enterprise* orbits Earth while undergoing repairs for damage sustained in its encounter with the Borg. Alexander, growing up on Earth without the support and affirmation of his surviving parent, has developed behavior problems. Worf's adoptive parents realize that the boy needs his father's supervision. Although Worf and Alexander eventually reconcile, this episode creates the image of the single-parent ethnic family as being a future reality. Though at first glance this may seem to be a revision of current media images of the female-headed ethnic family, *Star Trek*'s treatment of family, how it is accommodated and represented within Starfleet's command structure, may well deserve more specific study.

The point here is not to attack white foster parents but rather to ask why no other members of Worf's or K'Ehlyer's birth families have come forward to accept responsibility for the child. Instances of young transracial orphans usually result in the child being adopted by the ethnic side of the child's heritage. That is, inheritance, with all the attendant issues of property, wealth, power, and influence, as the right to the transfer of property, is jealously guarded and policed against transracial progeny, so that estates are maintained within the dominant culture. This principle is maintained here, as Alexander is exiled from both K'Ehlyer's white Terran familial and Worf's white Terran foster familial connections and forced to live with a father who is himself estranged from his people.

Relations Between Commanders and Ethnic Subordinates

At the conclusion of "Reunion," after Worf has killed Duras in revenge for his murdering K'Ehleyr, Worf is summoned to Picard for a reprimand. Worf justifies the murder of Duras by pointing out that it follows Klingon customs. Picard, speaking in his capacity as a Starfleet official, reveals much about his and the United Federation of Planets' attitudes toward ethnicity. Picard points out that there are many beings representing thirteen different planets, limited it seems to humanoid life-forms, serving on the *Enterprise,* that a smoothly running ship depends on all working together, and that Worf's independent act will result in an official negative evaluation being placed in his personnel file.[20]

Going further, Picard offers Worf the choice of resigning his commission in Starfleet or suppressing his cultural legacy, Klingon law and tradition, and pledging his allegiance to Starfleet by following its rules and regulations. Or, put another way, Terran white males remain unmarked; ethnic and alien males and females are marked, and their status as "Other" reverberates throughout their interactions and depictions. When these Other characters seek recognition and validation within a society such as Starfleet, they do so at the cost of renouncing their culture, values, and beliefs, suppressing their culture's worldview, and rejecting the vital, nourishing link between them and their culture. In contrast, Picard, for example, is referred to as French and even visits his brother who maintains the family winery in Lavaur, but French culture is never represented as being at odds with Federation culture or policy. Picard is not marked in any fashion and moves through Starfleet unencumbered, accepting its opportunities and rewards as if they should be just *naturally* his due for service rendered.

Roles and Actions

In both series, ethnic characters were included in a variety of roles as either continuing characters or featured players. Ethnic characters were depicted as engaged in a wide range of activities that were associated with their specific shipboard duties. However, instead of finding a wide range of occupations and activities that would reinforce the foundation mythology of Starfleet's future as one in which individuals are free and supported in their pursuit of professional and personal fulfillment, ethnic characters in this sample of programs were represented in a limited set of roles and actions. Unfortunately, to too large an extent, these representations reflect bias and the taint of past negative racial stereotypes.

The episodes from both series examined here revealed several modes for the depiction of ethnic characters. Some of the main themes related to ethnic characterization are identified in "Space Seed." Khan's first acts upon awakening from cryogenic suspension cast suspicion on his personality. Early in the episode, Khan eavesdrops on Dr. McCoy as he makes a medical log entry. Then, he responds to his new and puzzling circumstances with a threat of violence.

For series that are aimed in greatest part towards white male viewers between eighteen and thirty-nine years old, *Star Trek* episodes reflect a good deal of interest in romance and sexual practices among ethnic characters. Unfortunately, romantic encounters that feature ethnic characters are associated with violence and aggression.[21] In a later scene in "Space Seed," when Lieutenant McGivers questions Khan's plan to take control of the *Enterprise*, he reacts angrily and shoves McGivers away and to the floor, where she collapses into an emotional heap of sobs. Unable to deny her emotions, she confesses her love for Khan and he, crushing her hand in his far stronger one, forces her to join in his plan or face complete rejection (more than twenty years later, this scene would echo eerily when Worf and K'Ehleyr meet on the holodeck in "The Emissary").[22] These interactions depict the way a man like Khan courts a woman and how the balance of personalities in their relationship tilts. Near the episode's end, after Khan has taken over the *Enterprise*, Uhura refuses to obey orders from Khan, and one of her male captors slaps her face hard. Khan comments ironically, "I should have known that suffocating together on the bridge would create heroic camaraderie among you. But it is quite a different thing to sit by and watch it happening to someone else." After forcing Uhura to activate the view screen, the crew is forced to watch Kirk in the chamber suffering as its atmosphere is withdrawn.[23]

In "The Emissary," Ambassador K'Ehlyer's visit rekindles an old romance with Lieutenant Worf. Although viewer reaction to Klingon foreplay may vary, it must be recognized as a nearly exact copy of the scene with Khan and McGivers from the original series. There is an unmistakable connection between the ways each series represents ethnic sexuality. For northern Indians, Klingons, and Vulcans, pain and physical aggression are preludes to sexual intimacy. In *Star Trek*, these forbidden relationships are a sign foreboding the collapse of Starfleet order and civilization. Khan and his liaison obviously would challenge Starfleet's very existence; Worf's liaison undermines his official shipboard relationships. In each case, the women associated with these males earn death. In an episode from the original series, "Amok Time," Vulcan courtship rituals are depicted as including life-and-death combat between contesting males. This episode ends with Spock's rejecting marriage by spurning the designing Vulcan female, and in the process reinforcing Starfleet authority.

This idea of strenuous physical exercise or even aggression leading to sex is melodramatic, at best. Moreover, developing intimacy out of rigorous warrior training, mating ritual, or a flare of temper goes further than merely putting the emphasis on the physical side of ethnicity. What is operating here is an association of ethnic males with sexual excess and violence.[24] In these ways, the ethnic male is depicted as an untrustworthy sneak, a sexual predator towards white women, a sexual aggressor, and someone with a callous disregard for life.

Though the Klingon Empire was initially represented as the Federation's chief nemesis, more recent history has brought them within the Federation as an equal among equals. In both series, Klingons are the most familiar non-Terran, alien ethnic Other group. Unfortunately, *Star Trek*'s depiction of Klingons stresses only negative qualities to distinguish them from Terrans. Klingons have volatile tempers, value war over peace, eat uncooked invertebrates for food, shun comfort for Spartan hardship, and seem to apply the concept of conquest by force in all aspects of life. The only positive attributes recognized for Klingons is their parahuman strength and that side of their warrior aesthetic that values valor and honor.

This, of course, is just another variation on the mind/body duality in which the dominant group is identified with the mental aspects and the dominated group with the physical. Within this scheme, Klingons occupy a middle ground: exotic, superstrong, recently aligned with the Federation. Because of his mutinous intent, Khan is located at one end of this continuum. The Vulcan Spock occupies the opposite end: exotic; superstrong; long-term, family connection to the Federation; personally loyal; highly valued expert in science and computing.

To a large extent, these ethnic aliens' cultural identifications are represented as outside Starfleet. In Spock's case his Vulcan heritage is paramount, yet he is a dedicated Starfleet officer. Not only is Khan from another time, but he is a renegade with allegiance limited to those who follow his eugenics ideology. Because Worf was raised on Earth by Russian foster parents, his identification with Klingon culture is from a distance. He is onboard the *Enterprise* because his Terran acculturation is so complete that his primary identification is as a Starfleet officer and official of culture that dominates the galaxy. For Worf, reestablishing his Klingon heritage is crucial, but he may do so only to the extent that it does not conflict with Starfleet and the United Federation of Planets.

Despite being raised on Earth, his considerable efforts to blend within his personality Klingon and Terran cultures, and his years of sterling service aboard the flagship of the United Federation of Planets, when faced with a terrible personal challenge, he reverts to his violent nature. For example, when K'Ehlyer has been killed, Worf does not try to use guile or logic to ensnare Duras; instead, his aggressive Klingon temperament erupts in murderous violence. This kind of reaction resonates back to the scene in "Space Seed" when Uhura refuses to cooperate with Khan. These scenes present another instance of an ethnic male's violence toward a female; in this case, a genetically blended male slaps Lieutenant Uhura who is a female bridge officer of command rank. Khan's personal use of physical force, his endorsement of the use of force by others under his authority, and his use of both physical torture (Kirk in decompression chamber) and psychological terror (making the bridge crew watch Kirk suffer) mark the transracial man as cruel and barbaric.

Suspended between their cultures and those of Starfleet, ethnic types exist in a state of personal psychological tension. Dr. Daystrom and Lieutenant La Forge show how the impact of this tension is expressed within the *Star Trek* formula at the personal level. Both men are single, presumably so absorbed in their duties that romantic relations are precluded. Both are represented as workers who toil with machinery deep in the bowels of the *Enterprise*. They are glorified mechanics whose most intimate relations are with technology and whose authority is limited to that domain.

These two characters provide object lessons illustrating the integration of the technology within Starfleet. Daystrom's technology cannot be successfully incorporated because it is opposed to the fundamental premises behind Starfleet. Here the association of ethnic character with technology is brought to a logical conclusion. Just as M5 has overreached itself by trying to be more than a machine, Daystrom has overreached himself, not being content to enjoy Starfleet and the United Federation's recognition and awards for his previous invention, duotronics. Daystrom's is a sin of hubris that is all the more serious because it challenged the foundation ethos of Starfleet and the United Federation of Planets that put life at risk for the goal of interstellar exploration. Daystrom's basic failure is in not knowing his place, a lack of self-consciousness minorities can ill afford, and his mental collapse is linked to the stress this placed on him in trying to prove to everyone that his success was earned, not merely awarded to him because he was a clever, young Africanist scientist.[25]

An inference is lurking here about the nature of ethnic characters' mental capabilities. Daystrom is an object lesson about the limits of the ethnic characters' creativity. According to *Star Trek*, the tragic flaw in Daystrom's M5 computer stemmed from his use of his own brain patterns as the model for its circuits. The machine is doomed to failure because it originates from a flawed premise: an overwrought Daystrom trying to best a galaxy of scientists and make Starfleet obsolete. In the end, Daystrom's mental illness is a symptom of his inability to understand the way things are, an inability to come to grips with the status quo and his place within it. In this instance, we are told that the root cause of Daystrom's and M5's mental illness stems from either malformed or overstressed brain material donated by Daystrom. (In James Whale's *Frankenstein*, adapted by Francis Edwards Faragoh, the genesis of the monster is traced to using defective brain matter.)

La Forge, on the other hand, does not question Starfleet's basic philosophy. He functions comfortably within Starfleet and enjoys its benefits. Moreover, La Forge's engineering expertise is practiced within the boundaries of existing technology. This character incorporates the lesson Daystrom experiences. La Forge only runs into difficulty when he forgets that his relationship with technology is proscribed by his Starfleet engineering duties.

In two instances, La Forge tries to use high technology for no loftier aim than his own pleasure: when he uses the holodeck technology to create a beach setting for his romantic date and when he falls in love with the simulacrum of Dr. Brahms. The consequences of La Forge's unauthorized use of holodeck technology do not occur until "Galaxy's Child," when the trajectory of this narrative arc brings the real Dr. Brahms to the *Enterprise* and La Forge learns that there is no possibility for a romance with her because she is married.[26] These instances reinforce the implicit rule that ethnic characters may relate to technology only as sanctioned by the authority of the dominant culture. The problem does not arise from the technology; it is a problem linked to the psychology of these characters (their mental incapacity, their inability to think at a sufficiently sophisticated level), or they are represented as not being able to use technology outside their engineering training.

What ethnic characters do is important, but what they do *not* do is equally illuminating. In "Galaxy's Child," Brahms remarks that La Forge should write a paper and share his technological innovation for reinjecting plasma back in phase into the ship's engines with Starfleet and other propulsion scientists. La Forge says that writing is not his "strong suit" and declines. By refusing to document his invention, he perpetuates his separation from cerebral activities and continues his identification with manual labor.

Guinan, the mysterious space/time traveler, is another example of an ethnic character that has been reduced to the level of a servant. Despite the fact that she operates in her own portion of the ship and possesses unusual intuitive powers that allow her to sense temporal shifts and anomalies, Guinan is a bartender. Her position is associated with recreation (nothing related to the serious duties of running the ship occur in 10-Forward), her locus of activity is, as it were, in the ship's basement (like engineering), and so, like La Forge, she is a "downstairs" or serving person. The symbolic representation of this ethnic character associates Guinan with serving her patrons from behind the bar and limits her social mobility. The 10-Forward lounge, the bar itself, and her activities as hostess effectively segregate her from wider contact with more of the crew. This development of Guinan treats the character as a mere convenience to be brought into stories on an "as-needed" basis and reduces her to the level of a curiosity whose own story is never broached.[27]

Vestments and Anatomy

In the episodes from both series examined here, ethnic characters' physical appearance and the semiotic content of their clothing styles show a remarkable consistency (across the episodes). The clothing and anatomy of each of the ethnic characters in the episodes studied function to maintain social distance, to segregate them from even their shipmates.

Ethnic characters in the *Star Trek* series are marked in ways that make their recognition easy. Conversely, nonethnic characters are unmarked, so as to more seamlessly merge with the Starfleet/

Federation ideology whose "naturalizing" function supports its unquestioned dominance. Worf, like Spock, is identified as an alien by virtue of his physical features: horseshoe-crab-shaped cranium, dark brown skin, superhuman strength. Spock, in the earlier series, is often identified as alien by Kirk and McCoy who referred to his pointed ears, slightly green tinted skin, and superhuman strength as visible markers of difference.[28] Both are viewed with suspicion by their crewmates. Spock's and Worf's loyalties to Starfleet may be measured by the extent to which they refrain from displaying their superior physical capabilities. Through an act of denial, by rejecting aspects of their identity, Spock and Worf keep their colleagues comfortable by not bringing up humans' relative limitations. Worf's physical characteristics define him as "Other" and form a barrier, according to the dominant culture's aesthetics, to fraternization.

The Worf and Khan characters are depicted with long hair. In contemporary society, males wear long hair as a sign of rebelliousness and rejection of the dominant culture. For Khan, this of course coincides with his history of revolt against world order and his desire to establish an alternative cultural hegemony of the genetically enhanced over that of "normal" humanity. In terms of Worf, who longs to repair his connections with Klingon culture and its balance of barbarity and technological sophistication, wearing long hair is an easy way to identify with the Klingon warrior culture. The clothing and hair styles worn by Khan and Worf are also clearly derived from the conventions of representing buccaneers or outlaw sailors, particularly in motion pictures. However, we should note that inasmuch as the essential qualities of Khan and Klingon culture are so similar, long hair as a sign links together both as being outside the law and order of the Federation.

Star Trek's ethnic characters are often dressed in ways that make them distinctive, too. Deanna Troi, for example, is dressed in fashions that accent her sex and availability for coupling. As a female alien Other who is both light-skinned and identifies with the Federation, Troi's image combines femininity and healthy sexual appetite. Dr. Crusher, in contrast, is fully costumed with not a trace of décolleté. The difference is that Beverly Crusher is a white Terran female and, following the dominant culture's mythology about women, must be protected from the burden of sex and sexuality.[29]

Worf is rarely seen without a metallic sash.[30] The fact that Worf wears a visible marker and the fact of its diagonality serve as barriers and warning. This sash as sign simultaneously gives notice not to approach too closely; its wearer is different and should be regarded with caution, if not suspicion. The prior comment about costuming conventions for representing outlaw sailors applies to Worf's costuming. All he needs to complete the picture is an eye patch.

The character Geordi La Forge is described as blind from birth and able now to see because he wears a special prosthesis that converts the electromagnetic spectrum into impulses fed directly into his brain. La Forge's VISOR is a visual sign that marks him as different. Unfortunately, as much as La Forge's VISOR allows him to see, it keeps his colleagues—and the audience—from making eye contact with him. Oddly, even though his birth defect has been technologically corrected, La Forge is unique among *Star Trek*'s characters because he never generates a point of view shot. It seems not to matter that VISOR technology and the *Enterprise*'s remote sensor technology are compatible and would permit La Forge's enhanced view to be projected through the ship's view screens and computer monitors for everyone, including the audience, to share.[31] This inability to generate a point-of-view shot effectively reduces La Forge to the status of an object, forever the subject of another's gaze. As far as the development of episodes is concerned, the La Forge character is powerless to participate in the shaping of a televisual narrative, because that develops out of characters' abilities to generate images representing their point in relation to the plot. For all of his engineering skills, La Forge is essentially a powerless character in terms of being able to support a narrative. This inability to generate a narrative, this generative lack or incapacity, gets represented at the character level by La Forge's inability to engage in relationships that would lead to family, the projection of this generative lack to the genetic level. This may be the source of the failure of the series to conceive of La Forge as a human with emotional needs. Blocked from seeing others and from them seeing into his soul, unable to sponsor narratives, relegated to bachelorhood, a machine as his best friend, La Forge is a pitiful character indeed.[32] Is there lurking here in this model of genetic fading out of existence an attitude toward the fate of the physically challenged and ethnic people with physical challenges in the future?

Chapter 6

Looking back over *Star Trek* and *Star Trek: The Next Generation,*
we see that distinct patterns emerge in the representation of ethnic characters. Whether a loyal Starfleet officer or a maverick
product of a bygone world, ethnic and alien characters enjoy only
provisional acceptance, subject to revocation at any time. Ethnic
characters are depicted in terms of their superhuman physical
strength. Though superior strength may be an attractive or positive attribute, ethnic characters demonstrate a disturbing habit of
tying that physicality into a threat, particularly towards women.
Their inability to form meaningful relationships with women, either because they are too brutal or too inept, leads to their not being associated with intact nuclear families.

Ethnic characters are depicted in roles that emphasize an association with machines over human relations. When the roles of
ethnic characters bring them into frequent contact with others,
their specific roles as service or security personnel proscribe the
range of interactions to the more formal level that helps to ensure
predictable behavior and isolate them from the kind of social situations that could lead to friendship or more. These characters exist isolated from contact with others because of the environment
in which they work, or their cultural beliefs, or some physical limitation. These modes of representation bear a disturbingly strong
resemblance to an older and thoroughly discredited model for the
representation of ethnicity already documented in motion pictures and television. That they would be found in media productions that purport to fashion a vision of the future is all the more
disturbing.

Chapter 7

Conclusion

[T]he hope of doing without ethnicity in society as its sub-
groups assimilate to the majority group may be as utopian
and as questionable an enterprise as the hope of doing without social class in society.[1]

Threading through *Star Trek* and *Star Trek: The Next Generation* is
Gene Roddenberry's utopian vision of the future. In this utopia,
peace is maintained throughout the known galaxy by the United
Federation of Planets, whose diplomats are on hand to mediate local and regional disputes and hostilities on member planets. Roddenberry's future has found solutions to economic crisis, criminal
behavior, mental illness, and physical disease. Educational inequities, unemployment, homelessness, urban decay, religious
strife, poverty, race bias, and prejudice are relegated to humanity's past. The promise of *Star Trek* and *Star Trek: The Next Generation* is a world where social problems are no longer an impediment
to individual and social development.

When crises occur, they typically emerge from outside the Federation's comfortable family of civilizations: hostile renegade
worlds or intractable individuals with hyperactive egos. And
when these kinds of crises arise, Starfleet, the Federation's paramilitary service, is called upon to dispatch the problem. The key
issue of these series is the maintenance of order and stability. All
of the narratives across both series are conceived of as demonstrations of how crises may be managed so that Federation and
Starfleet authorities retain their unquestioned hegemony. Even

before the narratives express the ways Starfleet and the Federation's authority is challenged and reasserted, characters and relations among characters must be drawn upon which a foundation of stability can be set. These characters and their relationships with crewmates and those they encounter are the principal means by which *Star Trek*'s vision of the future is articulated. Given America's history of turmoil over race relations, which at the time of the original conception of *Star Trek* was especially noteworthy, among the main needs of series producers was a way to accommodate race relations within Starfleet and the Federation's ideology of stability.

Race and American Ideology in *Star Trek*

To their credit, the producers of *Star Trek* appreciated and adapted the controversy and drama of the national debate on civil rights, which was gathering considerable momentum by the end of the 1960s, to the developmental needs of their series. Although their interests may have led them to transform this theme into dramatic situations, a closer examination of these episodes reveals that these treatments did not include any indictment of America's race policies past or present.[2] What impact would including ethnicity have on the environment of peace and stability that is *Star Trek*'s vision of the future?

As noted earlier, the ethnic characters of the regular cast of *Star Trek* are uniformly depicted in subordinate roles. Whether as members of the *Enterprise* crew or as civilians that the *Enterprise* encounters during its travel, ethnic people are not represented as being on a par with the commander of the *Enterprise* or Starfleet Command. There were no instances in which an ethnic Starfleet ship commander was encountered. In only one instance (Commodore Stone in "Court Martial") was an ethnic character represented as part of Starfleet's upper-echelon command structure.[3] Within the repertoire of *Star Trek* roles, ethnic characters are relegated to the status of devoted servant, vicious criminal, knife toter, high-tech mechanic, mental inferior, sexual superman, violent savage, and, at every point, an individual prohibited from forming any romantic relationships.[4] Ethnic characters are depicted as lone individuals with no reference to their families or familial history. Whenever ethnic characters are situated in a setting outside the *Enterprise*, the cultural context of the scene always reflects aspects of Eurocentric culture rather than a context derived from the history, culture, and values of African Americans.

Ethnic characters on *Star Trek: The Next Generation* fare no better. Although it is true that the numerical presence of ethnics onboard the *Enterprise* has been broadened, the characters themselves show no more dimensionality. To the extent that ethnic characters are depicted as part of Starfleet Command's upper echelons, they are mere tokens, devices that move a plot point along; they are not developed and have no continuing identification with subsequent programs. That is, Captain La Forge (Geordi's father) and his wife (Geordi's mother), Captain Alvera K. La Forge (*Star Trek: The Next Generation* episode "Interface"),[5] Captain Turrell (*Star Trek II: The Wrath of Khan*), and Lieutenant Aquiel Uhnari (*Star Trek: The Next Generation* episode "Aquiel") are examples of ethnic characters who are brought into episodes, even at the level of a family member, and never return. On occasion, the *Enterprise* encounters Starfleet ship captains who are ethnic, but they, too, are infrequent and do not return for further development.

In other words, both series treat ethnic characters in featured roles as *fonctionnaires,* just a detail to move the plot along, and nothing in the corpus of these series demonstrates that any thought whatsoever has been given to using these characters to add dimension and texture to the representation of the lives of *Star Trek*'s recurring ethnic cast members.[6] The point is that no evidence from the material of either series examined here or from a survey of the entirety of *Star Trek*'s mass media products indicates that any consideration has been given to how the lives and cultures of ethnic people might contribute to understanding their relationship to the founding and vitality of Starfleet and the Federation of Planets.

In the last two seasons of *Star Trek: The Next Generation* there were several episodes that dealt with relationships among the *Enterprise's* captain and ethnic crewmembers. Examples from season six include "Aquiel" (airdate: 30 January 1993, episode 139) and "Lesson" (airdate: 3 April 1993, episode 145). In "Aquiel" La Forge comes to the defense of a beautiful and mysterious dark-skinned Starfleet Lieutenant who is accused of murder and falls in love with her. The episode ends with La Forge exonerating

Lieutenant Aquiel and the couple separating: La Forge returns to the *Enterprise*; Aquiel accepts reassignment within Starfleet. In "Lessons" Picard falls in love with a brilliant, mature female Starfleet research scientist and is torn between duty and love when he is forced to assign her to a life-threatening mission. When the rescue mission is completed, Picard breaks off the relationship because he realizes that he cannot command and love the same woman at the same time. In the seventh, and final, season there were three episodes that returned to this theme: "Parallels" (airdate: 27 November 1993, episode 163), "The Eye of the Beholder" (airdate: 26 February 1994, episode 170), and "All Good Things . . ." (airdates: 23 May and 30 May 1994, episodes 177 and 178). In "Parallels," Worf returns from a Bat'telh competition and flies into an alternate universe. In this story he jumps from one possible universe to another and discovers that in one of these he is married to Counselor Troi, that they have a family together, and that Alexander (Worf's son with K'Ehleyr) doesn't exist. This narrative's resolution, which involves returning Worf to his correct timeline, means that when this finally occurs, of course, Deanna Troi is merely a shipmate.

"The Eye of the Beholder" is the mirror opposite of "Parallels" with Troi experiencing strange empathetic visions and becoming romantically involved with Worf during her investigation of the circumstances surrounding a Starfleet officer's mysterious suicide. The episode concludes with Troi realizing that the "events" she has been experiencing are really psychic artifacts of this unique mystery, that her "experiences" are all hallucinations, and that her tumultous romantic relationship with Worf was actually a part of her mental metaphorization of events leading up to the death of the Starfleet officer and not reflective of anything between the real Troi and the real Worf.

The two-part finale, "All Good Things . . .", begins with an aged Picard being informed by Q, his old nemesis, that one of Picard's decisions as captain of the *Enterprise* has set in motion a series of effects that are rippling back through time and threaten humanity's earliest beginnings. In this episode, the taboos against crew intimacy appear to have been broken as we learn that Picard married Crusher and La Forge married Brahms. However, this story's plotline which involves a temporal paradox means that when Picard solves the mystery and saves humanity's past, he changes the future, including his and his crewmates'. Therefore, the entire episode is really a fantasy story and its events and relationship evaporate into the realm of possible universes well outside Starfleet and Federation norms.

Each of these episodes is really a different version of an alternative universe story that has been a regular feature of the series. In "Parallels" and "The Eye of the Beholder" when Worf returns to his proper place in time and space and when Troi regains her mind, the conclusion requires that any trace of the possibility of an interracial, transpecies relationship among crewmates is effectively structured out of Starfleet's reality. Turning to "All Good Things . . .", it is important to note that Picard's and Crusher's as well as La Forge's and Brahms's marriages take place outside the time of their service within Starfleet. Initially, it appears that the taboo against intimate relationships among Starfleet crewmates is effectively maintained in these episodes by situating these couples' marriages outside the narratives that are associated with the *Enterprise,* and beyond their Federation careers as explorers/researchers. However, it should be noted that once Picard figures out the answer to Q's riddle, not only is humanity saved, but the timeline (narrative) that resulted from his original erroneous decision is excised from time. This means that his marriage to Crusher and La Forge's to Brahms disappear like so much gossamer. In this way the prohibition against sexual relations among crewmates is held firm.

In the last two years of the series, after it had proven its success as a model of non-network syndication, after it had spawned two sequel series, and after a cross-over motion picture featuring the captains of both *Star Trek* television series was well into development, it seems clear that this series' producers, writers, and directors felt constrained to follow formula and eschewed any deviation that would have alluded to a future in which ethnicity could be harmonized within the larger society.[7]

No efforts seem to have been made to develop the ethnic members of the *Enterprise* crew that are continuing characters beyond their basic character sketches. La Forge and Guinan are two of the series' least developed characters. La Forge's parents were depicted once. And there has never been any mention of his culture, extended family, or personal history. Indeed, it remains unresolved as to whether he is a native of Jamaica or an African nation.

All that is known about Guinan could be summed up in a few words: she is a time traveling alien whose world was destroyed by the Borg and has joined the *Enterprise* crew as unofficial bartender. This potentially rich character is left insipid.

However, non-Terran ethnic characters do not seem to be barred from returning again and again or from having detailed observations about their cultures being incorporated within *Star Trek*'s mythology. Worf, perhaps because he represents a fantasy alien civilization, has experienced considerable development in the context of elaborating the image of a sometimes fierce Federation foe, sometimes ally. However, much of the development of this character actually relates to describing him in the context of an alien civilization that seems always on the verge of defecting from the Federation or tearing itself apart—hardly the description of a reliable ally. Worf, then, is a character that is treated with a good deal of suspicion and fear. Audiences never learn anything about Worf's personal history as a Klingon growing up in Russia, his friends, or his appreciation of Russian culture. Writers and producers seem content to use what little information is provided about this character's past to make explicit the earlier series' allusion of a comparison between our cold war nemesis, the Soviet Union and the Klingon Empire.

As for Troi, the series' continuing female Other, the little we know of her is learned from the infrequent episodes that feature her mother. After more than 180 episodes, we know that Troi grew up being overprotected by a mother, that her older sister died in a childhood drowning accident, that she has developed a high degree of integrity and maturity, and that she has a healthy sexual appetite. It is as if there is nothing to this character beyond her job, her relationship with her mother, and sex—hardly the formula for a three-dimensional character.

Featured non-Terran ethnic characters are brought back for further treatments that include intrigue, romance, family, rivalries, personal crises, command challenges, and heroic clashes and encounters with other aliens' civilizations. Among the non-Terran ethnic characters that recur in a number of episodes and through which viewers are exposed to increasing details about their extraterrestrial cultures and personal psychologies are Sarek, Mr. Spock's Vulcan father; Lwaxana Troi, Deanna Troi's Betazoid mother; K'Mpec, leader of the Klingon High Council; Duras, a

Klingon conspirator; Gowron, successor to K'Mpec; Sela, the half-Romulan daughter of Tasha Yar; Ro Laren, a Bajoran national; Gul Macet, a Cardassian military leader; and Gul Madred, a Cardassian military leader. Among the non-Terran ethnic groups that recur in a number of episodes and through which viewers are exposed to increasing details about their extraterrestrial cultures and psychologies are the Ferengi, a species of interstellar traders, and Romulans, a militaristic interstellar species opposed to the Federation.

Overall, Terran ethnic characters on *Star Trek: The Next Generation* tend to be one-dimensional, devoid of any human connections, isolated within their work, and limited by stereotypes about ethnicity that have long been part of American media. They tend to be what E. M. Forster would call flat characters, tending towards round.[8] However, those aspects of character development—romance, family, rivalries, personal crises, command challenges, heroic clashes, and encounters with alien civilizations—are deemed to be appropriate story lines for introducing secondary, irregularly recurring, supporting, non-Terran ethnic characters and for supplying additional information about the personal psychology or culture of the non-Terran ethnic Other.

The economics of television, particularly long-form, high-budget, independently produced programs such as *Star Trek: The Next Generation,* recommend international distribution to bring the production into profit. The decision to develop the character of Captain Picard as the focal point of audience identification and principal impetus for narrative development was made in a business context that appreciated the necessity of tapping into the post-first-run international television marketplace. In other words, the choice of a white, male European to act as the principal point of identification with the sequel series was undoubtedly a decision that was intended to improve the program's post-first-run international broadcast and videocassette sales—perhaps as important as any other creative consideration that brought this character into existence.

Proud of his French heritage, a culture that is dedicated to conserving and refining Western civilization, Picard represents Western ideological hegemony, especially as metaphorized through relationships with male and female whites, female and male Terran Others, and extraterrestrial Others. A closer examination of the relationship between this casting choice and the worldwide television market may prove illuminating. On a global basis, the United States is by far the dominant television market, with 1,469 stations generating billions of dollars in yearly revenues. Moreover, of sixteen international television markets, only four are not historically and politically aligned directly with the West.[9] Of these four, Hong Kong has been for years a British Crown Colony and straddles Western and Asian markets. This leaves Japan, the former states of the Soviet Union, and Czechoslovakia. By simply examining the international television marketplace, as displayed in table 7.1, it is clear that globally television exists within a Western institutional context. So the choice of using a male European as the focal point of audience identification turns out to be strategically correct, because it functions to facilitate the entry of the series into these post-first-run markets, which are Western countries or former Western colonies.

However, the characters Kirk and Picard serve an additional function in the way that *Star Trek* and *Star Trek: The Next Genera-*

Table 7.1

International Television Marketplace, 1991	
Country	*Channels/Stations*
France	10 channels
Italy	1404 stations
Portugal	2 stations
Spain	12 stations
Germany	16 stations
UK	18 channels
Australia	449 stations
New Zealand	3 networks
Canada	129 stations
USA	1469 stations
Mexico	57 stations
Brazil	196 stations
Hong Kong	4 stations
Japan	111 stations
USSR	148 channels
Czechoslovakia	3 channels

(Source: *Electronic Media*)

tion account for race and ethnicity. They are the node point for a system of relations that articulates, reconciles, and governs the ways races, genders, and classes interact in *Star Trek*'s vision of the future. American film and television have treated the representation of relations between the races problematically and according to a formulation that privileges white males at every turn. Historically, American media have formulated a series of complex interpersonal relations that support and mirror the larger society's codes for race relations, including relations of desire across gender.[10] With *Star Trek* and *Star Trek: The Next Generation*, these codes are projected onto the future and reveal the way added dimensions of class and miscegenation are accounted for and used to produce a new matrix of desiring relations.

This matrix is constituted by eight terms: non-Terran females, non-Terran ethnic males, Terran white females, biracial, Terran-ethnic males, Terran ethnic females, Starfleet personnel, and civilian elite leadership. The possible heterosexual relations among these terms have been illustrated in figure 7.1. This diagram shows the white male authority figures Kirk and Picard at the center of the four axes. Each of these axes has a positive and a negative pole. The positive and negative marks indicate whether relations of desire are allowed or prohibited. The result is a modification of a Greimasian-type semiotic rectangle.[11]

Along the x-axis, relations between civilians and Starfleet personnel are described. According to this graphic, relations of desire between Kirk/Picard (standing in for Starfleet Command and general staff) and lower ranks lie along the negative vector and are prohibited. But relations between Starfleet officials and civilians lie along the positive vector, such that the further one moves away from ordinary citizens into the area of civilian elites, the less opposition to a desiring relationship one faces.

Along the z-axis is the continuum of Terran women from ethnic Other to white. According to this axis, relationships of desire between Kirk/Picard and ethnic females are prohibited.[12] This diagram is also consistent with the forced intimacy between Kirk and Uhura in "Plato's Stepchildren," because that relationship occurred under duress and outside the aegis of Starfleet. Conversely, relationships between Starfleet officers and white women lie along the positive axis. In *Star Trek* episode "Requiem for Methuselah," Kirk discovers a world entirely owned by an enigmatic man

Race, Gender, and Class Axes in
Star Trek **and** *Star Trek: The Next Generation*

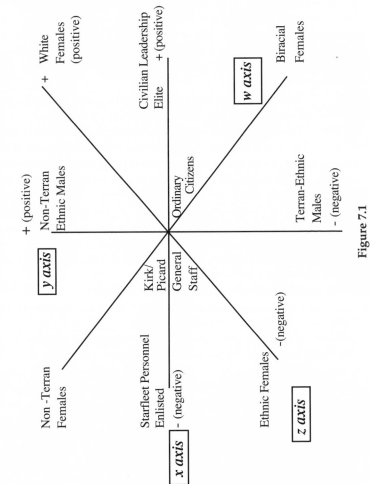

Figure 7.1

named Flint and attempts a romance with Flint's young female companion Rayna, whom Kirk assumes is the older man's daughter but is actually his robot creation. In "Wink of an Eye," Kirk actually is depicted as consummating a relationship with the Scalosian queen Deela. In "By Any Other Name," Kirk, in a familiar pattern, uses his sex appeal to spoil a Kelvan plan to use the *Enterprise* to travel back many light-years to the Kelvan Empire. In "The Mark of Gideon," Kirk is abducted from the *Enterprise* and falls in love with the daughter of the Gideon prime minister, Odona.

The y-axis describes male relationships between Terran and non-Terran ethnic males. According to this diagram, Terran ethnic males lie along the negative vector and are not candidates for heterosexual relationships of desire. La Forge demonstrates this in "Booby Trap" and "Galaxy's Child." Desiring relationships involving non-Terran ethnics lie along the positive portion of the y-axis and are therefore validated within *Star Trek*'s sociology. For example, Sarek, Spock's father, is revealed in "Journey to Babel" to be married to an aristocratic white, Terran female. The *Star Trek* episode "The Cloud Minders" illustrates this point for Mr. Spock, a non-Terran Other. Despite the legendary seven-year Vulcan mating period, there is every indication that Spock and Droxine, the daughter of the chief administrator of Stratos, would have become sexually involved had politics not intervened. Spock also turns the charm on in "The Enterprise Incident" and seduces a female Romulan commander.

The remaining w-axis describes possible relationships with biracial and non-Terran females. Biracial females lie along the negative portion of this continuum, and non-Terran females are located along the positive portion. K'Ehleyr and Troi in "The Emissary" and "Reunion" are examples of biracial females who are associated with Starfleet personnel in relationships that end in death or tragic separation. Non-Terran females fare substantially better, as shown in the *Star Trek* episode "Elaan of Troyius" and the *Star Trek: The Next Generation* episode "The Perfect Mate," in which Kirk and Picard have romantic encounters that conflict with their primary responsibilities but end only as bittersweet memories.

The continuing ethnic characters on *Star Trek: The Next Generation* are depicted as being personally and professionally isolated. One example of the precept is, of course, La Forge, whose blindness separates him from others. Worf is separated by his rough personality, life-threatening Klingon rituals, and lugubrious introspective distance from all but his most stout-hearted crewmates. Examples of *Star Trek* ethnic Others with limited personal dimensions include La Forge's perpetual bachelorhood and Worf's fiancée's death. These ethnic characters are further depicted as isolated from their crewmates by being stationed below decks and behind barriers. Worf, as security chief, is another example of an ethnic character who is isolated from others in a service role. Guinan is still another instance of ethnic Other who is physically separated from the crew by the 10-Forward bar. Therefore, the roles or occupations of *Star Trek*'s ethnic characters seem limited to such categories as mechanics, waiters, security officers, and without any romantic potential or ability to found and maintain a traditional family structure.

Moreover, Starfleet in *Star Trek* differentiates between whites and ethnics over the issues of technique and technology. Ellul understood that the intellectual process of conceptualizing problems was an aspect of cultural perspective that he identified with the term *technique*. He further pointed out that the materialization of this thought process takes the form of *technology*. In *Star Trek*, technique is associated with mind and technology with body. Technology, in this case, is metaphorized as the physical manipulation of matter, protective services, and general engineering (this opposition is familiar as another version of the mind-body duality).

The way Starfleet relates race and technique is shown in figure 7.2. In this Greimasian-style semiotic rectangle, the terms *white*, *ethnic Other*, *technique*, and *technology* are systematically linked. Whereas the white male Starfleet officer is directly associated with command (technique), the ethnic officer is only permitted control over technology.

Neither Kirk nor Picard are linked to any Terran ethnic character through friendship. From the point of view of process, Kirk and Picard are by training and education interested in cerebral pursuits and have no inclination toward engineering technologies.[13] The episodes "Ultimate Computer" (*Star Trek*) and "Booby Trap" (*Star Trek: The Next Generation*) epitomize these relations. In the first episode, the ethnic scientist who tries to go beyond technology into the arena of command techniques collapses into failure and humiliation. In the second episode, once La Forge has de-

Race and Technique

Terran White   Ethnic Other

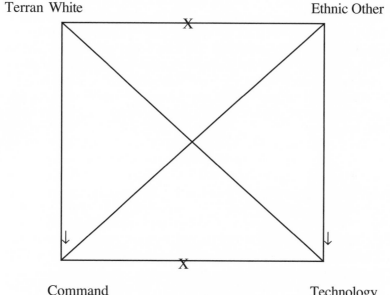

Command   Technology

An arrow (↓) indicates a socially sanctioned relation; an
X indicates a relation that is not socially sanctioned.

Figure 7.2

duced the proper solution to the energy-draining trap that im-
prisons the *Enterprise,* Picard insists that he pilot the vessel in a
successful application of La Forge's theory. La Forge may come up
with the plan—to shut down mechanical systems and manually
pilot the ship using thruster jets—but he is circumscribed from
acting on his insight. The rejection of technology serves to emphasize technique, and that area is Picard's, not La Forge's.

Star Trek, after almost thirty years of creative activity that includes the development of four long-form television series, not
only fails to carry forward the original series' interest in examining the social problems that surround the issue of race but actually
has retreated from even cursory treatments of this theme. Initially,

Star Trek developed characters, like Uhura, and social situations, like those found in "The Cloud Minders" and "Patterns of Force," that revisited the pain and tragedy that accompanies racial discrimination and exploitation and racially structured social policy. With *Star Trek: The Next Generation,* the number of regular cast members that are ethnically identified characters increased to three: Worf, La Forge, and Troi. But its stories that focus on the issues surrounding ethnicity have been shifted to emphasize extraterrestrial cultures and diminish any association with the historical or contemporary social situation ethnic people on Earth face daily.

Star Trek's ethnic representations, therefore, lean heavily on the old negative stereotypes that associate ethnic characters with body-service occupations, machine operation, violent behavior, and sexual aggression. These images of ethnicity date from the founding moments of American commercial film, their intention being to use the medium for the validation of white privilege and visual strategies for the stigmatization, marginalization, and containment of ethnicity. That is, the representation of ethnic characters is linked to American cultural values on race, gender, and class and frames the ways these categories participate in cultural and media context where discourse about these subjects takes place. Taken together, these relations form a consistent ideology of racial relations across the episodes in this study.

Race, this century's tragically misunderstood issue, is humanity's real final frontier. It seems clear from this analysis of two science fiction television programs spanning more than a quarter of a century that very little, if any, progress has been made in developing symbolic codes of representing ethnicity in the elaborate vision of the future woven across hundreds of hours of popular entertainment that counters our national legacy of abusive media stereotyping. Nor did either series attempt to address this legacy, by having an alien Other or a female, ethnic Commander or by having Kirk or Picard learn something from another culture that enriches his understanding of his position or that affirms life by discovering universal precepts in that Other character or civilization. Instead, aliens and ethnic Others are represented as civilized when they learn to blend with and support the Federation's model of paternalistic control and hegemony.

If predictions about a shrinking world community are accurate, technological, economic, public health, political, and environmental challenges will stretch beyond national borders and require international cooperation and understanding, if only to facilitate the dissemination of ideas and cultural products. There is a pressing need to create models for men and women of different cultures and backgrounds working cooperatively to solve problems and building a brighter future. The time meaning of these *Star Trek* series perpetuates into the future the privileged status of white male authority and values Western cultural ideology above others, with little sensitivity to providing a balanced view of the contributions that men and women of ethnic origin can make to resolve the growing challenges facing humanity. Ironically, these *Star Trek* programs, especially in the ways that they depict ethnicity, undermine imagination of how diversity contributes to the future they envision.

In the course of these two series, producers, writers, and make-up artists developed visions of several alien races and brought them into viewers' homes on a recurring basis, for instance Klingon, Romulan, Ferengi, and Borg. Romulans, the first of these alien "Others," were introduced to audiences during *Star Trek* in "Balance of Terror" (airdate: 15 December 1966, episode 14) and returned in "The Enterprise Incident" (airdate: 27 September 1968, episode 59). They return in *Star Trek: The Next Generation* in "Unification" Parts I and II (airdates: 9 and 16 November 1991, episodes 108 and 109). Klingons appear in *Star Trek* episodes "Errand of Mercy" (airdate: 23 March 1967, episode 26), "A Private Little War" (airdate: 2 February 1968, episode 48), and "Day of the Dove" (airdate: 1 November 1968, episode 62). Klingon characters, rivalries, politics, morality, and other cultural aspects returned in *Star Trek: The Next Generation* in entire episodes dedicated to them, including "Hearts of Glory" (airdate: 19 March 1988, episode 20), "A Matter of Honor" (airdate: 4 February 1989, episode 34), "The Bonding" (airdate: 21 October 1989, episode 53), "The Defector" (airdate: 30 December 1989, episode 58), "Yesterday's Enterprise" (airdate: 17 February 1990, episode 63), "Sins of the Father" (airdate: 17 March 1990, episode 65), "Reunion" (airdate: 3 November 1990, episode 81), "First Contact" (airdate: 16 February 1991, episode 89), "Redemption" Parts I and II (airdates: 15 June and 21 September 1991, episodes 100 and 101), "Unification" Parts I and II (airdates: 9 and 16 November 1991, episodes 108 and 109),

"Ethics" (airdate: 29 February 1992, episode 116), and "Rightful Heir" (airdate: 15 May 1993, episode 149).

During *Star Trek: The Next Generation* two new alien cultures were added to those populating Roddenberry's fictional universe: the Borg and the Ferengi. Borg culture is a cybernetic collective that is dedicated to assimilating every civilization they encounter. Ferengi civilization is based on a advanced capitalism freed of any regulation or other value beyond acquiring wealth. The Borg make their appearance about one-quarter of the way through the series' run, but constitute the Federation's greatest threat. Borg storylines fingure in "Q Who?" (airdate: 6 May 1989, episode 42), "The Best of Both Worlds," Parts I and II (airdates: 16 June and 22 September 1990, episodes 74 and 75), "The Descent," Parts I and II (airdates: 19 June and 18 September 1993, episodes 152 and 153), and "I, Borg" (airdate: 9 May 1992, episode 123). Ferengi characters and culture are highlighted in "The Last Outpost" (airdate: 18 October 1987, episode 5), "The Battle" (airdate: 14 November 1987, episode 9), "Ménage à Troi" (airdate: 26 May 1990, episode 72), "The Loss" (airdate: 29 December 1990, episode 84), "The Perfect Mate" (airdate: 25 April 1992, episode 121), and "Rascals" (airdate: 31 October 1992, episode 133).

Whether Klingon, Borg, or Ferengi, each of these fictional extraterrestrial cultures is represented as suspicious, amoral, barbarous, violent, predatory, cruel, irrational, unruly, and threatening. In fairness, these fictional aliens are conceived of as the regularly recurring villains and necessarily exhibit the more unsavory character traits. However, there is no hard and fast rule that malevolence must be one-dimensional, obvious, and predictable. That is, at no point in either series are any of these aliens represented as having a perspective or philosophy that could challenge the Federation's on its merits. It is as if these alien cultures are driven by only basic biological, emotional, territorial, and economic motivations. It is as if it were simply the case that Borg absorb whole worlds because that is what Borg do, Ferengi obsess about money because that is in their only nature, and Klingons shout, bluster, connive, and war because they know no other ways to react and settle disputes.

Both series devote considerable time and effort in developing presentations of these alien cultures as well-articulated and robust social systems that address the issues of life from unique perspectives. Yet Klingons, Borgs, and Ferengis are not portrayed as possessing any knowledge or point of view that would constitute an alternative to the Terracentric Federation's customs and values or challenge its traditions and ideology. Instead, Ferengi, Borg, and Klingon characters turn out to be a parade of personalities that runs the gamut from quirky to bizarre and not as representatives of complex, multilayered, powerful, space-faring civilizations. They are incapable, either as a society or as individuals, of leading the Federation or viewers to an expanded definition of humanity. To the extent that these series show these alien characters or fictional cultures developing, that evolution emulates Terran and Federation values. It is simply not the case that as a result of contact with any of these races the Federation, Starfleet, or its representatives grow emotionally, intellectually, or spiritually from their contact with alien Others.

If we reread these episodes as demonstrated heretofore, there is the strong impression that when alien cultures have contact with the Federation and Starfleet the consequences can be extremely unfortunate for the alien Other. Romulans are defeated and humiliated in both episodes by Kirk because they underestimate his intelligence and ingenuity and sacrifice individual initiative to technological sophistication and slavish obedience to military authority. The *Star Trek* episodes that feature Klingons consistently depict them as bad-tempered paranoids with delusions of galactic importance, clearly not the kind of psychology that melds well with others or whose perspectives one would place much confidence in. Vulcans are characterized as possessing superior minds trained in logic and subtle forms of telepathy. However, their emphasis on the rational limits their value for humans (who value intuition, empathy, and emotion).

The alien cultures that recur on *Star Trek: The Next Generation* reveal similar limitations which render them problematic candidates for augmenting humanity's sensitivity, intelligence, and capacities for affection, inclusion, and creativity. The Ferengi valorize every aspect of commerce over every other competing moral, political, familial, or ethical consideration or quality. By defining an entire fictional culture as one-dimensional in this way, producers effectively make it impossible for them to possess capacities that the Federation or Starfleet would want to learn about, much less emulate. The cybernetic collective known as the Borg is one of the Federation's and Starfleet's most aggressive and threatening adversaries. From their introduction in the second season of *Star Trek: The Next Generation* to the final season, Picard and crew knew no more unrelenting nemesis. At every point, the resolutions of their conflicts hinge on humans learning about some vulnerability in the Borg collective. It is as if, once the Borg are identified as hostile, every effort is made to demonize them to justify their eradication. This very fact could, but never does, raise the issue of the frequency of genocide in human history and beg the question of whether the Borg's techniques of individual and planetary absorption are worse than the human techniques of empire building through colonization, repression, murder, and genocide. Is it not possible to see the Borg as an image produced by holding a mirror up to human history and to learn from them something about ourselves? This prospect was never entertained by the series. Klingons, the fantasy alien culture most often revisited by the series, receive the most attention and development. They have gone from occasional villains in *Star Trek* to a trusted member of the *Enterprise's* senior staff and one of the more powerful, if temperamental, members of the Federation. In fact, several episodes of *Star Trek: The Next Generation* center on the political intrigue and social structure of the Klingon home world. Unfortunately, in each of these episodes the characters and situations are parsimoniously, illiberally drawn. Episode narratives do not go beyond what is necessary to relay their plots. This means that Klingon culture is given elaborate, even baroque treatment, but the details are superficial and so do not present any situations or characters that force human character to re-examine themselves or their motives.

There is a kind of cultural relativism running through both *Star Trek* series. The Alpha quadrant may contain a myriad of planets and civilizations, but they are not all created equal. This orientation may be a residue left over from the cold war climate that prevailed when the original series and its parameters were developed. It is unfortunate, indeed, that the other main impetus behind the series conception, the vision of racial understanding and harmony, never developed very far from its paternalistic, racially compromised origins. Another vision might allow for narratives in which aliens' point of view, at least momentarily, was validated and enriched the series' representation of the human condition.

Epilogue

Science fiction like *Star Trek* is not only good fun but it also
serves a serious purpose, that of expanding the human imagination. We may not be able to boldly go where no man (or
woman) has gone before, but at least we can do it in the mind.
We can explore how the human spirit might respond to future developments in science and we can speculate on what
those developments might be.[1]

Indeed, exploring the infinite possibilities the future holds—
including a world where humanity has overcome its myopic
international and racial tensions and ventured out to explore
the universe in peace—is part of the continuing wonder of
Star Trek.[2]

From our perspective at the end of the 1990s, W. E. B. Dubois' ad-
monishment about the centrality of race for the twentieth century
looks absolutely prescient and underscores the period's contradictions. Unprecedented prosperity exists side by side with crushing
poverty in every nation. Advances in medicine and health care
promise to banish age-old diseases and even conquer old age itself
as new plagues sweep the earth and the survival of the old and the
young is auctioned on the block of neoconservative budget bal-
ancing. International government agencies and public and private
companies cooperate across state sovereignty at the same time that
a nearly continuous succession of local and international conflicts,
wars, and campaigns of genocide render this the bloodiest century

in modern human history, at least. As empires collapse and spawn fervent new nations eager to express their freedom, the price of change seems to be plunging one new nation after another into the avaricious, vicious, and myopic control of a dictator, military junta, or president for life. At the moment that business, quasi-autonomous, non-governmental organizations, public and private nonprofit agencies, and the public are learning about the implications of ecology's diversity and individual empowerment as models of healthy and efficient systems, governments and politicians reject redefining the national identity and civic participation with campaigns designed to eradicate ethnicity, gender, and individual differences as categories of identification and mobilization. The new social sciences encourage a perspective that acknowledges the common needs, drives, and dreams among people, yet social reform, urban renewal, and publicly financed education find it hard to get a hearing for their agendas. Even the century's achievements in science, technology, and the arts, which have the potential to turn the globe into a village of neighbors, are exploited in a commercial environment that depends on markets of anonymous masses of interchangeable individuals defined by clinical demographic factors that insure mass media products address commodified, rather than actual needs.

This century has not only witnessed unprecedented industrial developments, technological innovations, and wealth, but its wars, regional conflicts, and economic disruptions have created widespread, long-term tumult. In other words, this century's accelerating velocity of change strains the ability of traditional social structures, like family, community, and nation, to keep pace and adapt. Mass media address this situation in two ways. First, one of mass media's roles is to reflect these changes back to audiences for their information, edification, and amusement. It is not surprising that our most popular entertainment mass media have responded with divertissements whose organizing principles are fantasy, romance, and the projection of morality (as a social cohesive) through power. These themes form the backbone of modern popular culture, especially American popular culture, which circulates around the globe. Second, mass media function as creative reinterpretations of society and social issues. By synthesizing change, they can illuminate problems and developments and bring the roles of individuals and groups as change agents before audiences. That is, part of mass media's creativity is its ability to portray an organized vision of society and explore the sociology of change: who introduces change, benefits from it, pays for it, and is excluded. Audiences engage media to the extent that they identify with and derive pleasure from engaging with favorite actors, their character portrayals, and types of story (as perversely derisory as that pleasure might be). In part, media products attract audiences with convincing depictions of social interactions that reflect events drawn from the larger social stage (whether the specific treatment tends toward fiction or documentary). In this context, it is hard to overstate the relationship of popular cultural products to society or their role in reflecting the social scene and its issues back to its audience (as metaphorized as they might be).

More than tides of immigrants fleeing conflict for peace and expanded human rights, the century's "huddled masses" represent new possibilities of social relations. For this country, new citizens, whether they came from other nations or from its own ethnic communities, represent the possibility of a continually evolving America: enriched and more cosmopolitan with the arrival of each new ethnic group.

From early in the century, when modern mass media shifted from entrepreneurial to corporate business models, the ability to identify male and female, black and white, native and foreign-born characters and set them in relation to each other, social institutions, values, and emotions was developed into a formula for financial success. Beyond these two basic prerequisites, mass media products are the result of integrating three factors: the aesthetic qualities of a medium, the producing agency (artist or studio), and the audience(s). From one perspective, the popular appeal of mass media is the result of a kind of alchemy. Public acceptance and success hang on familiarity with media aesthetics and other production qualities, recognizing directors, genres, and celebrities, and getting enough information about a specific cultural product into circulation to attract an audience.

Therefore, media production is a complex proposition made all the more problematic because it takes place in an environment where business policies, financial guidelines, aesthetics decisions, and public taste change from one year to the next. The downside for media producers is the lack of any scientific or organized business methods that could quantify these factors and add a measure of predictability to the industry. Among the advantages for film-makers is the chance to work in a profession that puts a high value on applying the complicated arts, crafts, and sciences of media production to create products that match contemporary tastes and trends.

Mass media throughout this century, especially motion pictures and broadcasting, have prospered, in part, due to their ability to fashion vehicles that foster strong audience identification. That is, audiences volunteer their time and attention to mass media entertainments to the extent that they contain ideas, emotions, characters, and situations that are familiar and satisfying. The variety of media products, such as comedies, fantasies, dramas, tragedies, westerns, and musicals, match fluctuations of public taste. Screenwriters and directors adapt the specific stories within these categories to reflect their interests and sensitivity to trends and issues in the media and society. Part of the allure of media products relates to their ability to continually renew their public relationship by pacing aesthetic and social developments and reflecting those changes through their depictions. If media are redemptive, then that quality arises from their ability to anticipate and adapt to shifts in audience and social attitudes and values. Therefore, one of media's strengths comes from their facility to continually reinvent themselves by reflecting fresh characters, revised myths and updated narratives, and new settings and situations back to a society in flux.

I have been engaged by media's chameleon-like nature for more than forty years, first as a consumer, then as a producer/teacher and now as a researcher/analyst. I have been drawn to media because they offer vivid, immediate ways to learn about and affect our society and the larger world. Whatever my specific role or relationship, my identification with media has its origins in the pleasure I found discovering the variety of emotional and conceptual experiences media afforded. These mass media experiences opened the vistas of my world by showing me people and places far distant from my suburban southeastern Baltimore ghetto neighborhood of Turners Station.

As I look back now, more than forty years later, it seems clear that my attraction to mass media cultural experiences originated out of a sense of curiosity about these powerful modes of communication. I was captivated, as were millions of my young peers, by media's exciting and glamorous trappings: the expensive production values, full-color advertising campaign, and visions of stunning men and women caught in intriguing and intricate stories, in exotic locales. Additionally, mass media spoke directly to my desire to stretch beyond my small town and to learn about other ways of life and people. I knew early on that I would not live my life within the narrow, socioeconomic constraints of my racially defined community and that I needed to appreciate and negotiate differences of individuals and cultures.

I may have been raised in a small town, but that community was connected to the city, nation, and world through mass media. My early experiences with media were rewarded as those imaginative scenarios permitted me to appreciate how characters negotiated a variety of social situations. This pastime became all the more important as the civil rights movement dramatically expanded the opportunities that I would face in the future. I believe that my engagement with broadcasting and motion pictures may be attributed in equal parts to a young person's natural curiosity and to a young African American's desire to learn more about the world of social interactions that the civil rights movement was transforming.

As a youthful and naive consumer of mass media, I sensed that there ought to be a connection between the world depicted in films and television programs and the actual world—and that as change occurred in the world around me, I would see and learn from media's evolution of its sociology the new social situations I might encounter and how I might face and deal with them.

My investment of time, emotions, and intellectual curiosity with mass media was rewarded and frustrated. I was often rewarded with mass entertainment vehicles that transported me to far-flung exotic real and fictional locales, dazzled with elaborate photographic and special effects, and introduced to extraordinary male and female actors playing an expanding list of characters. However, as much as I looked forward to the latest Matt Helm or Jules Verne or Jerry Lewis film and episodes of *The Adventures of Ozzie and Harriet, Hawaiian Eye, 77 Sunset Strip, Surfside 6, Colt .45,* and *Route 66,* I began to become aware of what I was not seeing. Mass media, like television and motion pictures, rarely showed me images that resonated with the people I knew in the community in which I lived. Certainly, there was *The Nat King Cole Show* which featured the African American jazz pianist in a variety show format. But this was the rare exception. I was increasingly aware of the social reform movement that was challenging the nation's customs and laws on race, and I was increasingly aware that mass media were not keeping pace or attempting to make this monumental effort anything beyond an occasional theme. If anthropologists from another world or our future were to examine these productions as artifacts of this era, they could easily come to the conclusion that the African American population of the United States was negligible and that the nation's history of enslaving tens of millions had no lasting effects for either race.

American broadcast media and films have a long history of making products that address the effects of social pressures on individuals and groups. This kind of theme is prevalent in disaster and science-fiction cultural products. While these media are quite distinct, they do share several traits. Both have an affinity for utopian/dystopian narratives, bring characters together that represent a wide cross-section of society (class and occupation), and confront situations that often involve cooperation across social distinctions to save lives. Thirty years after the nation's leaders resolved to institutionalize the agenda of the civil right movement in landmark legislation and court rulings, and public opinion shifted to support issues like equal accommodation, fair housing, and school desegregation, network and studio executives should have been able to make short work of incorporating those changes and African Americans into media treatments.

Instead, as I have engaged with American network and studio media, I have come away disappointed again and again. American media producers, who build their reputations on spotting new talent and bending the latest technology to create profitable, entertaining narratives, have demonstrated a singular difficulty and considerable hesitation about including the image of African Americans within this changing terrain. This fact of contemporary America would be understandable if the nation had decided to turn away from social reform and reaffirm its apartheid-like policies and attitudes. It, however, did not. Moreover, African American culture and personalities have helped to redirect and redefine the nation's new direction. And the impact of African American performers in several of the most popular mass media as contributors to this change of attitudes should not be minimized. For example, African American urban vernacular language styles as conveyed through recordings have added new expressiveness to American English. African American hip-hop fashions have migrated out of the urban centers and from MTV to suburban shopping malls nationwide. American couples have courted and fallen in love to the strains of African American recording artists from Nat King Cole to Luther Vandross. Something positive is happening when American language, fashion, advertising, and popular arts absorb African American influences and use them to transform the national identity and generate a profit, too. These are examples of African American culture helping the nation acquire the capacities it needs to go boldly into the uncharted realm of racial equality. Where are the examples of substantial change in network and studio media?

Something negative is happening when the same kind of acceptance, influence, and agency is not forthcoming in the broadcasting and motion picture dramatic arts. Something is wrong when year after year no NAACP Image Awards or Academy of Motion Picture Arts and Sciences Oscars are presented to African American actors in the major acting and directing categories. Something is wrong when media writing, craft guilds and related unions, and broadcast and studio corporate suites—more than thirty years after unions and management in nearly every other major American industry can point to a track record of bringing minorities into positions of leadership and influence—remain for all practical purposes devoid of minorities and questions still circulate about the creative and managerial abilities of minorities. Something is wrong when season after season neither motion pictures, nor movies of the week, nor episodes of weekly dramas, nor situation comedies bring audiences images of an integrated society to reinforce our common accomplishments and point toward our common future.

I have been waiting for more than two decades for the leaders of American media to turn their considerable business acumen to the issue of developing products that position this country in the vanguard of the issues of equality. I have been waiting for African American actors to move from the background as details used to flesh out a contemporary atmosphere to the middle and foreground as characters whose storylines affect the plot in consequential ways, for example, narratives that focus on integrating

African American history into a new vision of our common heritage and future. Where are the African American characters that are not hidebound by essentialist dogma or social pathology or limited to updating racialized stereotypes? Are African American characters destined to occupy business and social settings, like the up-scale corporate situations in American soap operas, without offering any appropriate critique when vestiges of inequality surface? In my experience as a media consumer, American media executives seem unable to conceive of this nation's experiences in rejecting racism as the source material for engaging and profitable media products.

This situation seems all the more difficult to understand since advances in communications technology have led to lower production and distribution costs and media market segmentation, that is the ability to profit from smaller audiences selected to match specific demographic parameters. The economics of contemporary media, especially broadcasting, cable, and syndication, make it highly desirable to identity and focus on distinct and coherent groups of potential viewers. American media corporations have already developed entertainment for African American and Hispanic audiences, and programming from Korea, Japan, France, England, and Germany is featured for a portion of the day on cable systems around the country.

It is ironic that at a time when communications technology and economics make it practical and profitable to link together people of similar cultural heritage regardless of distance as consumers of cultural products, American media producers seem bound to thoroughly discredited modes of representing minorities. Are American media unable or unwilling to be more courageous and challenging? Is it time to reevaluate whether the production of ethnic images has more to do with the unexamined attitudes on race and an uncritical reception legacy of American entertainment history than with business realities? How else can the marked difference between the ways ethnic models are employed in every aspect of American advertising to sell products from antiacids to automobiles and the attitude among American producers of entertainment media that ethnic actors cannot "open" or be the leading stars in a major dramatic motion picture or television series be reconciled. African American female and male models, as well as women of color from African countries, grace the haute conture

runways of this country and Europe, the covers of every important fashion magazine, and ensorcell their audiences with their talented operatic, folk, rhythm and blues, jazz, rock and roll, and
world music vocal stylings and physical beauty. Even if one could
prove that the American public's attitude towards race was irre-
deemably conservative, does such a situation absolve the leaders
of business and opinion from using the resources at their disposal
to bring before their audiences an enlightened point of view on a
subject of continuing national interest?

As disappointed as I have often been with American major media, I still find myself looking forward to each new season with
hope. In fact, I began watching *Star Trek: The Next Generation* because it was promoted as a continuation of *Star Trek* which I enjoyed. As the premier of the new series drew to a close, I recall an-
ticipating the way it would feature actors like LeVar Burton and
Michael Dorn and metaphorize contemporary issues about race to
space. I felt a certain amount of ambivalence, too. I had been disappointed so many times when science fiction cast African American actors only to veer away from dealing with the ways their ethnicity and cultural legacy could add subtlety and nuance to
narratives. I greeted the prospect of a new *Star Trek* series, like being reunited with an old friend who knew how to contact me but
chose for years to remain *incommunicado.* However, I readily admit to being a prisoner of hope and I believe in second and third
chances.

So, I tuned in that first season of *Star Trek: The Next Generation*
full of the expectation that I would find stories about brave star-
farers discovering bizarre alien worlds inhabited by a wide variety of non-humanoid beings and dealing with problems that reflected contemporary issues transposed to an extraterrestrial
location. I wanted to see characters representing a contemporary
vision of an integrated society solving these problems by employ-
ing their different aptitudes, cultural backgrounds, and personal
traits. I looked forward to finding in these new episodes characters that resonated back to the African American characters of the
earlier series, but because of the social changes in America and internationally on race, I expected that these characters would have
a wider range of interaction with the ship's command staff, technology, aliens, and Starfleet. At some point in the early seasons of
the sequel series, I had to admit that I was not engaging with the

kind of material that I anticipated. Gradually, the dream turned sour and I realized that I could no longer invest my hopes in *Star Trek: The Next Generation* because it was a system of cultural production governed by a political economy trapped in an ideology that reflected current conservative attitudes on race, not imaging a better future to go boldly toward.

I nonetheless tuned in each week to watch each episode of *Star Trek: The Next Generation*. I realized before long that I could not simply watch *Star Trek: The Next Generation* passively. Around the fourth season, I determined to study the series and to compare it with the original series, *Star Trek*. This research presented here is the result of that study and is my more comprehensive response to the implicit promise of *Star Trek*. Disappointed, but a prisoner of hope, I now tune in each week to watch the two latest additions to the *Star Trek* franchise: *Star Trek: Deep Space Nine* and *Star Trek: Voyager*. I am hopeful that these new series—one with an African American as the central character and commander of a space station deep in the Alpha quadrant and the other with a white American female as the central character and captain of a Starfleet vessel traveling back to Earth through the Delta quadrant—will reward my viewing. Now that these new series have established themselves in off-network syndication, I look forward to returning to this study and to conducting a more thorough examination of Roddenberry's mass media vision.

Notes

Introduction

1. *Race* as a term for identifying different population groups in society is used throughout this book interchangeably with *ethnicity.* Although *race* is freighted with emotion and a history of application against non-Western peoples, its popular acceptance makes substitution of alternative formulations problematic.

2. I have specifically decided against including the animated television *Star Trek* series and the seven *Star Trek* motion pictures because the differences between these media and live action television might make comparisons problematic. Although the recently launched *Star Trek: Deep Space Nine* and *Star Trek: Voyager* represent two new television series in the *Star Trek* tradition, at this writing they have been televised for two years and one year, respectively, and not enough episodes have been produced from which to select a sample for this study.

Chapter One

1. Interest in developing audiovisual media in service of civil rights and racial equality led William A. Washington and Frank J. Parker to charter in California the National Negro Foundation to try to get more African American actors into Hollywood productions. Their plans included developing original scripts for interracial film and television on African American figures, such as Booker T. Washington; Roland Hayes; Mary McLeod Bethune; historian Carter Woodson; surgeon Daniel Hill; engineer Archie A. Alexander; writers W. E. B. Dubois, James Weldon

Johnson, and Countee Cullen; lawyer Matt Bullock; and artist Henry Os-sawa. Among the group's early supporters were politicians, such as Sam Yorty and Mervyn Dymally.

2. William T. Bielby and Denise D. Bielby, "A Survey of the Employment of Writers in the Film, Broadcast, and Cable Industries for the Period 1987–1991," *The 1993 Hollywood Writers' Report* (West Hollywood: WGA/W, 1993); William T. Bielby and Denise D. Bielby, "Unequal Access, Unequal Pay," *The 1989 Hollywood Writers' Report* (West Hollywood: WGA/W, 1989); and William T. Bielby and Denise D. Bielby, "Pay Equity and Employment Opportunities among Writers for Television and Feature Films," *The 1987 Hollywood Writers' Report: A Survey of Ethnic, Gender and Age Employment Practices,* Summary Report (2 vols.) (West Hollywood: WGA/W, 1987).

3. "WGAW Prexy Nate Monaster Charges 'Conspiracy' by Unions against Negroes," *Daily Variety,* 1 July 1963, 1, 14.

4. Ibid., 14.

5. Michael Franklin estimates that there were no more than ten African American WGA members in 1963. Michael M. Fessier, Jr., "NAACP Charges '62 Promise of More Jobs Not Kept; Most Union Execs Disagree," *Daily Variety,* 6 June 1963, 4.

6. Bielby and Bielby, "A Survey of the Employment of Writers"; Bielby and Bielby, "Unequal Access, Unequal Pay"; and Bielby and Bielby, "Pay Equity and Employment Opportunities."

7. "Figure 1. Writers Added to WGA, West Membership Annually: 1936–1992," in William T. Bielby and Denise D. Bielby, "Unequal Access, Unequal Pay."

8. Ibid.

9. Writers Guild of America, compiled and edited by Lola Goelet Yoakem, *TV and Screenwriting* (Berkeley: University of California Press, 1958).

10. Six years before Lajos Egri wrote his style guide, the award-winning stage and screenwriter John Howard Lawson brought forward his survey of dramatic literature and approach to dramatic writing. Lawson's book, which was built around a case study method applied to dramatic literature, was revised and reprinted in 1949 in time for the commercial exploitation of television, but it went largely ignored until the mid-1980s when it was reprinted again. Unlike Egri, Lawson did not shy away from the relation between race and film but faced it directly. Lawson traced film's problematic relation to blacks to D. W. Griffith, the filmmaker who is generally regarded as the "father of American commercial cinema." Lawson balanced Griffith's "marvelous intuition . . . on the technical potentialities of the medium. . . . Those potentialities, as he correctly understood them, demanded that he interpret the living stuff of reality" against his lack of introspection about defining "reality as it was given him,

equating his own prejudices with the common prejudices of the time."
John Howard Lawson, *The Theory and Technique of Playwriting and Screen-writing* (New York: Putnam, 1936), 325. Lawson points out that when the motion pictures faced their next major technical challenge, the advent of synchronous sound, filmmaker King Vidor experimented in *Hallelujah* with African American subject matter as a solution to developing sound as integral with plot. As depicted in *Hallelujah*, "the life of the Negro in the South . . . achieves moments of artistic truth in depicting the labor and love and sorrow of plantation workers—the toil in the cotton fields, the families gathering in the evening, the tragedy of a child's death." Unfortunately, Lawson pointed out that Vidor believed "these humble actions lacked sufficient audience appeal . . . [and] tried to make the material picturesque, introducing scenes of hysteria and savage melodrama that dehumanized the characters and distorted their motives. . . . [T]he attitude toward the Negro community in *Hallelujah*, the acceptance of stereotypes, the dependence on artifice and violence stem from conceptual weaknesses that are evident in all of Vidor's films. In *The Crowd*, the individual is depicted as the victim of a fate that condemns him to mediocrity and indifference of his fellows. In *Hallelujah*, the Negroes are passionate children, driven by forces they cannot understand. Individuals emerge from the anonymous crowd only when blind fury or terror grips them." Lawson, *Theory and Technique*, 345–46. Lawson perceived a very limited change in studio policy toward African American images following World War II and wrote, "Some progress was made in eliminating the insulting characterizations of the Negro that had disgraced the American screen. But there was no attempt to portray the lives and activities of Negroes and other minority groups." Lawson, *Theory and Technique*, 356. Directly on the point of African Americans and films, Lawson generalized from his survey that "[t]he portrayal of Negroes, and members of other minority groups, is not merely a matter of good intentions and 'sympathetic' treatment. The problem is rooted in theme and structure. The Negro's vital contribution to American life is excluded from the social concepts on which films are built. The political pressures that limit the employment of Negro actors and assign them to insulting roles operate in the sphere of ideas, affecting the screenwriter's mode of thought and his approach to his material. Negro characters cannot be treated fully and honesty unless they are an organic part of the action, psychologically and socially integrated in the system of events. In the history of American industry, there are few pictures, possibly half a dozen, which present the Negro personality as a normal part of the action. The Negro doctor in *Arrowsmith* dies to help the advancement of science, and his death is an essential comment on the root-idea. The law student in *In This Our Life* has to be honest, hardworking and ambitious in order to highlight the neurotic woman's conduct toward him, and thus perform his

function in the story. The minister in *The Ox-Bow Incident* has depth as a person because he contributes to the depth of the whole concept. *Sahara* could not convey its message without the Senegalese soldier. Ben in *Body in Soul* is responsible for the decision that brings the films to a climax." Lawson, *Theory and Technique*, 436.

11. It is odd that Egri's book, which gestated during World War II, is silent on the subject of race. Egri, a Hungarian immigrant, seemed to be uninterested in the role that race could play in character and psychological development at precisely the moment in history when race theories were brought into play by the Axis powers in Europe, and the Pacific theaters of the war were igniting one of humanity's greatest and bloodiest conflicts. Lajos Egri, *The Art of Dramatic Writing: Its Basics in the Creative Interpretation of Human Motive* (New York: Simon & Schuster, 1946), 32–43.

12. Lewis Cole, "Screenplay Culture," *The Nation*, 4 November 1991, 560–66.

13. Lawson, *Theory and Technique*, 436.

14. Hollywood writers "work for hire" in a system that affords them none of the authorship rights they may have asserted as playwrights or writers of fiction, nonfiction, or humor. When studios obtain the rights to a literary property, its adaptation as a motion picture screenplay or teleplay is a separate work based on changes to the underlying work, even if completed by the original writer, that the studio owns and copyrights.

15. It is not necessary to assume a conscious conspiracy among media producers, directors, and writers to explain the limitations imposed on African American actors. As John Howard Lawson pointed out when he wrote about King Vidor's reliance on negative racial stereotypes in *Hallelujah*, "[t]he director may have been influenced by studio policy; he knew without any explicit statement from his employers, that the portrayal of Negro life would be tolerated only if it bowed to current prejudices. But it seems that Vidor himself was the unconscious victim of these prejudices, and that commercial pressures coincided with the limitations of his own understanding." In other words, media workers need never explicitly discuss the dos and don'ts of racial representation, because they are marinated in a culture that excludes any positive inference or treatment accruing to the credit of minorities. Lawson, *Theory and Technique*, 346.

16. "IA's Flaherty Is No Pessimist, Nor Optimist about Pix Jobs," *Daily Variety*, 6 February 1963, 3.

17. Actual unemployment rates for two union locals of grips and drivers reached 50 percent. Fessier, "NAACP Charges," 4.

18. To the extent that there were employment gains by African Americans, they may be counted on a badly maimed hand, and these were a few acting jobs secured by casting directors and studios. IATSE International representative Zeal Fairbanks reported weakly that "several"

African Americans were employed behind the camera. Fessier, "NAACP Charges," 4.

19. Fessier, "NAACP Ultimatum to Hollywood: Demonstrations Threatened Unless Negroes Get More Jobs; 15 'Lily-White' IA Locals Hit," *Daily Variety*, 26 June 1963, 1, 8.

20. Ibid., 8.

21. In addition, other civil rights organization appreciated the significance of the position that the NAACP took and began planning for their own direct actions. CORE met at Universal with Lew Wasserman on Monday, 10 June 1963, and discussed the African American employment situation at that studio. Also attending the meeting were Jay Kantor and Marlon Brando. Fessier, "Brando Sparks Anti-Bias Meet: Urges Stars Show Muscle to Aid Negroes," *Daily Variety*, 15 July 1963, 1, 9.

22. One example of the changing situation for African Americans was the initiation of an apprenticeship program by the International Brotherhood of Electrical Workers (IBEW) at Metro-Goldwyn-Mayer. In announcing this program, which followed the lead of the Revue-Universal program, the IBEW specifically sought African American applicants. Additional apprenticeship programs in plastering, wood working, carpentry, and scenic arts were under development for inauguration that fall. "One for Apprentices under Studio's IBEW Pact; Negro Applicants Being Sought," 11 July 1963, *Daily Variety*, 1, 4.

23. Fessier, "Negroes' H'wood Status Improving, Notes NAACP Rep," *Daily Variety*, 12 July 1963, 1, 13.

24. Ralph Clare, Teamsters Local 399 business agent, reported that his local was experiencing 50 percent unemployment and that this was a particularly inopportune time for the NAACP to pressure his union over jobs. Dave Kaufman, "IATSE Lamp Ops Take Dim View of NAACP Demands," *Daily Variety*, 1 August 1963, 1, 4.

25. Dave Kaufman, "Scenic Artists Nix Demand, Denounced by Other Labor Leaders as 'Arrogant,'" *Daily Variety*, 31 July 1963, 1, 4.

26. Fessier, "100% Integration of Films-Tv: That's NAACP Demand; IATSE Attack Renewed; Boren Sees an 'Area of Agreeableness,'" *Daily Variety*, 19 July 1963, 4.

27. "IA Lensers Nix NAACP Demand," *Daily Variety*, 30 July 1963, 4.

28. Kaufman, "IATSE Lamp Ops," 1, 4. Harold Minniear, IATSE Teachers Local 884 business agent, contradicted this position when he admitted that there were no African American members of his union. Ruth Compagnon, secretary for Culinary Local 639, claimed that her chapter supported IATSE International's antidiscrimination policy but that no African Americans had applied for membership. Ibid., 4.

29. Kaufman, "IATSE Lamp Ops," 1, 4.

30. "IA Lensers," 1, 4, and Kaufman, "More H'wood Unions Defy NAACP: Scenic Artists Nix Demand, Denounced By Other Labor

Leaders as 'Arrogant,'" *Daily Variety*, July 31, 1963, 1, 4; A.T. Dennison, Lamp Operators Local 728 business agent, stated that his chapter's objections were based on the poor employment situation in Hollywood and that adding minorities to crew rosters would constitute "featherbedding." See Kaufman, "IATSE Lamp Ops," 4.

31. Fessier, "NAACP Charges," 1, 4.

32. Fessier, "NAACP Ultimatum," 1, 8.

33. "Calif. FEPC Rap: Boothmen; Charge IA Projectionists' Frisco Local Refused Membership to Negro," *Daily Variety*, 28 June 1963, 1, 4.

34. In addition to forcing Set Designers and Model Makers Local 847 to adopt integration as its policy and to file official plans for its implementation, Tolbert admitted that it was the NAACP's strategy to use the set designers as an example to break the resistance of other recalcitrant unions. Fessier, "Plans Asking Decertification of Set Designers Local for Allegedly Barring Negro," *Daily Variety*, 2 August 1963, 1, 4.

35. "IA Publicists Support NAACP Pix Demands," *Daily Variety*, 8 August 1963, 1, 8.

36. Fessier, "Plans Asking Decertification," *Daily Variety*, 2 August 1963, 1, 4. In addition to these union objections, segregationist politicians denounced both the NAACP and anyone who would negotiate with them. For instance, U.S. Senator Strom Thurmond grilled CBS's president Frank Stanton before the Senate Communication Subcommittee on equal time and accused the "tiffany" network of following "the NAACP line" in its news coverage on civil rights. Another politician, California Assembly floor minority leader, Charles J. Conrad, known as the legislator-actor, backed with a concurring opinion from the office of the legislative counsel, declared that the NAACP's demands for adding an African American to each production crew was illegal. See "Dixie Sen. Thurmond Thunders; Sez CBS Toes 'NAACP Line,'" *Daily Variety*, 1 July 1963, 1, 14 and "Legislator-Actor Conrad Charges Some NAACP Demands on H'w'd Illegal," *Daily Variety*, 1 October 1963, n.p.

37. Fessier, "NAACP Charges," 4; and "NAACP H'wood Branch Meets Sunday as Pressure on Pix-TV Biz Mounts," *Daily Variety*, 13 June 1963, 1, 11.

38. "NAACP H'wood Branch," 1, 11. *Daily Variety* reported that another civil rights organization, CORE, was preparing its own program of actions in support of the cause of minority hiring and media representations. Ibid., 11.

39. "NAACP H'wood Branch," 1, 11; and Fessier, "NAACP Charges," 4.

40. Fessier, "Negroes' H'wood Status," 13.

41. Not every observer of the Hollywood scene held the same opinion on its response to minority employment. Phillip Waddell, spokesman for the Hollywood Race Relations Bureau, claimed that the industry had done a good job of minority hiring and that the NAACP was "very

wrong." See "Race Relations Bureau Hits NAACP, Says H'wood Doing 'Magnificent Job,'" *Daily Variety*, 25 June 1963, 1, 15.

42. "New NAACP Rap at Hollywood," *Daily Variety*, 1 July 1963, 1, 14.

43. "Names Spark Civil Liberties Union Drive to Get Negroes Better Break in H'wood," *Daily Variety*, 9 July 1963, 1,10.

44. Ibid., 10.

45. Kaufman, "Roles in Vidpix Not Cut on Bias: Producers Report Use of Negro Thesps Had Increased before Present Controversy," *Daily Variety*, 12 July 1963, 1, 13; and "NAACP Focuses on Madison Ave. in New Tack in Its Campaign against B'casting," *Daily Variety*, 20 August 1963, 7.

46. Kaufman, "Roles in Vidpix," 1, 13.

47. "Talent Guilds and Producers Harmonizing with NAACP, Which Sizzles at Unions," *Daily Variety*, 1 August 1963, 1, 4; and "IATSE Film Editors Join Other Unions Nixing NAACP," *Daily Variety*, 5 August 1963, 1, 10.

48. "Producers Urge Realistic Use of Negroes in Telepix," *Daily Variety*, 6 August 1963, 1, 12. For instance, Matthew Rapf, executive producer for Bing Crosby Productions, wondered, "What do you do on a 'Beverly Hillbillies' or 'Dick Van Dyke' show?" This query reveals that among television executives, the idea of introducing a black character as a financial adviser, stock broker, or professional on the side of the Clampetts against the slick city folk or of bringing a black client or song writer or comic into the world of Alan Brady to reveal another perspective on humor just never surfaced, or if it did, never became the subject of memoranda or experimentation. The limit of this conventional attitude as a guide for creativity is demonstrated by the fact that the African American actress Mimi Dillard was hired and featured on the *Dick Van Dyke Show* as reported by Lil Cumber, head of the largest African American talent agency in Hollywood. See "'Definite Increase' in Hollywood Jobs for Negro Performers Reported by Largest Colored Talent Agency," *Daily Variety*, 21 August 1963, 1, 14.

49. Kaufman, "Roles in Vidpix," 13.

50. Brando attributed the media's poor records to three main theories held by production executives: (1) "people aren't ready for it," (2) "we have a moral responsibility to the bankers," and (3) "40 percent of the market might be lost if more Negro actors are used." Fessier, "Brando Sparks," 1, 9.

51. In attendance at this meeting were Nate Monaster (WGAW), Phillip Dunne, James Whitmore, George Slaff, Mildred Walters, Tom Neusom, Stewart Stern, Toni Kimmel (William Schuller Agency), Bill Dana, and Charlton Heston. Ibid., 9.

52. "Negroes Break Blurb Barrier," *Daily Variety*, 2 August 1963, 1.

53. "NAACP Charges B'casting 'Openly Discriminating,' " *Daily Variety*, 12 August 1963, 1, 10.

54. Ibid., 10.

55. "NAACP Focuses on Madison Ave.," 1, 7.

56. " 'Definite Increase,' " 1, 14.

57. Fessier, "100% Integration of Films-TV: That's NAACP Demand," *Daily Variety*, 19 July 1963, 1, 4.

58. Fessier, "100% Integration," 1, 4.

59. None of the industry representatives would admit that any forms of discrimination were practiced in Hollywood, but through this meeting they sought to align themselves with the NAACP and African American actors and craftspersons' objectives. Ibid., 4.

60. Five African Americans were admitted to Theatre Projectionists Local 150 subsequent to NAACP pressure. Ibid., 4. Later that summer, a spokesman for IATSE Propman's Local 44 corrected Hill by pointing out that their union local never barred African Americans and had been completely integrated for years. See "IA Lensers," 4. Larry Kilty, business agent for Cartoonists IA Local 839, reported that the union local was integrated and did not discriminate. Harry Martinez, business agent for Plasterers Local 755, reported two African American members. Another integrated union was Local 724 International Hod Carriers, according to its business agent, Norval D. Jarrard. Two other business agents Max Krug, Local 174, and John A. Buchanan, Local 278 Janitors, went on record that their chapters were integrated. Fessier, "100% Integration," 4.

61. "TV Acad—East and West—Advocates More Integration in Video Industry," *Daily Variety*, 30 July 1963, 1, 9.

62. Ibid., 9.

63. "Projectionist Accepts Negro Applications," *Daily Variety*, 26 August 1963, 1, 4.

64. "Registration Up 115%; MPAA [sic] Spurs Drive," *Daily Variety*, 26 September 1963, 1, 4.

65. Ibid.

66. "17 Negroes Cast in Medical Roles in 'NEW Interns,'" *Daily Variety*, 7 September 1963, 1, 21.

67. "WB Joins Other Lots in NAACP Pledge," *Daily Variety*, 16 October 1963, 1, 9.

68. "IA Grips Local Admits 1st 5 Negroes; Aller Focuses Attack on NAACP," *Daily Variety*, 4 November 1963, 1, 4. Herb Aller, the union's representative for IATSE Cameramen's Local 659, objected vociferously to the NAACP program, saying, "The NAACP doesn't know what it's talking about. . . . I don't know why I always get condemned. I'm only here to protect members with seniority. . . . If the studio wants to hire a Negro let them hire one." Ibid., 4.

69. "NAACP Asks Studio-by-Studio Report on Just What Gains Negroes Have Made Here," *Daily Variety*, 13 December 1963, 1, 13.

70. Ibid.

71. Les Brown, "Television Off to the Races: Previews Reveal the Racial 'Mix,'" *Variety*, 14 September 1966, 1, 78.

72. Ibid., 78.

73. "H'wood NAACP in Stepped-Up Pitch for Negro Film-TV Prod. Employment," *Variety*, 28 July 1965, 1, 21.

74. The Congress on Racial Equality (CORE) found itself in the strange position of canceling its sponsorship of a San Francisco-area stage production because it presented interracial love affairs. The play, *What's Good for the Goose*, was written by Robert Sawyer and offered a satire of marital infidelity. Before its August 1965 opening in San Jose, the play had been cast as an all-black production but became integrated when white actors responded to advertisements for Negro-only actors. Still feeling the "shock waves" from the Los Angeles riots, CORE officials canceled the production because it ceased to offer acting opportunities for blacks. "L. A. Riots Kayo S.F. Negro Plays," *Variety*, 25 August 1965, 1, 60.

75. A. D. Murphy, "TV Progressing in Hiring Negroes, but Urge Speedup," *Variety*, 6 April 1966, 1, 48.

76. The seven Los Angeles television stations that were included in the study were KNXT (CBS-TV), KNBC (NBC-TV), KABC (ABC-TV), KTLA (Golden West Broadcasting), KHJ (RKO General), KTTV (Metromedia), and KCOP (Chris-Craft).

77. Murphy, "TV Progressing," 48.

78. Hill characterized union resistance to pressure for jobs for African Americans aspiring to crafts positions as "our toughest row to hoe." "Race Shut-Out Issue Still Rampant," *Variety*, 13 July 1966, 4.

79. "IA's Herb Aller Chides NAACP's 'Rabblerousing,'" *Variety*, 13 July 1966, 1, 54.

80. "LORE: Leonard on Racial Equality," *Variety*, 27 July 1966, 2.

81. "L. A. Riots Kayo," 1, 60.

82. "L.A. Riot Cost Ringling 300,000G," *Variety*, 25 August 1965, 60.

Chapter Two

1. Christopher H. Sterling and John M. Kitross, *Stay Tuned: A Concise History of American Broadcasting*, 2nd ed. (Belmont, CA: Wadsworth, 1990), 361–64, 399.

2. Several works have tried to provide a context for understanding the range of themes and issues expressed through science fiction literature. A partial list of these includes Isaac Asimov, Introduction to *More Soviet Science Fiction*, trans. Roza Prekofeva (New York: Collier, 1962); Basil Davenport, *The Science Fiction Novel: Imagination and Social Criticism* (Chicago: Advent, 1969); Violet L. Dutt, *Soviet Science Fiction* (New York: Collier, 1962); and Robert A. W. Lowndes, *Three Faces of Science Fiction: As Propaganda, Instruction and Delight* (Boston: New England Science Fiction Association Press, 1973).

3. This motto preceded each episode of the original *Star Trek* and was

spoken by the off-screen voice of the *Enterprise*'s white, male, American captain, James Tiberius Kirk. When *Star Trek: The Next Generation* was launched in the fall of 1987, the device of the motto was retained as each episode's formal introduction and boundary marking the "new territory" for exploration, but the wording was subtly changed. "No man" was replaced by "no one," so that the new series would not be tainted by Terran and masculine parochialisms. Nonetheless, the series retained the device of using the off-screen voice of the *Enterprise*'s white, male, French captain, Jean-Luc Picard.

4. Walter (Matt) Jefferies, a Desilu production designer, is credited with creating this identifying serial number for the spaceship [logo] for the series. See Joel Engel, *Gene Roddenberry: The Myth and the Man behind Star Trek* (New York: Hyperion, 1994), 55.

5. However, all Starfleet crew members and officers, when commissioned, pledged not to interfere with or to impose their values on any society they might encounter even at the point of death (this is the so-called "prime directive," which seems to have been adapted from Asimov's First Law of Robotics).

6. Examples of early science fiction programs for children include *Captain Midnight, Rocky Jones, Johnny Jupiter, Superman, Supercar, Thunderbirds, Joe 90, Captain Scarlet*, and *Fireball XL5*.

7. Quite early in the process, Roddenberry developed the habit and art of writing memos on all subjects related to the production of *Star Trek*. His memo to Gusman may have less to do with the way an executive producer supervises his various department heads and more to do with getting on record as being identified with a good idea. In this memo, Roddenberry says, "You may have been the one who suggested a week or so ago that this would have the side advantage of giving us a merchandising trademark." Roddenberry clearly seems content to leave the inference that the idea of the logo itself originated with him. See Memorandum from Gene Roddenberry to Pato Guzman, "Star Trek Emblem," 10 August 1964, in Gene Roddenberry Collection, Correspondence/General Files-Art Direction, box 27, folder 4, University of California at Los Angeles, University Research Library, Special Collections (hereafter UCLA-SC).

8. Adams Bryant, "Beam Me Up! I'm Out of Change!" *New York Times*, 29 September 1992, C5.

9. Traditionally, off-network syndication requires at least 100 individual programs for daily scheduling, so-called "stripping," and only seventy-nine episodes of *Star Trek* were originally produced.

10. Roddenberry explained the concept behind *Star Trek* to reluctant network executives by referring to the western explicitly. "Hell, it's just another horse opera except that they ride a spaceship instead of a nag . . . what's it like? *Wagon Train*? *Wagon Train* to the stars, get it?" Stephan E.

Whitfield and Gene Roddenberry, *The Making of Star Trek* (New York: Ballantine, 1971), 22–23.

11. Anthology television series that featured the fantastic and eldritch can be traced to radio series like *Lights Out, X Minus 1*, and *Suspense Theatre* and to television series like Rod Serling's *The Twilight Zone* which first aired on CBS 2 October 1959 and ran on CBS until 5 September 1965 and Leslie Steven's *The Outer Limits* which first aired on ABC 16 September 1963 and ran on ABC until 16 January 1965.

12. From 1963 to 1964, CBS had in its broadcast schedule a drama series based in the inner city called *East Side/West Side* on Monday nights that included Cicely Tyson as a regular cast member. Ironically, Greg Morris, one actor who benefited from Hollywood's accommodation to pressure for new opportunities for African Americans, was an outspoken opponent of the NAACP's protests, lobbying especially about a prospect of an NAACP picket at the 1963 Academy Awards. "Negro Actor Condemns Plan to Picket Oscar Tonight," *Daily Variety*, 8 April 1963, 1, 4.

13. The developments of prime-time opportunities for African Americans had a parallel in other parts of the television schedule. Programs such as *Daktari* and *Hogan's Heroes* contained running parts for African Americans. In addition, Brock Peters, Cicely Tyson, and James Earl Jones worked regularly on soap operas. Other minorities found roles on other series. For example, American Indians were included in frontier dramas such as *The Monroes*, about five orphans trying to set up housekeeping in the Wyoming territory, and *Daniel Boone*, about the title character's exploits in early colonial America.

14. "*I Spy* Clearance Grows in Dixie, Can't Snub a Hit," *Variety*, 21 September 1966, 1. Throughout the history of media in this country, the specter of obdurate and obstructionist Southern distributors has been raised as a bogeyman to warn media producers about the financial dangers of dealing with America's race controversy with liberal sympathy. For a discussion and analysis of the actual impact of the Southern box office on the financial health of motion pictures with race messages, see Thomas R. Cripps, "The Myth of the Southern Box-Office: A Factor in Racial Stereotyping in American Movies, 1920–1940," in *The Black Experience in America: Selected Essays*, ed. James Curtis and Lewis L. Gould (Austin: University of Texas Press, 1970), 116–44.

15. "New Research on Hits and Misses," *Variety*, 28 July 1965, 23, 53.

16. Kaufman, "Spy-Fi Gets Left in Cold," *Variety*, 25 January 1966, 26.

17. Ibid.

18. "Spy Spoofs Run Political Risks on Global Sales," *Variety*, 15 February 1966, 27.

19. "Next Season's 3 Net Schedule—First Round," *Variety*, 2 March 1966, 30; and "Next Season's 3 Net Schedule—14th Round," *Variety*, 16 March 1966, 37.

20. "Dear Old 'Nielsen Rule' Days: Top 3-R's Still Spell Ratings," *Variety*, 7 September 1966, 1, 62.

21. Murray Horowitz, "Frosh Open Weak Spy–Sci-Fi Next?" *Variety*, 28 September 1966, 31.

22. "Dear Old 'Nielsen Rule' Days," 1, 62.

23. Ibid.

24. Letter from Gene Roddenberry to Grant Tinker, 31 July 1964, box 29, folder 7, UCLA-SC.

25. "2nd Week Overnights," *Variety*, 21 September 1966, 22.

26. "'Star Trek' Gets NBC Nod for [Full] Slate," *Variety*, 12 October 1966, 35.

27. "75% of NBC-TV Sked to be Held Over in 1967–68; Set 'Danny Thomas Hour,'" *Variety*, 21 December 1966, 25.

28. Ibid.

29. During its premier season, *Star Trek* was regularly beaten by other programs in its time slot and finished the year fifty-second among all series.

30. In an effort to head off cancellation, Roddenberry attempted to organize an "impromptu" viewer demand to retain the show. He wrote Herb Schlosser, president, NBC-Burbank, that positive public reaction probably stemmed from the fact that *Star Trek* was the only "'tomorrow' drama on television" that uses the kind of high technology read about in news stories like Christian Bernard's heart transplant surgery. He went on to suggest how Schlosser could develop an eleven-point argument to use on NBC's New York executives. Letter from Roddenberry to Schlosser, 1 February 1968, box 29, folder 7, UCLA-SC.

31. Ibid.

32. Budget analyses for *Mannix, Mission: Impossible,* and *Star Trek,* three Paramount Pictures hour-long television programs in concurrent production, provide a basis for making comparisons of revenue. In their first and second seasons, these programs generated $4,399,896(1st)/4,621,728(2nd), $4,007,922(1st)/4,481,880(2nd), and $3,849,270(1st)/4,310,582(2nd), respectively. In these same seasons, they produced per episode $185,639(1st)/193,562(2nd), $181,941(1st)/193,567(2nd), and $166,065 (1st)/177,449(2nd) in profits. Although *Star Trek* showed improving trends for both of these categories into its third season, it was clear that its poor financial performance relative to other similar productions could not justify a renewal past a third season. See Budget Summaries of *Mannix, Mission: Impossible,* and *Star Trek,* box 35, folder 4, UCLA-SC.

33. Letter from Mort Werner, NBC vice president for Programs and Talent to Gene Roddenberry, 17 August 1966, box 29, folder 7, UCLA-SC.

34. Ibid.

35. Roddenberry's professional interest and association with civil rights subject matter dates back to his first job as a writer-producer on the

series *The Lieutenant* (NBC-TV, 1963–64). The series focused on the peacetime military life of Bill Rice, a recent graduate of the Annapolis naval academy who is assigned to Camp Pendleton. In one episode, entitled "To Set It Right," a black marine, played by Don Marshall, is stationed with his wife, played by Nichelle Nichols, at the camp and immediately attacks a young white marine, played by Dennis Hopper. When Rice investigates, he finds out that the two men knew each other from high school, that the Hopper character and the white gang he belonged to then made sport of beating up African Americans, and that the Marshall character was the victim of one of these race-hate beatings. Although the two Marines learn to respect and work with each other, the Pentagon so strenuously objected to the representation of racial problems within the military that it withdrew its support of the series on the basis of this episode. Engle, *Gene Roddenberry*, 27–28.

36. A public service announcement script that Roddenberry wrote in the early 1960s is evidence of his awareness of civil rights issues and his sympathetic attitude toward African-American pressure for reform. For a transcript of the public service announcement, see David Alexander, *Star Creator: The Autobiography of Gene Roddenberry* (New York: Penguin Books, 1994), 180–82.

37. The timeliness and fit of Roddenberry's approach to casting is demonstrated by the fact that Oscar Katz, a one-time head of CBS programming after he left Desilu Studio, where he worked with Roddenberry to bring *Star Trek* to viewers, worked as an agent for Irwin Allen who produced *Voyage to the Bottom of the Sea* (ABC-TV, 1964–68), *Lost in Space* (CBS-TV, 1965–68), *Time Tunnel* (ABC-TV, 1966–67), and *Land of the Giants* (ABC-TV, 1968–70). The aspects that these shows share with *Star Trek* are obvious. See Alexander, *Star Creator*, 194.

38. Whitfield and Roddenberry, *The Making of Star Trek*, 29.

39. Ibid.

40. This pilot was never broadcast as part of *Star Trek*. However, Roddenberry combined large portions from it with new material to fashion "The Menagerie," Parts I and II (airdates: 17 and 24 November 1966, episodes 15 and 16). In this form, "The Menagerie" provides details (called "back story") of the relationships among bridge crew members and, in particular, explores the personality of the ship's alien science officer, Mr. Spock.

41. Between Roddenberry's first conception of "Number One" and his realization of this character in the pilot episode commissioned by NBC, this female officer was transmogrified from a black to white female and was played by Majel Barrett, who would soon marry Gene Roddenberry.

42. Roddenberry first proposed a television series with an ethnically diverse crew in 1961 and may have been stimulated by the film *Master of*

the World (Warner Brothers, 1961), which was adapted from two Jules Verne stories: "Robur, the Conqueror" and "Master of the World." He envisioned the crew aboard a huge dirigible that would travel the globe searching out evil and championing right. See Alexander, *Star Creator,* 185.

43. The Uhura character is probably the original "Number One" character after being demoted. Roddenberry's persistence about the presence of a black female continuing cast member may actually predate *Star Trek* and stem from his earlier relationship with Nichelle Nichols. Before *Star Trek* and his marriage to Majel Barrett (Nurse Chapel), Roddenberry and Nichols were lovers. Confirmation of Roddenberry and Nichols' romance may be found in William Shatner with Chris Kreski, *Star Trek Memories* (New York: Harper/Collins, 1993), 294; Engel, *Gene Roddenberry,* 86; and Nichelle Nichols, *Beyond Uhura* (New York: Putnam, 1994), 128, 131–34.

44. The genesis for *Star Trek* probably stems from Roddenberry's combination of his previous ideas for other television series: *Hawaii Passage, APO 923,* and an adapted version of "Master of the World." The rapport among senior officers in *Star Trek* may be traced to *Hawaii Passage,* a show proposal about the adventures of a ship and its crew, and *APO 923,* a show proposal that centered on the relationship among three military officers. The multiracial crew may be traced to Roddenberry's interest in adapting Jules Verne's "Master of the World" for television. Roddenberry sought to secure this proposal for a science fiction television series by sending it to the Writers Guild on 24 April 1964. See Alexander, *Star Creator,* 188, and Engel, *Gene Roddenberry,* 38–39. Roddenberry's interest in developing a series around a multiracial cast of continuum characters indicates that he had matured beyond his childhood exposure and upbringing in his Southern father's racial biases. See Engel, *Gene Roddenberry,* 46.

45. Roddenberry's involvement with the international perspective from his last year in high school in Los Angeles. According to his school records, he was a member of the International Forum of Franklin High School, which was the local chapter of the World Friendship Club and was dedicated to fostering "better feeling among nations." See Alexander, *Star Creator,* 39, 41.

46. Early in the development process for *Star Trek,* it was suggested by one of the writing staff that regarding the female "Number One," writers be instructed to "make her a female computer." See Memorandum from Samuel A. Peoples, 6 September 1966, box 29, folder 14, UCLA-SC.

47. In fact, Roddenberry's argument about the necessity and appeal of Mr. Spock is really a paraphrasing of his description of "Number One." See Letter from Gene Roddenberry to Don Durgin, Vice President Television Network Sales-NBC, 19 July 1965, box 29, folder 7, UCLA-SC.

48. Roddenberry's interest in linking his series to larger social issues is

demonstrated by the fact that during its first season, *Star Trek* producers responded to a request for fund-raising support from a Los Angeles civil rights group by giving Nichelle Nichols permission to serve as chair of the event. Letter to Gene Roddenberry from Rev. Paul M. Martin, Project Supervisor, South-Central Project VISTA, 2 February 1967, box 30, folder 1, UCLA-SC.

49. In this episode, the race issue is displaced from a struggle between "monochromatic" Terrans to an interplanetary race that is divided between people who are "two-toned," in which skin colors are distributed bilaterally, and contend over whether it is a mark of superiority to be white on the left side.

50. Here the question of the Nazis' anti-Semitism is deflected by identifying the persecuted race as "Ekotians." In "Bread and Circuses" (airdate: 15 March 1968, episode 43), this same theme was revisited. However, in this program interference from space travelers threatens to derail the emergence of Christianity on a planet controlled by the alien equivalent of the Roman Empire.

51. In "Elaan of Troyius" (airdate: 20 December 1968, episode 57), the theme of interspecies romance was again featured. In this instance, however, Kirk falls in love aboard ship with the beautiful France Nuyen, a female Vietnamese actor, who plays a leader of an alien world whose proposed marriage is designed to end hostilities with her world's foe.

52. This episode and "Let That Be Your Last Battlefield" are examples of plots that refer equally well to consequences of the institutions of slavery in the United States and of apartheid in South Africa. Interestingly, however, the teleplay for this episode states that all of the denizens of Stratos are members of the same gene pool and appear phenotypically indistinguishable. Therefore, the issue of ethnic difference is deflected.

53. The strategy of using aliens (generally females) as paramours for the continuing characters of the *Enterprise* and to raise the issue of racial tolerance was used explicitly in several other episodes. Dr. McCoy fell in love with the Priestess of Ynodda in "For The World Is Hollow and I Have Touched the Sky" (airdate: 8 November 1968, episode 65). Kirk romanced his female drill instructor in "The Gamesters of Triskelion" (airdate: 5 January 1968, episode 46). Mr. Spock seduced a female Romulan commander in "The *Enterprise* Incident" (airdate: 27 September 1968, episode 59) and found himself strongly attracted to the daughter of the chief administrator of Stratos. In an unusual variation on this theme, a non-crew member, Zephram Cochrane, inventor of the warp drive, who was thought dead, falls in love with an energy entity that invades the body of a dying Federation ambassador to save the energy of the ambassador's life and to assume a form more acceptable to the Terran male's sensibilities ("Metamorphosis," airdate: 10 November 1967, episode 38).

54. Nichelle Nichols recalls meeting Dr. Martin Luther King, Jr., during

a personal and professional low point and discussing with him her intention to resign from *Star Trek*. As she recollects, "I met him in '66 I believe, or early '67, and I had said to him that I was leaving the show. . . . After he had said the show was in his home, their home, every week and how important I was to his family and made me very proud. He said, 'Think about this, Nichelle. You have changed the face of television forever. They can never undo what they've done. The door is open!'" Interview with Nichelle Nichols in *Star Trek: 25th Anniversary* (Los Angeles: Paramount Pictures, September 1991). See also Nichols, *Beyond Uhura*, 129–30.

55. The syndication deal that launched *Star Trek: The Next Generation* was precedent setting. Each episode was budgeted at $1.3 million in the first season, which meant that the series' executive producer Roddenberry and Paramount Pictures believed that they could recoup $130 million across the 100 episodes needed for stripping (after each had been shown twice in first release). William Mahoney, "Syndication: The Next Generation? 'Star Trek' Points First-Run toward Bold New World," *Electronic Media*, 15 February 1988, 1, 18.

56. In 1977, Paramount Pictures went so far as to build standing sets, commission scripts, and begin the process of bringing the original *Star Trek* with the original crew back as a first-run syndication program. This planning was part of Paramount's first steps towards creating a Paramount television service. The new service never came about, and planning for the return of the series stopped at that point. Mahoney, "Syndication," 1, 18, 36.

Chapter Three

1. Early in his administration, Nixon scribbled a note in the margin of a memo about the possibility of discovering a contingent of blacks who could be encouraged to vote for him that revealed his speculation of reaching the "30% who are potentially on our side." See Nicholas Lemann, *The Promised Land: The Great Black Migration and How It Changed America* (New York: Knopf, 1991), 203.

2. Research shows that Nixon, raised a Quaker pacifist, embraced many of the same racial prejudices of the "silent majority" that he claimed to speak for from the presidential podium. John Ehrlichman said, "He thought, basically, blacks were generally inferior. . . . In his heart he was very skeptical about their ability to excel except in rare cases. He didn't feel this way about other groups. He'd say on civil right things 'Well, we'll do this, but it isn't going to do any good.' He did use the words 'genetically inferior.' He thought they couldn't achieve on a level with whites." Ehrlichman cited in Lemann, *The Promised Land*, 204.

3. For a detailed analysis of the accomplishments and failures of the

Carter Administration and a discussion of Carter's moral ideology versus his rejection of a political ideology, I can recommend a speech by Hendrik Hertzberg, a Carter Administration speechwriter, entitled "Jimmy Carter's Character and Leadership," delivered at the LBJ Public Affairs Conference, Austin, Texas, C-SPAN, airdate: 17 February 1995.

4. "Minority Advocate Tenders Resignation after FCC Decision," *Variety*, 1 October 1986, 50; "FCC to Examine Minority Policy," *Variety*, 24 December 1986, 75, 78.

5. David Robb, "Minority Actors Are Still Slighted, Says a Report by SAG/AFTRA," *Variety*, 4 June 1986, 2.

6. Ibid., 130.

7. Ibid.

8. Paul Harris, "Minority Gains Screeching to a Halt," *Variety*, 10 December 1986, 45, 84.

9. William Mahoney, "Syndication: The Next Generation? 'Star Trek' Points First-Run toward Bold New World," *Electronic Media*, 15 February 1988, 18.

10. The Committee on National Television Audience Measurement (CONTAM), funded by the three networks, commissioned the first industry study of videotaping to answer advertisers' and sponsors' concerns that the new technology was being used by viewers to skip over, or "zap," commercials. The study indicated that more than half of the viewers (54 percent) fast forwarded on average two times an hour. This contrasted with a previous Nielsen study that reported 65 percent of viewers zapped commercials. "Home Tape Study Cues Webs Grins," *Variety*, 11 December 1985, 1, 143. As a category, science fiction accounted for 7 percent of prerecorded video rentals. Janet Stilson, "Programers Struggle for Fewer New Dollars," *Electronic Media*, 17 August 1987, 32.

11. Some industry insiders, like Henry McGee, HBO vice president for home video, disagreed with this projection and believed that by the end of the year, prerecorded video sales would reach $4 billion with no plateau in sight. Stilson, "Programers Struggle," 32; and Aljean Harmetz, "Big Gains for Video Cassettes: Revenue Nearing Box-Office Income," *New York Times*, 21 August 1995, C13.

12. William Mahoney, "Program Syndication Seminar Focuses on Cable's Importance," *Electronic Media*, 30 November 1987.

13. Ibid.

14. For insights into the way Hollywood producers, agents, studio, and other insiders regard the shifting ecology of television and the increasing opportunities in off-network syndication, see Michael I. Adler, Keith G. Fleer, and Michael Lauer, "Back to the Future™—Prognostications on the Future of the Motion Picture and Television Industries" (The Tenth Annual UCLA Entertainment Symposium), (Los Angeles: UCLA School of Law and UCLA Entertainment Symposium Advisory Committee, 1985), 146–220.

15. William Mahoney, "Stations Get Peek at New 'Star Trek,'" *Electronic Media*, 10 August 1987, 3, 61.

16. Confidence about the popularity of the *Star Trek* franchise, which had never been out of syndication since its network cancellation, led Paramount to offer the original series for syndication at the same time as it was about to launch its new sequel series. Less than two months before the two-part premiere on 3 and 4 October, Paramount announced that it had signed 151 stations, representing 90 percent national coverage, to a syndication deal for *Star Trek*. Marianne Paskowski, "Syndicators Cutting Into Network Turf," *Electronic Media*, 28 April 1987, 1, 47.

17. Ibid., 1.

18. Mahoney, "Syndication," 18.

19. Paramount Television Group must have viewed these figures with relief as they projected the costs of producing *Star Trek: The Next Generation* across the five years that would be necessary to accumulate a sufficient number of episodes for local broadcasters to broadcast a different episode each weekday. Marianne Paskowski, "Syndication Milestone: 'Cosby' Sales Close to $500 Million Mark," *Electronic Media*, 17 August 1987, 4.

20. Notwithstanding the emerging trend of hour-long network programs being contracted to cable for syndication, many in the television industry warned that long-form television should be offered to off-network broadcast syndication first and that local broadcasters still had a strong appetite for these programs. "Rethinking Hour-Long Shows," *Electronic Media*, 12 December 1987, 12; and Richard Mahler, "It Wasn't a Great Year for Syndicators," *Electronic Media*, 4 January 1988, 46.

21. After a year of speculation about the impact of the competition from alternative media and the new people metering on ratings, a somewhat more modest decline of 9 percent was reported by A. C. Nielsen Company. See William Mahoney and Adam Buckman, "ABC, CBS, NBC Battle New Erosion," *Electronic Media*, 28 April 1988, 1, 57.

22. Marianne Paskowski, "Syndicators Cutting into Network Turf," *Electronic Media*, 23 May 1988, 1, 47.

23. William Mahoney, "'Trek's Ratings Dropping," *Electronic Media*, 26 October 1987, 20.

24. Richard Mahler, "'Trek' Top New Show in First-Run," *Electronic Media*, 16 November 1987, 4, 86.

25. Ibid.

26. This figure may be arrived at by figuring that Paramount held back seven national barter spots per episode and that each episode is broadcast twice according to contract, equalling fourteen spots. Multiplying $70,000 by fourteen equals $980,000. Marianne Paskowski, "Growing Use of Barter Frustrating to Many Stations," *Electronic Media*, 22 February 1988, 70.

27. William Mahoney, "Network Pilots Reflect Interest in News, Sci-Fi," *Electronic Media*, 21 March 1988, 1, 31.

28. Motion pictures such as *Alien* (Fox, 1979), *Aliens* (Fox, 1986), *Amazing Stories* (MCA, 1986), **batteries not included* (MCA, 1987), *Blade Runner* (Warner Bros., 1982), *Brainstorm* (Metro-Goldwyn-Mayer, 1983), *The Brother from Another Planet* (Fox, 1984), *Capricorn One* (Fox, 1978), *Close Encounters of the Third Kind* (MCA, 1977), *Critters* (Columbia, 1986), *D.A.R.Y.L.* (Paramount, 1985), *Demon Seed* (MGM, 1977), *Dune* (MCA, 1984), *The Empire Strikes Back* (Fox, 1980), *E.T.: The Extra-Terrestrial* (MCA, 1982), *The Fly* (Fox, 1986), *Highlander* (HBO, 1986), *Innerspace* (Warner Brothers, 1987), *The Last Starfighter* (MCA, 1984), *The Philadelphia Experiment* (HBO, 1984), *Return of the Jedi* (Fox, 1983), *Star Trek* (Paramount, 1980), *Star Trek II* (Paramount, 1982), *Star Trek III* (Paramount, 1984), *Star Trek IV* (Paramount, 1986), *The Terminator* (HBO, 1984), and *The Thing* (MCA, 1982) demonstrated the popular acceptance of science fiction.

29. According to Nielsen Media Research's "Television Audience 1987" report on American television viewing, viewing went down by twenty-eight minutes in 1986 for the first decline in viewing by Americans in twenty years. Households watched forty-nine hours and forty-eight minutes less television. Men watched television forty-two minutes less per week, and women viewed thirty-four minutes less per week. These results were reported for a year when the total number of households with television increased by 1.2 million and the number of stations in operation increased from 401 to 451. Adam Buckman, "Nielsen Reports 1st Drop in Viewing," *Electronic Media,* 4 January 1988, 1, 2. See also, William Mahoney, "Networks Plot Strategies to Stop Ratings Erosion," *Electronic Media,* 9 November 1977, 6, 60; Marianne Paskowski, "The Good, Bad, and Ugly of the New People Meters," *Electronic Media,* 4 January 1988, 48; and Janet Stilson, "Cable Networks Pulling Viewers from Broadcast," *Electronic Media,* 9 November 1987, 6, 60.

30. Cable subscription among all television households climbed from 18 percent in the last quarter of 1986 and the first quarter of 1987 to 32 percent in July and August 1987. Stilson, "Cable Networks," 6; and Janet Stilson, "Study: Meters Show Improved Cable Ratings," *Electronic Media,* 4 January 1988, 4. This improvement in cable's finances was linked directly to FCC deregulation of the medium, which allowed cable operators to discount fees and entice new consumers to switch from over-the-air television. See Janet Stilson, "Deregulation Spurs Cable Industry to Boom Year," *Electronic Media,* 4 January 1988, 43, 118.

31. Pay television viewing went up 13 percent as compared with 1986 to total two hours and forty-nine minutes. Ibid., 6.

32. Diane Mermigas, "Analysts Foresee More Changes in the Industry," *Electronic Media,* 4 January 1988, 48.

33. Diane Mermigas, "Cap Cities See a Soft Ad Market," *Electronic Media,* 23 May 1988, 2.

34. Alternative media used audience familiarity and acceptance of

science fiction and the perennial popularity of feature-length movies on television to successfully tease enough audience away from network programs to outscore their broadcast competitors in key markets such as Los Angeles, Chicago, and New York. Richard Mahler, "Movies Score Well vs. Big Three," *Electronic Media,* 14 March 1988, 14.

35. Marianne Paskowski, "Upfront Barter Heats Up: Syndicators Worried about Sluggish Demand," *Electronic Media,* 28 March 1988, 3, 33.

36. Ibid., 3.

37. Richard Mahler, "Industry Becoming One of Have, Have Nots," *Electronic Media,* 22 February 1988, 1, 56, 72. This article also reported a survey by the Association of Independent Television Stations that found 86 percent of distributors agreeing that fewer syndicators would survive to do business in the 1990s, that 500 jobs in Hollywood's first-run syndication community were phased out, and that 28 percent predicted price improved against 15 percent who foresaw declines.

38. By mid-June 1988, the Writers Guild of America had been on strike against film and television for more than 100 days. Richard Mahler, "On Strike: Out-of-Work Writers Try to Make Ends Meet," *Electronic Media,* 20 June 1988, 1, 40.

39. Marianne Paskowski, "Syndicators Begin Closing Upfront Deals," *Electronic Media,* 20 June 1988, 4.

40. Ibid.

41. William Mahoney, "New Syndicated Series Ready for Fall Launches Despite Strike," *Electronic Media,* 25 July 1988, 3, 38.

42. William Mahoney, "Paramount Set to Launch Never-Aired 'Star Trek' Pilot," *Electronic Media,* 26 September 1988, 4.

43. In *Star Trek,* the *Enterprise*'s captain was clearly supposed to be associated with America. Even before Kirk, the *Enterprise*'s first captain, Christopher Pike reveals in the episode "The Menagerie," that he is an American, enjoys horseback riding, and if he were not in Starfleet, would most want to own a small ranch in the American West. In *Star Trek: The Next Generation,* the *Enterprise*'s captain is unmistakably French. In the fourth season, Picard returns to his ancestral home ("Family;" airdate: 29 September 1990, episode 75) in the French wine country (the village of Lavaur, near Toulouse) and is reconciled with his older brother, who is a vintner. Clearly, these personal, even familial, background details of the characters evoke associations with national traditions and popularly held myths about America and France. The backstories of these leading characters are one of the first indications of the scope of dissemination (broadcast and syndication markets) envisioned by producers. In the case of *Star Trek,* the original series emerged when the legal and financial structure of television allowed independent studios to produce programming for first and second run on the national broadcast networks with subsequent local market syndication reverting to the ownership and control of the orig-

inating independent. Under the terms of this structure, independent studios were able to deficit finance production and enter profitability when their programs were syndicated. However, by the mid-1980s, developments in television technology (cable television, videocassette recorders, and prerecorded videocassettes) were eroding the aggregate audience for network television by as much as 12 percent. This new situation made it incumbent upon independent producers (such as Paramount Pictures Company and Roddenberry) to look beyond traditional domestic markets and to place fresh emphasis on videocassette sales and syndication to international markets. Therefore, a program's leading character—and in these cases, the shift from a white American to white European leading man—may reflect the producers' efforts to create a point of identification between the series and its perceived audience after its first-run syndication in the United States.

44. This character, which was not envisioned as an original member of the continuing cast, has little beyond a bare sketch of attributes. Moreover, in many ways this character, her function aboard the *Enterprise,* and her lack of meaningful contact with other shipmates or inclusion in significant plots reminds this researcher of the Isaac Washington character, another black bartender, on *The Love Boat.* This point will be expanded upon in discussing the ways in which the *Star Trek* formula marks ethnic characters.

45. In fact, the *Star Trek: The Next Generation Writer's/Director's Guide '89–'90,* emphasizes in its list of story line "do's" that writers should "emphasize science fiction and futuristic sociological stories" and under "don'ts" that they should "not write a story which does not principally involve our continuing characters." Taken together these two admonitions mean that teleplays that get the green light should explore the implications of encountering alien life for the multicultural crew of the *Enterprise.*

46. These figures were determined by referring to the "unofficial" and "official" synopses of all of the episodes through the fifth season. For years 1 through 4, see Mark A. Altman, "Episode Guide," *Cinefantastique,* September 1990, 26–51. For the fifth year, see Mark A. Altman, "Episode Guide," *Cinefantastique,* October 1991, 19–51. For an "official" cumulative summary of years 1 through 5, see Michael Okuda and Denise Okuda, *Star Trek Chronology: The History of the Future* (New York: Pocket Books, 1993), 79-149.

47. Two episodes from *Star Trek: The Next Generation*—"The Vengence Factor" (airdate: 18 November 1989; episode 57) and "The Perfect Mate" (airdate: 2 May 1992; episode 121)—are reiterations of plotlines from the parent series, but with ethnicity drained from them. "The Vengence Factor" is "Let That Be Your Last Battlefield" without the makeup effects that focused the earlier story line on race. "The Perfect Mate" is an almost exact retelling of "Elaan of Troyius," except that in this version the irresistible female is no longer identifiably a woman of color.

48. This character's fictional origin is a subject of considerable ambiguity. As the series was getting under way, the "bible" stated that Geordi was from Jamaica. *The Star Trek Chronology* lists Geordi as "born in the African Confederation on planet Earth." Since these two documents, *The Star Trek Encyclopedia* has appeared and drops the subject of La Forge's birthplace altogether. This lack of clarity, among other reasons, suggests the use of a more inclusive term such as *Africanist* for identifying this character.

49. "Kitameer" is a variation on this spelling, which is found in some sources.

50. This is an intriguing phrase that betrays a rather biased attitude toward miscegenation, race mixing, or intermarriage between humanoid species. *Hybrid* is commonly applied to the artificial manipulation of genomes to produce an offspring that would not occur without intervention in nature. Terms such as *hybrid, breed, mongrel, mulatto, quadroon,* and so forth seem to be part of a uniquely American vocabulary for ethnic blending. There are no similar special terms to describe the child of a Briton and a Saudi Arabian, the offspring of Irish and Polish Catholic parents, or the product of sexual relations between a French and Amerindian couple. This description of K'Ehlyer as a transpecies character was written by Altman, "Episode Guide," 38.

51. When Worf's son, Alexander, is introduced, he is older than can be accounted for by the duration of the couple's separation. This anomaly is left unexplained.

52. See Adams Bryant, "Beam Me Up! I'm Out of Change!" *New York Times,* 29 September 1992, C5.

53. This information was culled from an on-line Internet archive file server dedicated as a storage and retrieval device for E-mail messages generated by discussion groups on several specific aspects of *Star Trek* within the general ".rec.arts" newsgroup, Otto E. Heuer, "Star Trek Outside North America," Archive-Name: f(requently)a(sked)q(uestions) l(ist).rec.arts.startrek.abroad., 15 November 1993.

Chapter Four

1. See David Alexander, *Star Creator: The Autobiography of Gene Roddenberry* (New York: Penguin, 1994), 243–45; and "Writer/Director Guide," Roddenberry Collection, UCLA-SC.

2. While visiting the planet Stratos, Spock tells the chief administrator's daughter that while he has a first name, she would not be able to pronounce it. This strategy of naming, or rather not completely naming, this character not only served to deny viewers a glimpse of Vulcan culture (at least at the level of the cultural significance of names) but imposed a formal distance and withheld intimacy, which can been seen to be in keep-

ing with the character's conception. Moreover, the effect of this omission preserves the alien, Spock here, as exotic and tantalizingly unattainable for both the chief administrator's daughter and viewers.

3. Gene Roddenberry collected his advice for character development in a manual that in the media industry is referred to as a show's "bible." In this writer's guide he points out again and again that "*people* must be believable." Among their character traits, "[t]he crewmembers of the Enterprise are intelligent, witty, thoughtful, compassionate, caring human beings. They do have human faults and weaknesses, but not as many or as severe as in our time." See Gene Roddenberry, *Star Trek: The Next Generation Writer's/Director's Guide '89–'90* (Los Angeles: Paramount Pictures, 1989), 33.

4. Ibid.

5. Ibid., 16–17.

6. The term *Klingon* is used to designate an extraterrestrial race that values aggression, uses rituals to valorize behaviors and attitudes related to combat at every level of social intercourse, and seems to privilege emotional excess over rationality at crucial individual and group decison points. The origin of this term may be traced to Roddenberry's career as a Los Angeles policeman and one of his fellow officers, Wilbur Cligman. See Alexander, *Star Creator*, 131.

7. However, in the episode "Time's Arrow," it was revealed that Guinan's friendship and closeness with Picard stems from his time-travel adventure back to nineteenth-century San Francisco and rescue of her when she was trapped in an underground cave and injured. At considerable risk that he might not return to his proper time, Picard nursed Guinan and waited there until help, in the form of Samuel Clemens, arrived to convey her to medical attention.

8. In the 1994 feature-length motion picture *Star Trek: Generations,* Captain Picard reveals that he is descended from Auguste Piccard.

9. Joel Engel, *Gene Roddenberry: The Myth and the Man Behind Star Trek* (New York: Hyperion, 1994), 19.

10. This name can be traced back to Roddenberry's writing on the television series *Mr. District Attorney* (ABC-TV, 1951–52; first-run syndication from 1954–55) and an episode he wrote called "Defense Department Gambling." In the episode, he created a character named "Sergeant Ryker." This was the first complete script that Roddenberry ever sold for television. See Alexander, *Star Creator*, 128. This last name next appears in an idea for a series entitled "The Man from Lloyds" that he registered with the Writers Guild. The name of its main character was Anthony Riker. See Alexander, *Star Creator*, 154.

11. Norman Moss, *The British/American Dictionary* (London: Hutchinson, 1973), 115.

12. The "official" explanation for this character and his name holds that it memorializes a physically challenged *Star Trek* fan named George

La Forge. While this solution has the benefit of being traced to an actual person, it should not be taken in any way as an invalidation of the symbolism revealed by the name's analysis.

13. The other non-Terran member of the new *Enterprise*'s bridge crew is a Klingon named Worf. Inasmuch as this character's naming is in Klingonese and there are no references to Terran history or symbolism, no practical analysis is offered here.

14. Worf is the *Enterprise*'s chief of security. Because Worf is from the fictional planet Klingon, neither are there any Terran symbolic referents related to this name, nor have the series producers provided any backstory details that would provide an insight relating his name to Klingon history or mythology.

15. Until his death in 1991, Roddenberry was an active consultant on *Star Trek: The Next Generation, Star Trek: Deep Space Nine,* and six *Star Trek* motion pictures.

16. The series' "bible" features a great deal of material that illustrates the basic environment of the *Enterprise,* Starfleet gadgets, and a glossary of terminology. For example, the *Enterprise* is depicted in one drawing as would be seen in front, side, and rear views. In another, the ship's outline is projected over an aerial view of Paramount Pictures studio lot for comparative purposes. There is a schematic of the bridge with labels giving detailed information about its various features, their functions, and markings that relate the bridge to other aspects of the larger ship ("exit to turbolift: direct to battle bridge"; "to conference lounge and head"). The bible's glossary extends to twenty-four pages (nearly a third of the total pages), and its terminology ranges from definitions of orbit to dilithium crystals and how they help power starflight.

17. The first thirty numbered pages of Roddenberry's bible for *Star Trek: The Next Generation* introduce these characters and lay the ground rules for their relationships with other principal characters. See *Star Trek: The Next Generation Writer's/Director's Guide, '89–'90,* 1–30.

18. This name may be traced to Roddenberry himself, whose full name was Eugene Wesley Roddenberry. Roddenberry used his middle name for a character as far back as the script entitled "Defense Department Gambling" that he wrote for the series *Mr. District Attorney* in 1954. See Alexander, *Star Creator,* 128.

Chapter Five

1. William Gibson, "The Gernsback Continuum," in *Burning Chrome* (New York: Ace Books, 1986), 33–34.

2. It is not my goal to assert that some version of the *Star Trek* concept has more importance or is closer to Roddenberry's "vision" or to assert the

primacy of one series over the other for any reason. Neither is it any part of this project to develop any criteria, values, or qualities, whether aesthetic or otherwise, to put forth some notion about what is proper to the *Star Trek* concept and what is beyond the pale. Roddenberry's concept at this time may be described as generating at least 365 hours of mass media programming across seven motion pictures, a cartoon series, and four television series (not to exclude for a moment other narrative forms such as comic books and novels). Therefore, the notion of trying to reduce all of these sources of data to some more basic premises is one that not only is too daunting for this researcher but a project whose merits seem dubious.

3. A wealth of material, from posters to fanzines, from computer bulletin boards to conventions, from comic books to novels, is excluded here but could form the basis of an expanded treatment and analysis of the *Star Trek* phenomenon.

4. A number of researchers have examined the representation of ethnicity in American media from several points of view. A partial list of these include Lawrence Reddick, "Educational Programs for the Improvement of Race Relations: Motion Pictures," in *The Black Man on Film*, ed. Richard Maynard (Rochelle, NJ: Hayden Book, Inc., 1974); Harry Allan Potamkin, *The Compound Cinema: The Film Writings of Harry Alan Potamkin*, selected, arranged, and introduced by Lewis Jacobs (New York: Teachers College Press, 1977); Donald Bogle, *Toms, Coons, Mulattoes, Mammies and Bucks* (New York: Bantam Books, 1974); Thomas Cripps, "Black Stereotypes on Film," in *Ethnic Images in American Film and Television*, ed. Randall M. Miller (Philadelphia: Balch Institute, 1978); Thomas Cripps, *Slow Fade to Black: The Negro in American Film, 1900–1942* (New York: Oxford University Press, 1977); Allen L. Woll and Randall M. Miller, *Ethnic and Racial Images in American Film and Television*, Historical Essays and Bibliography Series (New York: Garland Publishing, 1987); Daniel Leab, *From Sambo to Superspade: The Black Experience in Motion Pictures* (Boston: Houghton Mifflin Company, 1978); James Robert Parish and George H. Hill, *Black Action Films* (Jefferson, NC: McFarland, 1989); Mark A. Reid, *Redefining Black Film* (Berkeley: University of California Press, 1993); and James Snead, *White Screens, Black Images: Hollywood from the Dark Side* (New York: Routledge, 1994).

5. Roland Barthes, *S/Z: An Essay*, trans. Richard Miller (New York: Hill & Wang, 1974), 3–4.

6. Indeed, sometimes stated (but always implied) in their reviews, critics evaluate media according to their own or generally held assumptions about what constitutes a perfect realization within a specific genre or category. This might prove interesting and stimulating for film reviewers (who are finally involved in selling media to readers/viewers) and diverting as a gambit for media enthusiasts (intent upon displaying an encyclopedic knowledge of film minutia). Barthes, *S/Z*, 3.

7. Jacques Derrida, "The Supplement of Copula: Philosophy Before Linguistics," in *Margins of Philosophy* (Chicago: University of Chicago Press, 1976).

8. Christopher Norris, *Deconstruction and the Interests of Theory* (Norman, OK: University of Oklahoma Press, 1989),187–98, 213–26.

9. Barthes, *S/Z*, 12–15.

10. Barthes warns here about the dangers of being over-objective and literal. Linguists and semiologists differ chiefly over this point. Linguistics, he argues, is interested in "reducing language to the sentence, its lexical and syntactical components." Semiology, in contrast, is ambiguous about the heirarchy of denotation and connotation and regards dictionary definitions (denotation) as just another system of meanings to be analyzed. Ibid., 4–11.

11. In fairness, I should probably state here that in many ways I regard both series (and certainly the episodes that I selected for analysis) as two instances of unified pictorialization and, indeed, that they function as a single text. This position is not only supported by the fact of Roddenberry's supervision of both but is further indicated by the lengths to which producers of *Star Trek: The Next Generation* went to bring characters from the original series onto that one and the considerable efforts expended to construct a history (a kind of deep-space back story) that explicitly links Kirk's period (the end of hostilities with the Klingon Empire and the Klingon's peaceful inclusion within the Federation) to the enlarged Federation of Picard's era. Moreover, throughout the early discussions between Roddenberry and Paramount about creating a new sequel series, the project was characterized as "catching lightning in a bottle for a second time" and Roddenberry self-consciously set out to duplicate the process he used to create, promote, and implement his "vision." See Alexander, *Star Creator*, 498–502; and Engel, *Gene Roddenberry*, 219–22.

12. The methodology of this research combines the analytical methods of Barthes in *S/Z* and Bernadette J. Bucher in "The Savage European: A Structural Approach to European Iconography," *Studies in the Anthropology of Visual Communication* 2 (Fall 1975): 80–86. The present analysis renounces the temptation to develop a new structure or reading based on interpretations/evaluations of large portions of these texts, such as acting, direction, set design, lighting, editing, mise-en-scène, or cinematography, to pursue the examination of the video/text at a more minute level—individual pictorial and aural symbols. The aim of this study, however, is to produce a "gradual reading" or analysis of the video/text. Accordingly, this analysis shuttles back and forth through the episodes to yield a commentative discourse that relates the individual episodes' diachronic, denotative meanings to the recurring symbols found in specific episodes that comprise the larger synchronic, connotative meanings of the episodes.

13. Barthes, *S/Z*, 3–35.

14. Bucher, "The Savage European," 81.

15. Perhaps Spock's ambivalence toward these strangers of altered genetic stock (he defends, then opposes the space travelers) stems from the fact that his own status as a Starfleet officer and his loyalty to the Federation are questioned because of his own mixed genetic heritage (Sarek his father is Vulcan, and Amanda his mother is Terran). A Starfleet command-level officer with this kind of mixed biological heritage and family background must appreciate at least semi-consciously that his status within that organization as well as the perception of his loyalty is viewed as conditional and contingent upon his unquestioned support of Starfleet ideology.

16. The ship's designation *S.S. Botany Bay* provides yet another example of the program producers' self-consciousness bought to their work. Botany Bay, of course, is a reference to Australia and the initial landing place of English convicts who were banished there as colonists. In making the name "Botany Bay" a significant part of the first information that the *Enterprise* crew (and the audience) discovers about the mysterious ship, a context relating to historical criminals is established. Moreover, this association is picked up and resonates as Kirk and Spock try to figure out the identity of the leader of their unexpected guests.

Chapter Six

1. Nicholas Meyer interviewed in the made-for-television documentary that commemorates Roddenberry's vision. See *Star Trek: 25th Anniversary Special* (Los Angeles: Paramount Pictures, 1991).

2. Bernadette Bucher, "The Savage European: A Structural Approach to European Iconography," *Studies in the Anthropology of Visual Communication*, 2 (Fall 1975): 81–84.

3. Roddenberry laid down the formula for this teaser in a memorandum, dated 2 May 1966, that was supposed to supplement omissions and oversights in the series' Writer/Director Guide. See David Alexander, *Star Creator: The Autobiography of Gene Roddenberry* (New York: Penguin, 1994), 240.

4. In *Star Trek*, the text of this introduction stated, "Space, the final frontier. These are the voyages of the starship *Enterprise*. Its five-year mission to explore strange new worlds, to seek out new life and new civilizations, to boldly go where no man has gone before."

5. Noël Carroll, *Mystifying Movies: Fads and Fallacies in Contemporary Film Theory* (New York: Columbia University Press, 1988), 159.

6. It is interesting that both of the ethnic characters in *Star Trek* play musical instruments and that this has been carried forward to Data in *Star*

Trek: The Next Generation. Musicianship is one of the few areas in which minorities are allowed to create a space for excellence in white patriarchy. In mass media, however, this creative capacity has been transformed into a rather hackneyed stereotype of the minority as musical entertainer. The popular assumption that all African Americans have rhythm derives from this.

7. See *Star Trek: The Next Generation, Writer's and Director's Guide '89–'90,* 7–30.

8. Ibid.

9. Although the episodes selected for this analysis did not feature the Data character, it should be pointed out that the white-gold android is the locus of many race and gender issues. As I have already pointed out, *Star Trek* writers related this character to African Americans in "Measure of a Man." That identification with minorities is at the center of "The Naked Now" when Tasha Yar picks Data as her ideal lover and explores the previously taboo issues of her sexuality, sexual needs, and sexual stamina with him. For a discussion of this character as an ersatz minority, see Rhonda V. Wilcox, "Dating Data: Miscegenation in 'Star Trek: The Next Generation,'" *Extrapolation* 34 (1993): 265–75.

10. At some point after the writer's and director's guide was written, La Forge's birthplace was changed from Jamaica to the African Confederation. See Michael Okuda and Denise Okuda, *Star Trek Chronology: The History of the Future* (New York: Pocketbooks, 1993), 82; and Michael Okuda, Denise Okuda, and Debbie Mirek, *The Star Trek Encyclopedia* (New York: Pocket Books, 1994), 168.

11. In the episode "The Emissary," the success of K'Ehleyr's mission revolves around Worf's integration and adaptation of Terran gaming culture and values to convince a shipful of ancient Klingons to surrender to Federation control.

12. In the last two years of the series, two separate episodes were dedicated to stories about female bridge officers, Dr. Crusher and Counselor Troi, and the issue of females commanding the *Enterprise.*

13. Roddenberry seems to have been interested in basing dramatic action aboard a ship for some time, perhaps as a response to James Michener's highly successful book *Return to Paradise* and the television series it spawned. In Roddenberry's concept, dated 20 June 1956, action takes place aboard a cruise ship, and possible alternative titles for the series pointed to his future series *Star Trek: Star Passenger* and *Of Ships and Stars.* His description of the concept of the series shares a great deal in common with another series, *The Love Boat,* and his own *Star Trek.* In a letter posted to himself, to protect his copyrights, and dated 20 June 1956, he wrote that the show would be structured as "a series of stories which take place mainly aboard an ocean liner, a cruise ship which travels between the mainland and Hawaii and possibly other pacific ports. Although the be-

ginning or close of the story might be set in any stateside or island city, the major setting is the ship itself." More to the point on relationships being discussed here, Roddenberry envisioned that "[t]he continuing main characters in the series outside of the ship itself, are the ship captain, purser, and/or deck-officer. The stories are of a general anthology nature. They will concern passengers and the ship's personnel, separately and in combination." Letter from Roddenberry to Roddenberry, dated June 20, 1956, box 29, folder 7, UCLA-SC; and Alexander, *Star Creator*, 149–50.

14. Troi was originally conceived as "a four-breasted, oversexed hermaphrodite." In this light, her clothing, which emphasized her bosom, may be a vestigial remnant that can be traced back to that earlier description/conception. Joel Engel, *Gene Roddenberry: The Myth and the Man behind Star Trek* (New York: Hyperion, 1994), 226.

15. Several studies of both series point out, however, that the "prime directive" is regularly violated by both Kirk and Picard.

16. In this sample, there were no examples of male-male or female-female romantic involvements.

17. In the episode "Elaan of Troyius," Kirk's command authority is thrown into jeopardy when he touches the tears of the Dohlman of Elas and falls "head over heels" in love with her because of the intoxicating effects of the chemicals in those tears. Here, again, something extraordinary happens that dissolves Kirk's authority and absolves him of responsibility for his actions. This appears to be a *Star Trek* formula that allows the white male authority figure to succumb to a romantic liaison with an ethnic woman with impunity.

18. This is another instance or variation of nineteenth-century sexual theory that held that black females' sexual urges were abnormally strong and not at all feminine, therefore removing them from the protection of gentility and making them fair game for the lusts of white males.

19. No non-humanoid life-forms serve onboard the *Enterprise*.

20. Although this survey of programs from the original *Star Trek* did not include "Amok Time," it may be noted that in that episode the onset of Mr. Spock's seven-year reproductive sexual cycle causes him to act violently: break objects, disobey orders, and nearly kill his commanding officer and friend, Kirk. The plot of this episode needs to be appreciated as part of *Star Trek*'s (both series') formula for depicting ethnic sexuality as an alien and dangerous threat to white male order and authority.

21. See my earlier discussion of the prelude to intimacy between K'Ehlyer and Worf.

22. When Spock takes control of the *Enterprise* in "The Menagerie," Parts I and II he accomplishes this feat through guile and logic, not force. This is another of the ways *Star Trek* differentiates between "good aliens/ethnics" and "bad aliens/ethnics."

23. This is a familiar and discredited Western myth in which white

women are restricted from experiencing their sexuality. Civilization places the white female on a pedestal, according to nineteenth-century theories of sexuality, so that she need not experience her coarse, debasing sexual nature except in procreation. In this myth, white and black males are brutish, sexual animals. However, white males are able to hold themselves in check with Western values. Black males, not having title to these values of culture, such as Judeo-Christian religion, have to be contained by strong laws and punishments for sexual expression outside the purview and control of white owners. This myth authorizes liaisons between white males and ethnic females as an aspect of white male privilege and as a way for white males to express their sexual drives with a kind of female who cannot be damaged because she is not recognized as a civilized human. Sexual relationships between ethnic males and white females are not sanctioned, because uncoupling sexual desire from moral and legal repressions threatens white male authority and white male paternity (i.e., inheritance).

24. Dr. Daystrom's position is reminiscent of General Othello's plight and tragedy. In Shakespeare's drama, Othello's suspicion of Cassio and murder of Desdemona come about because he thinks of himself as a Venetian, not a Moor, and as being due the honors bestowed on him by the state. He has subsumed his identity within that of his adopted country and forgotten the central fact of his life: that being Other marks him as a target for the envy of even those closest to him, like Iago. The result of forgetting that he is always under suspicion himself, of accepting Desdemona as a trophy bride, and failing to appreciate his double-consciousness, as state official and Other, is that Iago can use Othello's longing to be accepted as the foundation of his scheming. In other words, Iago uses Othello's mind against him. This is precisely analogous to the situation of Daystrom in "Ultimate Computer." For a discussion that follows this approach to Shakespeare's play, see Caryl Phillips, "A Black European Success," in *The European Tribe* (London: Faber and Faber, 1987), 45–51.

25. This is a view of romance that daytime dramas, for instance, do not subscribe to and regularly violate.

26. In the episodes "Time's Arrow, Parts I and II," which ended the fifth and opened the sixth seasons, it is revealed that Guinan is a member of the race of time-and-space-traveling aliens. In the second season episode "Q Who?" Guinan reveals that her planet was completely destroyed and that her people were nearly exterminated by the Borg. Despite Guinan's many irregular appearances, these few facts are the extent of the information allowed viewers.

27. That the character Worf's forehead is so prominent deserves additional commentary because in *Star Trek* Klingons are not depicted with such a gross anatomical feature. In the idiom of science fiction, sorcery, and fantasy, and superhero comic books in particular, character alter egos

(their Other personalities that put on the tights and do daring deeds) are represented as possessing extremely well-developed musculature. In this fashion, present-day fictional heroes and their villainous opponents armor themselves after the fashion of medieval knights centuries removed. Armor both encapsulates and separates. Therefore, a social distance is maintained by Worf's physical difference. The semiotic import of Worf's protruding skull resounds with these meanings and marks him as a man of actions, not thoughts. Because the frontal lobe is the seat of much intellectual and emotional activity, this kind of representation effectively hides Worf's different mind and culture from exposure. Additionally, armor protects vital weaknesses; no less so in Worf's case. It is also the case in *Star Trek* mythology that a forceful and direct blow to a Klingon's forehead is a "death blow."

28. *Star Trek's* mythology about the sexuality of white male and female of command rank illustrates how this theme has been developed regarding Commander Riker and Dr. Crusher. The episodes "The Outcast" and "The Host" center on romantic liaisons between alien Others and Riker and Crusher, respectively. In "The Outcast," Riker falls in love with a J'-naii who presents as a female. Even after his lover has been psychologically adjusted to reflect the J'naii preference for expressing neither male nor female sexuality, Riker's emotional attachment leads him to attempt to rescue his lover. One the other hand, Crusher in "The Host" falls in love with Ambassador Odan, whose humanoid body hosts a Trill symbiant. When Odan dies, Riker temporarily hosts the Trill, and Crusher and Riker/Odan resume their romance. However, when the new host arrives, Crusher refuses to acknowledge the possibility of continuing their relationship in any form, because the new Trill host is female.

29. Klingon characters as far back as the original series—Kor ("Errand of Mercy") and Kang ("Day of the Dove")—display a similar sash as part of their uniform.

30. In more than 180 episodes, Geordi La Forge's VISOR was linked to the ship's monitor in only one episode, "Heart of Glory," so that the bridge crew could share his enhanced acuity. The experiment was never repeated.

31. "The Mind's Eye" stands out as the single episode in which the La Forge character is at the center of the plot. On route to planet Risa to attend an artificial intelligence seminar, La Forge is captured, tortured, brainwashed by Romulans, and returned to the *Enterprise* programmed to kill. At several points during the episode, audiences see through La Forge's VISOR. Although this episode was not one of the ones selected for study here, it is worth noting that the one occasion when La Forge can generate a point of view is only when those shots are under the direction of yet another "Other," Romulans, a long-time Federation nemesis and, obviously, for nefarious purposes.

Chapter Seven

1. Nathan Glazer and Daniel P. Moynihan, eds., *Ethnicity: Theory and Practice* (Cambridge, MA: Harvard University Press, 1975), 23.

2. Joel Engel, Roddenberry's unofficial biographer, alludes to this lack of attention to developing the social, economic, and political contexts of the future in *Star Trek: The Next Generation*. The vacuum that this created was filled, perhaps by default, with rather conventional Judeo-Christian values and attitudes. See Engel, *Gene Roddenberry: The Myth and the Man behind Star Trek* (New York: Hyperion, 1994), 247.

3. An expanded sample from *Star Trek: The Next Generation*—one, for example, that included "Code of Honor," "Identity Crisis," "Suddenly Human," "The Best of Both Worlds, "Parts 1 and 2, "The Price," "Menage à Troi," "Data's Day," "The Defector," "The Enemy," "Contagion," "Conspiracy," "Sins of the Father," "The Bonding," "A Matter of Time," and "Heart of Glory"—might reveal the ways *Star Trek* mythology treats ethnicity across a definition of the term that was broadened to encompass all alien characters and cultures that have been represented.

4. Lawrence Reddick, in *The Black Man on Film: Racial Stereotyping*, ed. Richard A. Maynard (Rochelle Park, NJ: Hayden, 1974), vi, 2–17.

5. As a case in point, Geordi La Forge's family was treated with a casualness that was atypical of the series' treatment of the backgrounds of continuing characters. His father, played by Ben Vereen, has no first name, and his mother (no actor listed) is listed first with the first name Alvera which was changed to Silva. See Michael Okuda, Denise Okuda, and Debbie Mirek, *The Star Trek Encyclopedia* (New York: Pocket Books, 1994), 168.

6. I am indebted to Thomas Cripps and his late wife, Alma, for their patience in listening to my thoughts about these collateral characters as their guest at breakfast in one of their favorite Fells Point restaurants in Baltimore and to Thomas Cripps for suggesting the French term *fonctionnaire* for identifying the way African American actors are used in so many films and television programs.

7. This second season episode was entitled "The Jem 'Hadar'" (airdate: 11 June 1994).

8. Forster wrote that "[f]lat characters were called 'humours' in the seventeenth century, and are sometimes called types, and sometimes caricatures. In their purest form, they are constructed round a single idea or quality; when there is more than one factor in them, we get the beginning of the curve toward the round. . . . [F]lat characters are very useful to him [the writer], since they never need reintroduction, never run away, have not to be watched for development, and provide their own atmosphere." E. M. Forster, *Aspects of the Novel* (New York: Harcourt, Brace & World, 1954), 103–5.

9. "Media Markets around the World: *Electronic Media's* Annual International Market Survey," *Electronic Media*, 13 May 1991, 30, 32–33.

10. This analysis constitutes a revision of a recent schema proposed by Nick Browne that was limited to race and gender relations in American film. However, important elements of the social and sexual relations in *Star Trek* and *Star Trek: The Next Generation* fail to be addressed by Browne's discussion. The schema offered here is more complex, because it is meant to recover for discussion the variety of social interactions in media the omitted categories of class and biracial relations. Nick Browne, "Race: The Political Unconscious in American Films," *East-West Film Journal*, 6 (Spring 1991): 5–16.

11. A. J. Greimas, *On Meaning: Selected Writings in Semiotic Theory* (Minneapolis: University of Minnesota Press, 1987).

12. In this connection, we should note that once-married Engineer Miles O'Brien and Keiko Ishikawa have effectively broken this prohibition, although they are close to each other in rank and status, and must leave the *Enterprise* and Starfleet. This vector analysis helps to explain their reemergence on *Star Trek: Deep Space Nine*, a non-Starfleet environment.

13. Going further, it could be stated that Picard endures his greatest humiliation and challenge to his ego when the Borg capture him and transform him into one of them by surgically implanting him with various computer devices. This intimate association with technology with the embodiment of technique nearly results in Picard's total mental collapse. Indeed, in a later episode it becomes clear that he will perhaps never fully recover his previously secure sense of self.

Epilogue

1. Stephen Hawking, "Foreword," in Lawrence M. Krauss, *The Physics of Star Trek* (New York: Basic Books, 1995), xi-xii.

2. Krauss, *Physics of Star Trek*, xv.

References

Alexander, David. 1994. *Star Creator: The Autobiography of Gene Rodden-berry*. New York: Penguin Books.

Alexander, Francis W. 1976. "Stereotyping as a Method of Exploitation in Film." *The Black Scholar*, May, 7:8, 25–29.

Allen, Robert C., ed. *Channels of Discourse: Television and Contemporary Criticism*. Chapel Hill: University of North Carolina Press, 1987.

Amis, Kingsley. 1961. *New Maps of Hell*. New York: Ballantine Books.

Altman, Mark. 1990. "Episode Guide." *Cinefantastique*, September 1990, 26–51, 1991.

———. "Episode Guide." *Cinefantastique*, October 1991, 19–51.

Asimov, Isaac. 1962. *Visitor from Outer Space: Soviet Science Fiction*. New York: Collier Books.

———. 1962. "Introduction." In *More Soviet Science Fiction*, by Roza Prekofeva, Jr. New York: Collier Books.

Auletta, Ken. 1991. *Three Blind Mice*. New York: Random House.

Bailey, James Osler. 1947. *Pilgrims Through Space and Time: Trends and Patterns in Utopian Fiction*. New York: Argus Books.

Balsley, David F. 1959. "A Descriptive Study of References Made to Negroes and Occupational Roles Represented by Negroes in Selected Mass Media." Unpublished dissertation, University of Denver.

Barnouw, Erik. 1990. *Tube of Plenty*. New York: Oxford University Press.

Barron, Neil, ed. 1987. *The Anatomy of Wonder*. New York: R. R. Bowker Company.

Barthes, Roland. 1974. *S/Z: An Essay*. Trans. by Richard Miller. New York: Hill and Wang.

Bielby, William T. and Denise D. Bielby. 1993. "A Survey of the Employment of Writers in the Film, Broadcast, and Cable Industries for the

Period 1987–1991," *The 1993 Hollywood Writers' Report.* Beverly Hills: Writers Guild of America/West.

————. 1989. "Unequal Access, Unequal Pay," *The 1989 Hollywood Writers' Report.* Beverly Hills: WGA/W.

————. 1987. "Pay Equity and Employment Opportunities Among Writers for Television and Feature Films," *The 1987 Hollywood Writers' Report: A Survey of Ethnic, Gender and Age Employment Practices.* Summary Report (2 vols). Beverly Hills: WGA/W.

Biskind, Peter. 1983. "War of the Worlds." *American Film.* December, 37–42.

Black, Jay and Frederick C. Whitney, 1983. *Introduction to Mass Communication.* Dubuque: Wm. C. Brown Company Publishers.

Blum, Richard and Richard Lindheim. 1987. *Primetime: Network Television Programming.* Boston: Focal Press.

Bronson, John. 1978. *Future Tense: The Cinema and Science Fiction.* New York: St. Martin's Press.

Brooks, Tim and Earl Marsh. 1992. *The Complete Directory to Prime Time Network TV Shows.* New York: Ballentine Books.

Brown, Les. "Television Off to the Races: Previews Reveal the Racial 'Mix,'" *Variety,* September 14, 1966, 1 & 78.

Browne, Nick. 1987. "The Political Economy of the Television (Super) Text." In *Television: The Critical View.* Ed. by Horace Newcomb. 613–627. New York: Oxford University Press.

Bryant, Adams. 1992. "Beam Me Up! I'm Out of Change!" *The New York Times.* September 29, C5.

Bucher, Bernardine J. 1975. "The Savage European: A Structural Approach to European Iconography." *Studies in the Anthropology of Visual Communication.* 2:2, 80–86.

"Calif. FEPC Rap: Boothmen; Charge IA Projectionists' Frisco Local Refused Membership to Negro," *Daily Variety,* June 28, 1963, 1 & 4.

Carroll, Noel. 1988. *Mystifying Movies: Fads and Fallacies in Contemporary Film Theory.* New York: Columbia University Press.

Clareson, Thomas D. 1987. "The Emergence of Science Fiction: The Beginning to the 1920s." In *The Anatomy of Wonder.* Ed. by Neil Barron. New York: R. R. Bowker Company.

Cole, Lewis. "Screenplay Culture," *The Nation,* November 4, 1991, 560–566.

Corcoran, Farrel. 1987. "Television as Ideological Apparatus: The Power and the Pleasure." In *Television: The Critical View.* Ed. by Horace Newcomb. 533–552. New York: Oxford University Press.

Cripps, Thomas R. 1970. "The Myth of the Southern Box-Office: A Factor in Racial Stereotyping in American Movies, 1920–1940." In *The Black Experience in America: Selected Essays.* Ed. by James C. Curtis and Lewis L. Gould. 116–144. Austin: University of Texas Press.

Dates, Jannette L. 1990. "Commercial Television." In *Split Images: African Americans in the Mass Media*. Ed. by Janette L. Dates and William Barlow. 253–302. Washington, D. C.: Howard University Press.

Davenport, Basil. 1969. *The Science Fiction Novel an Social Criticism*. Chicago: Advent Publishers.

"Dear Old 'Nielsen Rule' Days: Top 3-Rs Still Spell Ratings: Not a Tight Race; Rather How Wide the Separation Between Nets?" *Variety*, September 7, 1966, 1, 62.

De Bolt, Joe and John R. Pfeiffer. 1987. "The Early Modern Period: 1938–1963." In *The Anatomy of Wonder*. Ed. by Neil Barron. New York: R. R. Bowker Company.

"'Definite Increase' In Hollywood Jobs For Negro Performers Reported By Largest Colored Talent Agency," *Daily Variety*, August 21, 1963, 1 & 14.

Dempsey, John. "Dear Diary: I'll See You In September: Nielsen Vamps on Fall Meters," *Variety*, May 21, 1986, 53 & 83.

"Dixie Sen. Thurmond Thunders; Sez CBS Toes 'NAACP Line,'" *Daily Variety*, July 1, 1963, 1 & 14.

Dutt, Violet L. 1962. *Soviet Science Fiction*. New York: Collier Books.

Easthope, Anthony, ed., 1993. *Contemporary Film Theory*. London: Longman.

Ellis, John. 1987. "Broadcast Television Narration." In *Television: The Critical View*. Ed. by Horace Newcomb. 553–565. New York: Oxford University Press.

Egri, Lajos. 1946. *The Art of Dramatic Writing: Its Basis in the Creative Interpretation of Human Motivation*. New York: Simon and Schuster.

Engel, Joel. 1994. *Gene Roddenberry: The Myth and the Man Behind Star Trek*. New York: Hyperion.

Equal Employment Opportunity Commission. 1968. "Hearing Before the United States Equal Employment Opportunity Commission on Discrimation in White Collar Employment," New York: The Commission, January 15–18.

Equal Employment Opportunity Commission. 1969. "Hearing Before the United States Equal Employment Opportunity Commission on Utilization of Minorities and Women Workers in Certain Major Industries," Los Angeles: The Commission, March 12–14.

Erickson, Hal. 1989. *Syndicated Television: The First Forty Years, 1947–1987*. Jefferson, N.C.: MacFarland and Company, Inc.

Fessier, Michael M. Jr. "NAACP Charges '62 Promise of More Jobs Not Kept; Most Unions Execs Disagree," *Daily Variety*, June 6, 1963, 4.

———. "NAACP Ultimatum to Hollywood: Demonstrations Threatened Unless Negroes Get More Jobs; 15 'Lily-White' IA Locals Hit," *Daily Variety*, June 26, 1963, 1 & 8.

———. "Urges Stars Show Muscle To Aid Negroes; WGA Prez Would Waive Pay Minimum For Cause," *Daily Variety*, July 15, 1963, 1 & 9.

————. "Negroes' H'wood Status Improving, Notes NAACP Rep," *Daily Variety*, July 12, 1963, 1 & 13.

————. "Demonstrations Threatened Unless Negroes Get More Jobs; 15 'Lily-White' IA Locals Hits," *Daily Variety*, June 26, 1963, 1 & 8.

————. "Plans Asking Decertification of Set Designers Local for Allegedly Barring Negro," *Daily Variety*, August 2, 1963, 1 & 4.

————. "100% Integration of Films-TV: That's NAACP Demand; IATSE Attack Renewed; Boren Sees an 'Area of Agreeableness,'" *Daily Variety*, July 19, 1963, 1 & 4.

————. "Brando Sparks Anti-Bias Meet: Urges Stars Show Muscle To Aid Negroes; WGA Prez Would Waive Pay Minimum for Cause," *Daily Variety*, July 15, 1963, 1 & 9.

Fiske, John and John Hartley. 1978. *New Accents: Reading Television*. London: Methuen.

Forster, E. M. 1954. *Aspects of the Novel*. New York: Harcourt, Brace and World.

Gras, Vernon W., ed., 1973. *European Literary Theory and Practice: From Existentialism to Structuralism*. New York: Dell Publishing Co., Inc.

Gates, Henry Louis Jr. "Tv's Black World Turns—But Stays Unreal." *New York Times*. November 12, 1994. 2: 1 & 40.

Gibberman, Susan R. 1991. *Star Trek: An Annotated Guide to Resources on the Development, the Phenomenon, the People, the Television Series, the Films, the Novels and the Recordings*. Jefferson, N. C.: MacFarland and Company, Inc.

Gibson, William. 1986. "The Gernsback Continuum." In *Burning Chrome*. New York: Ace Books.

Gitlin, Todd. 1987. "Prime Time Ideology: The Hegemonic Process in Television Entertainment." In *Television: The Critical View*. Ed. by Horace Newcomb. 507–532. New York: Oxford University Press.

Glazer, Nathan and Daniel P. Moynihan, eds. 1975. *Ethnicity: Theory and Practice*. Cambridge: Harvard University Press.

Gunn, James E. 1975. *Alternative Worlds*. Englewood Cliffs, N. J.: Prentice Hall.

Hardy, Phil (with Denis Gifford). 1986. *The Encyclopedia of Science Fiction Movies*. London: Octopus Books.

Hooks, Bell. 1992. *Black Looks: Race and Representation*. Boston: South End Press.

Horowitz, Murray. "Frosh Open Weak Spy-Sci-Fi Next?" *Variety*, September 28, 1966, 31.

————. 1991. *Science Fiction*. London: Aurum Press.

"H'wood NAACP in Stepped-Up Pitch for Negro Film-TV Prod. Employment," *Variety*, July 28, 1965, 1 & 21.

"'I Spy' Clearance Grows in Dixie, Can't Snub a Hit," *Variety*, September 21, 1966, 1.

"IA's Flaherty is No Pessimist, Nor Optimist About Pix Jobs," *Daily Variety*, February 6, 1963, 3.

"IA Grips Local Admits 1st 5 Negroes; Aller Focuses Attack On NAACP," *Daily Variety*, November 4, 1963, 1 & 4.

"IA's Herb Aller Chides NAACP's 'Rabblerousing,'" *Variety*, July 13, 1966, 1 & 54.

"IA Lensers Nix NAACP Demand," *Daily Variety*, July 30, 1963, 1 & 4

"IA Publicists Support NAACP Pix Demands," *Daily Variety*, August 8, 1963, 1 & 8.

"IATSE Film Editors join Other Unions Nixing NAACP," *Daily Variety*, August 5, 1963, 1 & 10.

Jefferson, Margo. "Seducified by a Minstrel Show." *The New York Times*. May 22, 1994, 2: 1 & 40.

Jenkins, Henry. 1992. *Textual Poachers: Television Fans and Participatory Culture*. London: Routledge.

Kaufman, Dave. "IATSE Lamp Ops Take Dim View of NAACP Demands," *Daily Variety*, August 1, 1963, 1 & 4.

———. "Scenic Artists Nix Demand, Denounced By Other Labor Leaders As 'Arrogant,'" *Daily Variety*, July 31, 1963, 1 & 4.

———. "More H'wood Unions Defy NAACP: Scenic Artists Nix Demand, Denounced By Other Labor Leaders as 'Arrogant,'" *Daily Variety*, July 31, 1963, 1 & 4.

———. "Spy-Fi Gets Left in Cold," *Variety*, January 25, 1966, 26.

———. "Roles in Vidpix Not Cut on Bias: Producers Report Use of Negro Thesps Had Increased Before Present Controversy," *Daily Variety*, July 12, 1963, 1 & 13.

Ketterer, David. 1974. *New Worlds for Old: The Apocalyptic Imagination, Science Fiction, American Literature*. Garden City, N.Y.: Anchor Press.

Kaminsky, Stuart M. (with Mahan, Jeffrey H.). 1985. *American Television Genres*. Chicago: Nelson-Hall.

"L. A. Riot Cost Ringling 300,000G," *Variety*, August 25, 1965, 60.

"L. A. Riots Kayo S.F. Negro Plays," *Variety*, August 25, 1965, 1 & 60.

Lawson, John Howard. 1949. *Theory and Technique of Playwriting and Screenwriting*. New York: G. P. Putnam.

"Legislator-Actor Conrad Charges Some NAACP Demands on H'w'd Illegal," *Daily Variety*, October 1, 1963, n.p.

Lentz, Harris M. 1994. *Science Fiction, Horror and Fantasy Film and Television Credits*. Jefferson, N.C.: MacFarland and Company, Inc.

Lentz, Harris M. 1989. *Science Fiction, Horror and Fantasy Film and Television Credits*. Supplement: Through 1987. Jefferson, N.C.: MacFarland and Company, Inc.

Lentz, Harris M. 1994. *Science Fiction, Horror and Fantasy Film and Television Credits*. Supplement 2: Through 1993. Jefferson, N.C.: MacFarland and Company, Inc.

Lewis, Lisa A., ed. 1992. *The Adoring Audience : Fan Culture and Popular Media*. London: Routledge.

"LORE: Leonard on Racial Equality," *Variety*, July 27, 1966, 2.

Lowndes, Robert A. W. 1973. *Three Faces of Science Fiction: As Propaganda, Instruction, and Delight*. Boston: The NESFA Press.

Lundwall, Sam. 1971. *Science Fiction: What It's All About*. New York: Ace Books.

MacDonald, J. Fred. 1992. *Blacks and White TV: African Americans in Television Since 1948*. 2nd Edition. Chicago: Nelson-Hall Publishers, Inc.

Magill, Frank N., ed., 1979. *Survey of Science-Fiction Literature*. 5 vols. Englewood Cliffs: Salem Press.

"Management Brief." *The Economist*. December 10, 1994, 70 & 75.

Molson, Francis J. 1987. "Children's and Young Adult Science Fiction." In *The Anatomy of Wonder*. Ed. by Neil Barron. New York: R. R. Bowker Company.

Moss, Norman. 1973. *The British/American Dictionary*, London: Hutchinson.

Murphy, A.D. "TV Progressing in Hiring Negroes, But Urge Speedup," *Variety*, April 6, 1966, 1 & 48.

"NAACP Asks Studio-By-Studio Report on Just What Gains Negroes Have Made Here," *Daily Variety*, December 13, 1963, 1 & 13.

"NAACP Charges B'casting 'Openly Discriminating,'" *Daily Variety*, August 12, 1963, 1 & 10.

"NAACP Focuses On Madison Ave. In New Tack In Its Campaign Against B'casting," *Daily Variety*, August 20, 1963, 1 & 7.

"NAACP H'wood Branch Meets Sunday As Pressure On Pix-TV Biz Mounts," *Daily Variety*, June 13, 1963, 1 & 11

"Names Spark Civil Liberties Union Drive to Get Negroes Better Break in H'wood," *Daily Variety*, July 9, 1963, 1 & 10.

"Negro Actor Condemns Plan to Picket Oscar Tonight," *Daily Variety*, April 8, 1963, 1 & 4.

"Negroes Break Blurb Barrier," *Daily Variety*, August 2, 1963, 1.

"New NAACP Rap at Hollywood," *Daily Variety*, July 1, 1963, 1 & 14.

"New Research on Hits and Misses," *Variety*, July 28, 1965, 23 & 53.

"Next Season's 3 Net Schedule—First Round," *Variety*, March 2, 1966, 30 and "Next Season's 3 Net Schedule—14th Round," *Variety*, March 16, 1966, 37.

Nicholls, Peter and John Clute, eds. 1993. *The Encyclopedia of Science Fiction*. New York: St. Martin's Press.

Nichols, Nichelle. 1994. *Beyond Uhura*. New York: G. P. Putnam & Sons.

Norris, Christopher. 1989. *Disconstruction and the Interests of Theory*. Norman: Oklahoma University Press.

Okuda, Michael and Denise Okuda. 1993. *Star Trek Chronology: The History of the Future*. New York: Pocket Books.

Okuda, Michael, Denise Okuda, and Debbie Mirek. 1993. *The Star Trek Encyclopedia*. New York: Pocket Books.

"One For Apprentices Under Studio's IBEW Pact; Negro Applicants Being Sought," July 11, 1963, *Daily Variety*, 1 & 4.

Penley, Constance, ed. 1991. *Close Encounters: Film, Feminism, and Science Fiction*. Minneapolis: University of Minnesota Press.

"Plans Asking Decertification of Set Designers Local for Allegedly Barring Negro," *Daily Variety*, August 2, 1963, 1 & 4.

"Producers Urge Realistic Use of Negroes In Telepix," *Daily Variety*, August 6, 1963, 1 & 12.

"Projectionist Accepts Negro Applications," *Daily Variety*, August 26, 1963, 1 & 4.

"Race Relations Bureau Hits NAACP, Says H'wood Doing 'Magnificent Job,'" *Daily Variety*, June 25, 1963, 1 & 15.

"Race Shut-Out Issue Still Rampant," *Variety*, July 13, 1966, 4.

"Registration Up 115%; MPAA (sic) Spurs Drive," *Daily Variety*, September 26, 1963, 1 & 4.

Roddenberry, Gene. 1989. *'Star Trek: The Next Generation' Writers'/Directors' Guide*, (Third Season). Hollywood: Paramount Pictures Company.

Sampson, Robert. 1983. *Yesterday's Faces: A Study of Series Characters in Early Pulp Magazines. Glory Figures*. Vol.1. Bowling Green: Bowling Green University Press.

———. 1983. *Yesterday's Faces: A Study of Series Characters in Early Pulp Magazines. Strange Days*. Vol. 2. Bowling Green: Bowling Green University Press.

Screen Reader 2. 1981. London: The Society for Education in Television and Film.

"2nd Week Overnights," *Variety*, September 21, 1966, 22

"17 Negroes Cast in Medical Roles In 'NEW Interns,'" *Daily Variety*, September 7, 1963, 1 & 21.

"75% of NBC-Tv Sked to be Held Over in 1967–68; Set 'Danny Thomas Hour,'" *Variety*, December 21, 1966, 25.

Shatner, William (with Chris Kreski). 1993. *Star Trek Memories*. New York: HarperCollins Publishers.

Silverman, Kaja. 1983. *The Subject of Semiotics*. New York: Oxford University Press.

Sklar, Robert. "Is Television Taking Blacks Seriously?" *American Film*, September 1978, 25–29.

Snead, James. 1994. *White Screens, Black Images*. New York: Routledge.

Snorgrass, J. William and Gloria T. Woody. 1985. *Blacks and Media: A Selected, Annotated Bibliography 1962–1982*. Tallahassee: University Presses of Florida.

"Spy Spoofs Run Political Risks on Global Sales," *Variety*, February 15, 1966, 27.

Stableford, Brian. 1987. "Science Fiction Between the Wars: 1918–1938." In *The Anatomy of Wonder*. Ed. by Neil Barron. New York: R. R. Bowker Company.

———. 1987. "The Modern Period: 1964–1986." In *The Anatomy of Wonder*. Ed. by Neil Barron. New York: R. R. Bowker Company.

"'Star Trek' Gets NBC Nod for Full Slate," *Variety*, October 12, 1966, 35.

Star Trek: 25ᵗʰ Anniversary Special. 1991. Los Angeles: Paramount Pictures Company.

Strick, Philip. 1976. *Science Fiction Movies*. London: Octopus Books.

"Talent Guilds And Producers Harmonizing With NAACP, Which Sizzles at Unions," *Daily Variety*, August 1, 1963, 1 & 4

Tymn, Marshall B. and Mike Ashley. 1985. *Science Fiction, Fantasy and Weird Fiction Magazine*. Westport, Conn.: Greenwood Press.

"TV Acad—East and West—Advocates More Integration In Video Industry," *Daily Variety*, July 30, 1963, 1 & 9.

"TV Progressing in Hiring Negroes, But Urge Speedup," *Variety*, April 6, 1966, 48.

Warren, Bill (with Bill Thomas). 1986. *Keep Watching the Skies: American Science Fiction Movies of the Fifties*. Jefferson, N.C.: McFarland.

"WB Joins Other Lots In NAACP Pledge," *Daily Variety*, October 16, 1963, 1 & 9.

"WGAW Prexy Nate Monaster Charges 'Conspiracy' By Unions Against Negroes," *Daily Variety*, July 1, 1963, 1 & 14.

Whitfield, Stephen E. and Gene Roddenberry. 1971. *The Making of Star Trek*. New York: Ballantine Books, Inc. Hollywood: Paramount Pictures Corporation.

Weinberg, Robert. 1977. *The Weird Tales Story*. West Linn, Ore.: Fax Collector's Editions.

Writers Guild of America, 1958. Comp. and ed. by Lola Goelet Yoakem, *TV and Screenwriting*. Berkeley: University of California Press, 1958

Zizek, Slavoj. 1992. *Enjoy Your Symptoms: Jacques Lacan in Hollywood and Out*. New York: Routledge.

Zook, Kristaal Brent. 1995. "Trekking for Tolerance: Voyager's Radical Vision for the Future." *LA Weekly*. February 3–9, 39–40.

Index

241

About the Author

Micheal Charles Pounds is professor and chair of the Department of Film and Electronic Art at California State University, Long Beach. He regularly teaches courses in media studies (history, aesthetics, criticism, and critical studies) and production (audio and video). His research interests center on the relationship between audience and media, including examination of the role race plays in shaping radio, television, and film products for audiences.